Monks, Bishops and Pagans

UNIVERSITY OF PENNSYLVANIA
SOURCES OF MEDIEVAL HISTORY,
EDITED BY EDWARD PETERS

The First Crusade: The Chronicle of Fulcher of Chartes and Other Source Materials

Christian Society and the Crusades, 1198–1229. Sources in Translation, including The Capture of Damietta by Oliver of Paderborn

The Burgundian Code: The Book of Constitutions or Law of Gundobad and Additional Enactments, translated by Katherine Fischer Drew

The Lombard Laws, translated with an introduction by Katherine Fischer Drew

Ulrich Zwingli (1484–1531), Selected Works, edited by Samuel Macauley Jackson. Introduction by Edward Peters

From St. Francis to Dante: Translations from the Chronicle of the Franciscan Salimbene (1221–1288), G. G. Coulton. Introduction by Edward Peters

The Duel and the Oath. Parts I and II of Superstition and Force, Henry Charles Lea. Introduction by Edward Peters

The Ordeal. Part III of Superstition and Force, Henry Charles Lea. Introduction by Edward Peters

Torture. Part IV of Superstition and Force, Henry Charles Lea. Introduction by Edward Peters

Witchcraft in Europe, 1110–1700. A Documentary History. Edited by Alan C. Kors and Edward Peters

The Scientific Achievement of the Middle Ages, Richard C. Dales. Introduction by Edward Peters

History of the Lombards, Paul the Deacon. Translated by William Dudley Foulke. Introduction by Edward Peters.

Monks, Bishops and Pagans

Christian Culture in Gaul and Italy, 500–700

Sources in Translation, including *The World of Gregory of Tours*, edited and translated by William C. McDermott

Edited, with an Introduction
by Edward Peters

University of Pennsylvania Press
Philadelphia

Contents

Introduction

The transformations of the western Eurasian world between the second and the eighth centuries have taken on many forms to contemporaries and later historians who have tried, for a thousand years, to define and analyze them. To the humanists of the fifteenth and sixteenth centuries, as to Edward Gibbon in the eighteenth, these changes seemed to be adequately and exhaustively summed up in the phrase *ab inclinatione imperii*, a humanist commonplace which became the title for Gibbon's great work, *The Decline and Fall of the Roman Empire*.[1] Nineteenth and twentieth century historians, although equipped with more sophisticated methodologies and possessed of more data, both literary and non-literary, also spent much time and effort in the fields of economic and social history, political history, and the history of religions. Few have escaped from Gibbon's influential model or from the consequently defensive attitude which adherence to that model requires when examining the spiritual and intellectual culture of the period between the mid-sixth and the mid-eighth centuries.

The texts whose translations are printed in this volume illustrate several aspects of the transformation of the late antique world. Their authors, educated and frequently highly literate, no longer belong even to the brilliant intellectual community of the fourth and early fifth centuries whose most impressive representatives are Sts. Augustine and Jerome.[2] Nor are they, in most cases, the literary equals of the scholars who surrounded Charlemagne in the late eighth and ninth centuries and whose labors on vellum, stone and metalwork produced the intense but fragile culture of the ninth and tenth centuries.[3] Yet these writers (from Gregory of Tours to Bede) invested their altered legacy with an attraction for peoples at widely differing levels of cultural and material development, offered new avenues for the development of individual and collective world-views, and created an image of the self between a material and an immaterial world that has done much to shape the concept of the personality between their day and our own. When they themselves held power or wrote for those who did, their instructions were literal, specific and generally full of good sense. Ironically, between the ruthlessly maladministered world of the late Roman Empire in the West and the irregularly and often brutally underadministered world of the early Germanic kingdoms, it is often in the guise of superbly logical and conscientious administrators that we first meet such figures as Gregory of Tours and Gregory the Great. Yet even their sense of practicality is invested with a transcending spiritual significance, just as their sense of the immanence of the supernatural world is often directed to mundane, practical ends. In a sense, the writers and ecclesiastical rulers of Europe between the fifth and the ninth centuries made a heroic effort to rejoin the practical and the contemplative lives in a new vision of the human community and the place of the self in that community.

Once again the poor, the defenseless and the weak had claims to justice exerted on their behalf. The early Germanic rulers, invested, to be sure, with orthodoxy, were yet endowed with none of the enormously weighty and increasingly empty forms of political authority and ceremonial display that characterize some of the worst of the later Roman emperors. Gregory of Tours could still direct his *History of the Franks* in the sixth century against the shenannigans of the royal grandchildren of Clovis and attempt to call them back to what he mistakenly pictured as the idyllic Christian ways of their grandfather's day. New ideal personality types, new heroes, emerged in the saints and holy men of this period and, less frequently noticed, new heroic ideals indicated subtly transformed social values and social ideas as well. It is not as destroyers of or epigones following a brilliant intellectual culture that we should regard these writers and the figures they describe, but as engineers of a new culture—responsible colonial administrators of an empire that existed only in the mind and spirit and the traditions from the past they shaped and adapted to present conditions.[4] Separated from the precocious and fragile learning of the Christian Empire of the fourth century—the empire of Augustine the sceptic, Jerome the inventor of monastic chic and the politically-minded Eusebius—these thinkers were also separated from the surviving East Roman Empire on linguistic, theological, cultural, and administrative levels. During the late seventh and eighth centuries they also became separated from large segments of what Cyril Toumanoff has called "the ancient Christian Mediterranean world,"—Africa, Spain, Egypt, the Levant, and Armenia falling under the domination of western Christendom's sister civilization, Islam.[5]

Yet with all these separations and their measurable and immeasurable consequences, there also opened up new avenues, avenues formerly closed through inability or indifference to the older culture. The early Middle Ages, whatever else that unfortunate label designates, witnessed the final settlement of Europe by its historical populations, and the history of that settlement and the new political, cultural, and economic structures that it produced is the real focus of early medieval history. Too much attention paid to the faded glories of ancient Rome may make one forget that those glories were faded long before the fifth century, and even in their heyday in full color there were certain lacunae in their dealings with the rest of the world and their own population. The dignity of labor, the linking of different societies by common spiritual experience and practices, the balance between asceticism and action, the responsibility of converting the pagan, and the insistence on the responsibilities of ecclesiastical and political power were the contributions of these post–empire writers, not only to the history of early Europe, but to modern Europe as well. Their world and their work also touch on other areas: the history of the decline of slavery, the rise of technology, new explorations in the visual arts and new ideas about such fundamental social units as the individual, the child, and the family.

There is no better introduction to the importance of the work of churchmen and the laypeople who cooperated with them during this period than Gabriel Le Bras' brilliant study, "The Sociology of the Church in the Early Middle Ages."[6] Suggesting that the sociology of Christianity "operates in three sectors, it defines and explains the lines of internal organization within the Church, its external ties with the World, and its higher relations with the Beyond." Le Bras focuses on three significant areas of analysis:

dispersion and coordination, Christianization and laicization, and individualism and fellowship. In the first area he sees the fragmentation of ecclesiastical structures, the development of local practices, cults, forms of existence and at the same time, the grouping of larger coordinated units (from the diocese to the national church council), the importance of pilgrimages and the role of saints who appeal to wider and wider circles of devotees. In the second area, Le Bras identifies the increasing ecclesiastical control of lands, the style of organization on ecclesiastical property, the insistence on what another historian has called "orthopraxy, rather than orthodoxy"—the imposition of external forms of behavior and worship, not in place of, but before instruction concentrating on orthodox interior belief and the spiritual growth of the individual—and the differentiation between clergy and laity.[7] At the same time, new relationships are established between lay rulers, patrons and ecclesiastical establishments. Finally, Le Bras suggests the importance of the concept of individuation and fellowship in changing liturgical practices such as Baptism and Penance, and in the role of ecclesiastical structures in redefining the relationships among members of other kinds of communities. Such an approach as this will bring us to a much sharper appreciation and understanding of the culture represented by the writers in this book.

This book of readings is divided into three general sections and a concluding excerpt. The first, drawing upon the writings of Pope Gregory the Great (590-604) and Bede (c. 672-735), suggests the important role played by the great pope in defining the spheres of different forms of religious life. Describing the complex and dangerous universe in which supernatural powers touch everyday life, often with malevolence and great force, Gregory gives a shape to the world of human time by bracketing it between the Incarnation and the vision of the afterlife with the last judgement. The materials come from sources that reflect Gregory's great energy and dedication. His advice on pastoral care is derived from his book of that title, one of the most influential works on clerical life ever written. The second selection, on the sinful monks, comes from his *Dialogues*, a volume of miracle stories that did much to shape Christian consciousness and literary expression for centuries to come. Gregory's anticipation of the last judgement, which colors the eschatological tone of much of his work, comes from a conflated passage in one of his letters and one of his sermons. Bede's description of the vision of the afterlife is from his great work *The Ecclesiastical History of the English People*.

The second section of the book focuses upon the theme of monks and their place in early European society. *The Benedictine Rule*, one of the most remarkable documents ever to direct any human organization, touches on aspects of the self, personality, society, technical matters of diet, work and administration with a depth that is something quite new in the world. Paul the Deacon's poems in honor of St. Benedict reflect the growth of Benedict's legend, especially after Gregory the Great devoted the whole of Book II of the *Dialogues* to recounting Benedict's life. Jonas' *Life of St. Columbanus* tells the story of another kind of monk, one of the wandering Irish monks who were contemporaries of Gregory the Great, but followed non–Benedictine rules. The concluding section from the *Life of St. Gall*, one of Columbanus' companions, suggests some of the common features that Celtic monasticism shared with Roman.

The third section of this book presents another world, that of the bishops—specifically that of Gregory of Tours, the sixth–century bishop whose *History of the Franks* is his best known work, but whose "minor writings," some of which are here reprinted, reveal the mental world of a Gallo–Roman aristocrat dealing with a new and violent society. Gregory's heroes are mostly bishops themselves, and their interests suggest some of the cultural variety of the sixth century.

The concluding selection, the story of St. Barbatus, takes us to a different part of Europe, southern Italy, and to a different Germanic society, that of the Lombards.[8] St. Barbatus is concerned with backsliding, the long-term problem of keeping converts converted, and the book ends, as it began, with holy men seeking solutions to practical problems. The way they envisioned the problems and the variety of solutions they used constitute one of the best windows.on early European culture.

The bibliography at the end of the volume is not exhaustive, but it attempts to suggest the most useful directions for further reading, citing extensively works in translation as well as recent research into the culture and society of the period 500–700. The editor would like to thank Dr. William C. McDermott for his generosity and advice; and Mr. Alfred J. Marion for extensive contributions to the bibliography.

Edward Peters
Philadelphia, 1974

A Note on the Contents

Although the original locations of the selections printed below are indicated with each selection, it is proper to note that the following works from the University of Pennsylvania series *Translations and Reprints from the Sources of European History* are included in the specified edited forms. D. C. Munro, *The Life of St. Columban*, Vol. II, no. 7 (1895), excluding editorial material, is complete. W. C. McDermott, *Gregory of Tours: Selections from the Minor Works*, Third Series, Vol. IV (1949) is complete, excluding the dedication, foreword, preface, and the index. A new bibliography has been added.

Notes

1. For the development of European history *ab inclinatione imperii Romani*, see Denys Hay, "Flavio Biondo and the Middle Ages," *Proceedings of the British Academy* 45 (1959), pp. 97–127; Wallace K. Ferguson, *The Renaissance in Historical Thought* (Cambridge, Mass., 1948); Erwin Panofsky, *Renaissance and Renascences in Western Art* (rep. New York, 1972). For Gibbon, see Lynn White, ed., *The Transformation of the Roman World: Gibbon's Problem After Two Centuries* (Berkeley and Los Angeles, 1966). The standard edition of Gibbon's history is that by J. B. Bury, 7 vols. (London, 1896–1900).

2. See R. A. Markus, *Saeculum: History and Society in the Theology of St. Augustine* (Cambridge, 1970); A. Momiglkano, ed., *The Conflict Between Paganism and Christianity in the Fourth Century* (Oxford, 1963); Peter Brown, *The World of Late Antiquity* (New York, 1970). On the development of Christianity, see now Karl Baus, *From the Apostolic Community to Constantine* (London, 1965).

3. In general, see Donald Bullough, *The Age of Charlemagne* (New York, 1966); David Talbot Rice, ed., *The Dark Ages* (London, 1965); Heinrich Fichtenau, *The Carolingian Empire* (New York, 1964). The most recent reassessment of the scholarship is Donald Bullough, "*Europae Pater:* Charlemagne and His Achievement in the Light of Recent Scholarship," *English Historical Review* 85 (1970), pp. 59–105.

4. Two fine introductions to this period are William C. Bark, *Origins of the Medieval World* (Stanford, 1958), and the superb anthology of texts and commentary by J. N. Hillgarth, *The Conversion of Western Europe, 350-750* (Englewood Cliffs, 1969).

5. See Brown, *The World of Late Antiquity*; F. Gabrieli, *Muhammad and the Conquests of Islam* (New York, 1968); J. M. Hussey, *The Byzantine World* (New York, 1961); Cyril Toumanoff, *Studies in Christian Caucasian History* (Washington, 1963).

6. Reprinted in Sylvia Thrupp, ed., *Early Medieval Society* (New York, 1967), pp. 47-57; in general, see the papers by Le Bras and others in *Caratteri del secolo VII in Occidente, Settimane di studio del centro italiano di studi sull'alto Medioevo*, No. V, 2 vols. (Spoleto, 1958), as well as other volumes in this series.

7. The felicitous distinction between orthopraxy and orthodoxy, as well as many other useful observations about the transformation of Christian culture may be found in Janet L. Nelson, "Society, Theodicy and the Origins of Heresy: Towards a Reassessment of the Medieval Evidence," in D. J. Baker, ed., *Schism, Heresy and Religious Protest*, Studies in Church History, Vol. IX (Cambridge, 1972), pp. 65-77.

8. For the Lombards, see Katherine Fischer Drew, trans., *The Lombard Laws* (Philadelphia, 1973) and Paul the Deacon, *History of the Lombards*, trans. William Dudley Foulke, (rep. Philadelphia, 1974).

I
The Shaping of
Christian Culture

1
Pope Gregory the Great

The following selections from Gregory's Dialogues, Pastoral Care, Letters, *and* Sermons *are all taken from James Harvey Robinson,* Readings in European History, *Vol. I (Boston, 1904), pp. 75-77, 80-82, 90-97. For complete translations of these works, see the Bibliography.*

1. from *Pastoral Care*

It is hard for a preacher who is not loved, however right may be his warnings, to be heard gladly. He, therefore, who is over others ought to study to be loved, that he may be heard; and yet not to seek his own popularity for itself, lest he be found by a secret usurpation in thought to oppose Him whom by his office he appeareth to serve. This Paul well signifieth, when he maketh manifest to us the secrets of his desires, saying, "Even as I please all men in all things"; who nevertheless saith again, "If I yet pleased men, I should not be the servant of Christ." Paul therefore pleaseth and pleaseth not, because in that he desireth to please, he seeketh not that he himself, but that through him the Truth, should please men.

The spiritual guide ought also to know that vices for the most part feign themselves to be virtues. For niggardliness often cloaketh itself under the name of frugality; and lavishness, on the other hand, hideth itself under the title of bounty. Often an inordinate forgiveness is thought to be kindness, and unbridled wrath is reckoned the virtue of spiritual zeal. Often headlong action is supposed to be the efficiency of speed, and slowness apes the deliberation of seriousness.

Hence the ruler of souls must needs distinguish with watchful care between virtues and vices; lest either niggardliness take possession of his heart, and he be delighted to appear frugal in his distributions; or when a thing is lavishly expended, he should boast himself as bountiful in showing mercy; or by forgiving that which he ought to smite, he should drag his subjects to eternal punishments; or by smiting ruthlessly that which is wrong, he do more grievous wrong himself; or by unreasonably hastening that which might have been done duly and seriously, he should render it of no esteem; or by putting off the merit of a good action, he should change it for the worse.

Inasmuch, then, as we have shown what manner of man the pastor ought to be, let us now make known after what manner he teacheth. For, as Gregory Nazianzen of reverend memory hath taught long before us, one and the same exhortation is not suited to all, because all are not bound by the same manner of character. For ofttimes the things which profit some are bad for others. Inasmuch as for the most part the herbs also which feed some animals kill others; and a gentle whistling which stilleth horses setteth dogs astir; and the medicine which abateth one disease giveth force to another; and the bread which strengtheneth the life of the vigorous putteth an end to that of babes.

The speech, therefore, of teachers ought to be fashioned according to the condition of the hearers, that it may both be suited to each for his own needs, and yet may never depart from the system of general edification. For what are the attentive minds of the hearers but, as I may so say, certain strings stretched tight on a harp which he that is skillful in playing, to the end that he may produce a tune which shall not be at variance with itself, striketh in various ways? And therefore the strings give back harmonious melody because they are beaten with one quill indeed but not with one stroke. Whence also every teacher, to the end that he may edify all in the one virtue of charity, ought to touch the hearts of his hearers out of one system of teaching but not with one and the same address.

2. from the *Dialogues:* On Monks.

There was in my monastery a certain monk, Justus by name, skilled in medicinal arts. . . . When he knew that his end was at hand, he made known to Copiosus, his brother in the flesh, how that he had three gold pieces hidden away. Copiosus, of course, could not conceal this from the brethren. He sought carefully, and examined all his brother's drugs, until he found the three gold pieces hidden away among the medicines. When he told me this great calamity that concerned a brother who had lived in common with us, I could hardly hear it with calmness. For the rule of this our monastery was always that the brothers should live in common and own nothing individually.

Then, stricken with great grief, I began to think what I could do to cleanse the dying man, and how I should make his sins a warning to the living brethren. Accordingly, having summoned Pretiosus, the superintendent of the monastery, I commanded him to see that none of the brothers visited the dying man, who was not to hear any words of consolation. If in the hour of death he asked for the brethren, then his own brother in the flesh was to tell him how he was hated by the brethren because he had concealed money; so that at death remorse for his guilt might pierce his heart and cleanse him from the sin he had committed.

When he was dead his body was not placed with the bodies of the brethren, but a grave was dug in the dung pit, and his body was flung down into it, and the three pieces of gold he had left were cast upon him, while all together cried, "Thy money perish with thee!". . .

When thirty days had passed after his death, my heart began to have compassion on my dead brother, and to ponder prayers with deep grief, and to seek what remedy there might be for him. Then I called before me Pretiosus, superintendent of the monastery, and said sadly: "It is a long time that our brother who died has been tormented by fire, and we ought to have charity toward him, and aid him so far as we can, that he may be delivered. Go, therefore, and for thirty successive days from this day offer sacrifices for him. See to it that no day is allowed to pass on which the salvation-bringing mass [hostia] is not offered up for his absolution."[1] He departed forthwith and obeyed my words.

We, however, were busy with other things, and did not count the days as they rolled by. But lo! the brother who had died appeared by night to a certain brother, even to Copiosus, his brother in the flesh. When Copiosus saw him he asked him, saying, "What is it, brother? How art thou?" To which he answered: "Up to this time I have been in torment; but now all is well with me, because today I have received the communion." This Copiosus straightway reported to the brethren in the monastery.

Then the brethren carefully reckoned the days, and it was the very day on which the thirtieth oblation was made for him. Copiosus did not know what the brethren were doing for his dead brother, and the brethren did not know that Copiosus had seen him; yet at one and the same time he learned what they had done and they learned what he had seen, and the vision and the sacrifice harmonized. So the fact was plainly shown forth how that the brother who had died had escaped punishment through the salvation-giving mass.

3. from the *Dialogues:*
On Holy Men and Demons(I)

Andrew, by God's mercy bishop of Fondi, was a man of most holy life, but the ancient enemy of mankind sought to tempt him, by causing him to think evil thoughts.

Now one day a certain Jew was coming to Rome from Campania, and he traveled by the Appian Way. When he reached the hill of Fondi he saw that the day was darkening toward evening, and he did not know at all where he might sleep. He was near a temple of Apollo, and he decided to stay there.

He feared the sacrilegious character of the place, so, though he had not the faith of the cross, he took care to protect himself with the sign of the cross. In the middle of the night he was disturbed by the very fear of solitude, and lay awake. Suddenly he looked up, and saw a crowd of evil spirits. He who was in authority over the rest took his place in the midst of them and began to discuss the deeds of each spirit, and to ask how much evil each one had accomplished.

One of the spirits told how he had caused Bishop Andrew to think an unholy thought. Then the evil spirit and enemy of the human race exhorted that spirit to carry out what he had begun in Andrew's soul.

Then the spirit who commanded the rest ordered his followers to find out who had presumed to sleep in that temple. But the Jew made the sign of the cross, and all the throng of evil spirits, crying out "Woe, woe!" disappeared.

4. from the *Dialogues:*
On Holy Men and Demons (II)

In Campania, upon Mt. Marsicus, a venerable man called Martin lived for many years the solitary life, shut up in a very small cave. Many of us knew him, and were witnesses of his deeds. I myself have heard much of him both from Pope Pelagius, my predecessor, and from other religious men who related anecdotes of him. His first miracle was this: hardly had he established himself in the cleft of the mountain, when from the very rock which was hollowed out to make his narrow cave burst forth a stream of water just sufficient to supply the daily need of the servant of God, and there was never too much or too little. . . .

But the ancient enemy of mankind envied the man's strength, and labored with his wonted skill to drive him forth from the cave. For he entered into the beast that is his friend—the serpent—and sought to make the monk afraid, and to drive him from his dwelling. He came at twilight, and stretched himself out before the holy man when he was praying, and lay down with him when he went to rest.

The holy man was entirely unafraid. He would hold to the serpent's mouth his hand or his foot, and say to him, "If thou hast leave to smite me, I do not say thee nay." After these things had taken place continually for three years, on a certain day the ancient enemy of mankind, vanquished by such great endurance, groaned; and the serpent let himself glide over the steep mountain side to a precipice. And the flame that went out from him burned all the trees in that place. Almighty God constrained him to burn the mountain side, and so compelled him to show forth the great virtue of the man from whom he had departed, conquered.

5. from the *Letters* and *Sermons:*
Eschatology

With all my heart I have wished to answer you better, but the burden of my pastoral calls so overpowers me that I would rather weep than speak,—as your reverence undoubtedly gathers from the very character of my correspondence when I am remiss in addressing one whom I warmly love. In fact, so beaten about am I

by the billows in this corner of the world, that I can in no wise bring
to harbor the ancient, rolling ship at whose helm I stand through
God's mysterious dispensation.

Now the waves break over us from the front, now at the side the
foaming mountains of the sea swell high, now in the rear the
tempest pursues us. Beset by all these perils, I am forced first to
steer directly in the face of the storm, again to swerve the vessel
and to receive obliquely the onset of the waters. I groan, because I
know that if I am negligent the bilge water of vice is deepening,
and that if the storm assails us furiously at that instant the decaying
planks forebode shipwreck. Fearful, I remember that I have lost
my quiet shore of peace, and sighing I gaze toward the land which,
while the wind of circumstances blows contrarily, I cannot gain.
So, dearest brother, if you love me, stretch forth the hand of prayer
to me amid these floods, and, as you aid me in my troubles, thus as a
reward shall you come forth more valiantly from yours. . . .

[Of all the signs described by our Lord as presaging the end of
the world], some we see already accomplished; the others we
dread as close upon us. For we now see that nation rises against
nation, and that they press and weigh upon the land in our own
times as never before in the annals of the past. Earthquakes
overwhelm countless cities, as we often hear from other parts of
the world. Pestilence we endure without interruption. It is true that
as yet we do not behold signs in the sun and moon and stars; but
that these are not far off we may infer from the changes in the
atmosphere. Before Italy was given over to be desolated by the
sword of a heathen foe, we beheld fiery ranks in heaven, and even
the streaming blood of the human race as it was afterwards spilt.

2
Bede

from *The Ecclesiastical History:*
The Vision of the Afterlife

At this time [Bede writes] a memorable miracle, and like to those of former days, was wrought in Britain; for, to the end that the living might be saved from the death of the soul, a certain person, who had been some time dead, rose again to life, and related many remarkable things he had seen; some of which I have thought fit here briefly to take notice of.

There was a master of a family in that district of the Northumbrians which is called Cunningham, who led a religious life, as did also all that belonged to him. This man fell sick, and his distemper daily increasing, being brought to extremity, he died in the beginning of the night; but in the morning early he suddenly came to life again, and sat up, upon which all those that sat about the body weeping fled away in a great fright: only his wife, who loved him best, though in a great consternation and trembling, remained with him. He, comforting her, said, "Fear not, for I am now truly risen from death, and permitted again to live among men; however, I am not to live hereafter as I was wont, but from henceforward after a very different manner."

Then rising immediately, he repaired to the oratory of the little town and, continuing in prayer till day, immediately divided all his substance into three parts, one whereof he gave to his wife, another to his children, and the third, belonging to himself, he instantly distributed among the poor. Not long after he repaired to the monastery of Melrose, which is almost inclosed by the winding of the river Tweed, and having been shaven, went into a private dwelling which the abbot had provided, where he continued till the day of his death in such extraordinary contrition of mind and body that, though his tongue had been silent, his life declared that he had seen many things, either to be dreaded or coveted, which others knew nothing of.

Thus he related what he had seen. "He that led me had a shining countenance and a bright garment, and we went on silently, as I thought, towards the northeast. Walking on, we came to a vale of great breadth and depth, but of infinite length; on the left it appeared full of dreadful flames; the other side was no less horrid for violent hail and cold snow flying in all directions; both places were full of men's souls, which seemed by turns to be tossed from one side to the other, as it were by a violent storm; for when the wretches could no longer endure the excess of heat, they leaped into the middle of the cutting cold; and finding no rest there, they leaped back again into the middle of the unquenchable flames.

"Now whereas an innumerable multitude of deformed spirits were thus alternately tormented far and near, as far as could be seen, without any intermission, I began to think that this perhaps might be hell, of whose intolerable flames I had often heard talk. My guide, who went before me, answered to my thought saying, 'Do not believe so, for this is not hell, as you imagine.'

"When he had conducted me, much frightened with that horrid spectacle, by degrees, to the farther end, on a sudden I saw the place begin to grow dusk and filled with darkness. When I came into it, the darkness, by degrees, grew so thick that I could see nothing besides it and the shape and garment of him that led me. As we went on through the shades of night, on a sudden there appeared before us frequent globes of black flames, rising, as it were, out of a great pit, and falling back again into the same.

"When I had been conducted thither, my leader suddenly vanished, and left me alone in the midst of darkness and this horrid vision, whilst those same globes of fire, without intermission, at one time flew up and at another fell back into the bottom of the abyss; and I observed that all the flames, as they ascended, were full of human souls, which, like sparks flying up with smoke, were sometimes thrown on high, and again, when the vapor of the fire ceased, dropped down into the depth below. Moreover, an insufferable stench came forth with the vapors, and filled all those dark places.

"Having stood there a long time in much dread, not knowing what to do, which way to turn, or what end I might expect, on a sudden I heard behind me the noise of a most hideous and wretched lamentation, and at the same time a loud laughing, as of a rude multitude insulting captured enemies. When that noise, growing plainer, came up to me, I observed a gang of evil spirits dragging the howling and lamenting souls of men into the midst of the darkness, whilst they themselves laughed and rejoiced.

"Among those men, as I could discern, there was one shorn like a clergyman, also a layman, and a woman. The evil spirits that dragged them went down into the midst of the burning pit; and as they went down deeper, I could no longer distinguish between the lamentation of the men and the laughing of the devils, yet I still had a confused sound in my ears.

"In the meantime some of the dark spirits ascended from that flaming abyss, and, running forward, beset me on all sides, and much perplexed me with their glaring eyes and the stifling fire which proceeded from their mouths and nostrils; and they threatened to lay hold on me with burning tongs, which they had in their hands; yet they durst not touch me, though they frightened me. Being thus on all sides inclosed with enemies and darkness, and looking about on every side for assistance, there appeared behind me, on the way that I came, as it were, the brightness of a star shining amidst the darkness, which increased by degrees, and came rapidly towards me: when it drew near, all those evil spirits that had sought to carry me away with their tongs dispersed and fled.

"He whose approach put them to flight was the same that had led me before; who, turning then towards the right, began to lead me, as it were, towards the southeast, and having soon brought me out of the darkness, conducted me into an atmosphere of clear light.

"While he thus led me in open light, I saw a vast wall before us, the length and height of which, in every direction, seemed to be altogether boundless. I began to wonder why we went up to the wall, seeing no door, window, or path through it. When we came to the wall, we were presently, I know not by what means, on the top of it, and within it was a vast and beautiful field, so full of fragrant flowers that the odor of its delightful sweetness immediately dispelled the stench of the dark furnace, which had penetrated me through and through.

"So great was the light in this place that it seemed to exceed the brightness of the day, or of the sun in its meridian height. In this field were innumerable assemblies of men in white and many companies seated together rejoicing. As he led me through the midst of these happy people, I began to think that this might, perhaps, be the kingdom of heaven, of which I had often heard so much. He answered to my thought, saying, 'This is not the kingdom of heaven, as you imagine.'

"When we had passed those mansions of blessed souls and gone farther on, I discovered before me a much more beautiful light, and heard therein sweet voices of persons singing; and so wonderful a fragrancy proceeded from the place that the other, which I had before thought most delicious, then seemed to me but very indifferent, even as that extraordinary brightness of the flowery field, compared with this, appeared mean and inconsiderable. When I began to hope we should enter that delightful place, my guide on a sudden stood still; and then, turning round, led me back by the way we came.

"When we returned to those joyful mansions of the souls in white, he said to me, 'Do you know what all these things are which you have seen?' I answered that I did not; and then he replied, 'That vale you saw, so dreadful for its consuming flames and cutting cold, is the place in which the souls of those are tried and punished who, delaying to confess and amend their crimes, at length have recourse to repentance at the point of death, and so depart this life; but nevertheless because they, even at their death, confessed and repented, they shall all be received into the kingdom of heaven at the day of judgment by the prayers, alms, and fasting of the living, and more especially by masses.

" 'That fiery and stinking pit which you saw is the mouth of hell, into which whosoever falls shall never be delivered to all eternity. This flowery place, in which you see these most beautiful young people, so bright and gay, is that into which the souls of those are received who depart the body in good works, but who are not so perfect as to deserve to be immediately admitted into the kingdom of heaven; yet they shall all, at the day of judgment, see Christ and

partake of the joys of His kingdom; for whoever are perfect in
thought, word, and deed, as soon as they depart the body immediately enter into the kingdom of heaven; in the neighborhood
whereof that place is, where you heard the sound of sweet singing,
with the fragrant odor and bright light.

" 'As for you, who are now to return to your body and live among
men again, if you will endeavor nicely to watch your actions, and
to direct your speech and behavior in righteousness and simplicity,
you shall, after death, have a place of residence among these joyful
troops of blessed souls; for when I left you for a while, it was to
know how you were to be disposed of.' When he had said this to
me I much abhorred returning to my body, being delighted with
the sweetness and beauty of the place I beheld and with the
company of those I saw in it. However, I durst not ask him any
questions; but in the meantime, on a sudden, I found myself alive
among men."

II
Monks

The following selections are reprinted from these sources: The
Rule of St. Benedict, *from* E. F. Henderson, Select Historical
Documents of the Middle Ages *(London, 1896), pp. 274–314, with
the first few paragraphs translated by the editor of this volume;
Paul the Deacon,* Poems in Honor of St. Benedict, *from William
Dudley Foulke, trans.* Paul the Deacon's History of the
Langobards *(Philadelphia, 1907), pp. 393–414; Jonas,* Life of St.
Columbanus, *from D. C. Munro,* Life of St. Columban, *University
of Pennsylvania Translations and Reprints from the
Sources of European History, Vol. II, no. 7 (Philadelphia, 1895);*
The Life of St. Gall, *from J. H. Robinson,* Readings in European
History, *Vol. I (Boston, 1904), pp. 90–91.*

The italicized passages in the Prologue and text of the Rule of St.
Benedict *indicate quotations from Scripture, woven into the
abbot's text. Benedict himself used several different versions of
Scripture, and since Henderson's translation omits many references, it seemed appropriate in the Prologue to give some sense
of the richness of scriptural allusions in Benedict's Rule. The
complex questions of language and style in this period may be
illuminated by consulting Erich Auerbach,* Mimesis *(Princeton,
1953), and his* Literary Language and Its Public in Late Latin
Antiquity and the Middle Ages *(New York, 1965). A good introduction to the Latin of the period is Karl Strecker,* Introduction to
Medieval Latin, *trans. and rev. by Robert B. Palmer (Berlin,
1963).*

On the study and use of Scripture, *see Beryl Smalley,* The Study
of the Bible in the Middle Ages *(rep. Notre Dame, 1964) and* The
Cambridge History of the Bible, *Vol. II, ed. G. W. H. Lampe
(Cambridge, 1969).*

3
The *Rule of St. Benedict*

The translation of the Prologue *is based on the text of* Cuthbert Butler, *Sancti Benedicti Regula Monachorum (Freiburg, 1912), pp. 1–8. Henderson's text is based on that in Migne, Patrologia Latina, Vol. 66. Italicized passages indicate quotations from Scripture.*

Prologue

Listen, my son, to the teachings of your master, and incline the ear of your heart; receive joyfully the warnings of your loving teacher and perform them usefully, so that you may return to him through the works of obedience, from whom you strayed through the vice of disobedience. I direct my teaching to you, who, by renouncing your own will and enrolling in the army of Christ the true King, assume the most powerful and brightest armor of obedience.

First, whatever good task you undertake, pray God most intensely to bring it to perfection, so that He who deigns to count us among the number of His children ought never to sorrow for any of our wicked acts. For He must always be served by His good things that He has given us, so that He will never, like an angry father, disinherit His children. Nor, like a fearsome master, angered by our evil deeds, deliver to perpetual punishment His wicked servants, who do not wish to follow Him into glory.

Let us rise up then, Scripture urging us, saying: *Now is the hour for us to rise out of sleep.* Let us open our eyes to the divine light, for we hear the divine voice daily imploring, which warns us saying: *Today, if you should hear His voice, harden not your hearts,* and further: *Let him who has ears to hear, hear what the*

Spirit says unto the churches. And what does the Spirit say? *Come, O my son, listen to me; I will teach thee the fear of God. Run, while you still have the light of life, lest the shadow of death overtake you unawares.*

And God, seeking His workman in the midst of the people, cries out to him saying: *Which of you is the man who desires life and wishes to witness good days?* And you, if you hear Him and respond "I am he," then God says to you: *If you wish to have true and perpetual life, forbid thy tongue from wickedness, keep your lips from speaking lies. Turn away from evil and do good. Seek after peace and follow it.* And when you shall have done these things, My eyes shall be upon you and My ears will listen to your prayers. And even before you invoke Me, I say to you: Behold, I am here. What can be sweeter to us than the voice of God inviting us? Behold, in His love the Lord shows us the way of life.

Our loins, therefore, are bound up by faith and the observance of good works; let us walk in His path by the guide of the Gospel, so that we may merit the vision of Him who calls us into His kingdom. If we wish to live in the tabernacle of His kingdom, we shall not, save by our good acts alone. Let us ask the Lord, with the prophet saying: *Lord, who shall dwell in Thy house, and who shall rest in Thy holy Mountain?* After this question, let us hear God responding and showing us the way to His tabernacle, saying: *He only who walks without a stain and does justice; who speaks only the truth in his heart; who does not speak in lies; who does no injury to his neighbor; who shares no reproach against his neighbor.* Whoever has denied the malign demon, spewing him forth from his heart with all his wicked counsels and has taken his wicked thoughts while they were still new and cast them before Christ, he and others like him, fearing God, not taking excessive pride in their good works, knowing that the good in them is not of their own creation but from God, praise God who works in them saying: *Not to us O Lord, not to us, but to Thine own name give the glory.* Thus the Apostle Paul imputed nothing of his preaching to himself saying: *Thanks be to God that I am what I am,* and *Let whoever rejoices rejoice in the Lord.*

And as the Lord says in the Gospel: *Whoever hears these words of Mine and does what they direct, I will make him like the wise man who builds his house upon a rock, and when the rivers flooded and the winds blew and the rains pounded against it, it did not fall, because it was built upon a rock.* The Lord, having given us these assurances, awaits us daily to respond by our deeds to His holy commands. Therefore the days of our life are extended because it is necessary that we change our evil ways. As the Apostle says: *Do you not know that God's kind waiting invites you to repent?* For the merciful God says *I wish not the death of the sinner, but that he should turn again to Me and that he should live.*

Since we have asked the Lord about those who shall dwell in His tabernacle, we have heard His instructions for those who will dwell there. Let us fulfill the duties of such citizens! Therefore our hearts and our bodies must be trained and drilled under the holy precepts of obedience, and whatever shortcomings we have by nature, let us ask God out of His grace to complement by His aid. And if, fleeing the punishments of Gehenna, we wish to reach eternal life while there is yet time remaining, while we are still in the flesh, and while there remains yet light along the way to fulfill these instructions, we must all hasten and act now in such a way that we may win eternity. We are about to found, therefore, a school for the Lord's service; in the organization of which we trust that we shall ordain nothing severe and nothing burdensome. But even if, the demands of justice dictating it, something a little irksome shall be the result, for the purpose of amending vices or preserving charity;—thou shalt not therefore, struck by fear, flee the way of salvation, which can not be entered upon except through a narrow entrance. But as one's way of life and one's faith progress, the heart becomes broadened, and, with the unutterable sweetness of love, the way of the mandates of the Lord is traversed. Thus, never departing from His guidance, continuing in the monastery in His teaching until death, through patience we are made partakers in Christ's passion, in order that we may merit to be companions in His kingdom.

1. *Concerning the kinds of monks and their manner of living.* It is manifest that there are four kinds of monks. The cenobites are the first kind; that is, those living in a monastery, serving under a rule or an abbot. Then the second kind is that of the anchorites; that is, the hermits,— those who, not by the new fervour of a conversion

but by the long probation of life in a monastery, have learned to fight against the devil, having already been taught by the solace of many. They, having been well prepared in the army of brothers for the solitary fight of the hermit, being secure now without the consolation of another, are able, God helping them, to fight with their own hand or arm against the vices of the flesh or of their thoughts.

But a third very bad kind of monks are the sarabaites, approved by no rule, experience being their teacher, as with the gold which is tried in the furnace. But, softened after the manner of lead, keeping faith with the world by their works, they are known through their tonsure to lie to God. These being shut up by twos or threes, or, indeed, alone, without a shepherd, not in the Lord's but in their own sheep-folds,—their law is the satisfaction of their desires. For whatever they think good or choice, this they call holy; and what they do not wish, this they consider unlawful. But the fourth kind of monks is the kind which is called gyratory. During their whole life they are guests, for three or four days at a time, in the cells of the different monasteries, throughout the various provinces; always wandering and never stationary, given over to the service of their own pleasures and the joys of the palate, and in every way worse than the sarabaites. Concerning the most wretched way of living of all of such monks it is better to be silent than to speak. These things therefore being omitted, let us proceed, with the aid of God, to treat of the best kind, the cenobites.

2. *What the Abbot should be like.* An abbot who is worthy to preside over a monastery ought always to remember what he is called, and carry out with his deeds the name of a Superior. For he is believed to be Christ's representative, since he is called by His name, the apostle saying: *Ye have received the spirit of adoption of sons, whereby we call Abba, Father.* And so the abbot should not—grant that he may not—teach, or decree, or order, any thing apart from the precept of the Lord; but his order or teaching should be sprinkled with the ferment of divine justice in the minds of his disciples. Let the abbot always be mindful that, at the tremendous judgment of God, both things will be weighed in the balance: his teaching and the obedience of his disciples. And let the abbot know that whatever the father of the

family finds of less utility among the sheep is laid to the fault of
the shepherd. Only in a case where the whole diligence of their
pastor shall have been bestowed on an unruly and disobedient
flock, and his whole care given to their morbid actions, shall that
pastor, absolved in the judgment of the Lord, be free to say to the
Lord with the prophet: *I have not hid Thy righteousness within
my heart, I have declared Thy faithfulness and Thy salvation, but
they despising have scorned me.* And then at length let the
punishment for the disobedient sheep under his care be death
itself prevailing against them. Therefore, when any one receives
the name of abbot, he ought to rule over his disciples with a
double teaching; that is, let him show forth all good and holy
things by deeds more than by words. So that to ready disciples he
may propound the mandates of God in words; but, to the hard-
hearted and the more simple-minded, he may show forth the
divine precepts by his deeds. But as to all the things that he has
taught to his disciples to be wrong, he shall show by his deeds that
they are not to be done; lest, preaching to others, he himself shall
be found worthy of blame, and lest God may say at some time to
him a sinner: *What hast thou to do to declare My statutes or that
thou should'st take My covenant in thy mouth. Seeing that thou
hatest instruction and casteth My words behind thee; and why
beholdest thou the mote that is in thy brother's eye, but
considerest not the beam that is in thine own eye?* He shall make
no distinction of persons in the monastery. One shall not be more
cherished than another, unless it be the one whom he finds
excelling in good works or in obedience. A free-born man shall
not be preferred to one coming from servitude, unless there be
some other reasonable cause. But if, justice demanding that it
should be thus, it seems good to the abbot, he shall do this no
matter what the rank shall be. But otherwise they shall keep their
own places; for whether we be bond or free we are all one in
Christ; and, under one God, we perform an equal service of
subjection; for God is no respecter of persons. Only in this way is
a distinction made by Him concerning us: if we are found humble
and surpassing others in good works. Therefore let him (the
abbot) have equal charity for all: let the same discipline be
administered in all cases according to merit. In his teaching

indeed the abbot ought always to observe that form laid down by the apostle when he says: *reprove, rebuke, exhort.* That is, mixing seasons with seasons, blandishments with terrors, let him display the feeling of a severe yet devoted master. He should, namely, rebuke more severely the unruly and the turbulent. The obedient, moreover, and the gentle and the patient, he should exhort, that they may progress to higher things. But the negligent and scorners, we warn him to admonish and reprove. Nor let him conceal the sins of the erring: but, in order that he may prevail, let him pluck them out by the roots as soon as they begin to spring up; being mindful of the danger of Eli the priest of Shiloh. And the more honest and intelligent minds, indeed, let him rebuke with words, with a first or second admonition; but the wicked and the hard-hearted and the proud, or the disobedient, let him restrain at the very beginning of their sin by castigation of the body, as it were, with whips: knowing that it is written: *A fool is not bettered by words.* And again: *Strike thy son with the rod and thou shalt deliver his soul from death.* The abbot ought always to remember what he is, to remember what he is called, and to know that from him to whom more is commmitted, the more is demanded. And let him know what a difficult and arduous thing he has undertaken,—to rule the souls and aid the morals of many. And in one case indeed with blandishments, in another with rebukes, in another with persuasion—according to the quality or intelligence of each one,—he shall so conform and adapt himself to all, that not only shall he not suffer detriment to come to the flock committed to him, but shall rejoice in the increase of a good flock. Above all things, let him not, dissimulating or undervaluing the safety of the souls committed to him, give more heed to transitory and earthly and passing things: but let him always reflect that he has undertaken to rule souls for which he is to render account. And, lest perchance he enter into strife for a lesser matter, let him remember that it is written: *Seek ye first the kingdom of God and His righteousness; and all these things shall be added unto you.* And again: *They that fear Him shall lack nothing.* And let him know that he who undertakes to rule souls must prepare to render account. And, whatever number of brothers he knows that he has under his care, let him know for certain that at the day of judgment he shall render account to God for all their souls; his own soul without doubt being included. And thus, always fearing the future interrogation of the shepherd concerning the flocks entrusted to him, while keeping free from foreign interests he is rendered careful for his own. And when, by his admonitions, he administers correction to others, he is himself cleansed from his vices.

3. *About calling in the brethren to take council.* As often as anything especial is to be done in the monastery, the abbot shall call together the whole congregation, and shall himself explain the question at issue. And, having heard the advice of the brethren, he shall think it over by himself, and shall do what he considers most advantageous. And for this reason, moreover, we have said that all ought to be called to take counsel: because often it is to a younger person that God reveals what is best. The brethren, moreover, with all subjection of humility, ought so to give their advice, that they do not presume boldly to defend what seems good to them; but it should rather depend on the judgment of the abbot; so that whatever he decides to be the more salutary, they should all agree to it. But even as it behoves the disciples to obey the master, so it is fitting that he should providently and justly arrange all matters. In all things, indeed, let all follow the Rule as their guide; and let no one rashly deviate from it. Let no one in the monastery follow the inclination of his own heart; and let no one boldly presume to dispute with his abbot, within or without the monastery. But, if he should so presume, let him be subject to the discipline of the Rule. The abbot, on the other hand, shall do all things fearing the Lord and observing the Rule; knowing that he, without a doubt, shall have to render account to God as to a most impartial judge, for all his decisions. But if any lesser matters for the good of the monastery are to be decided upon, he shall employ the counsel of the elder members alone, since it is written: *Do all things with counsel, and after it is done thou wilt not repent.*

4. *What are the instruments of good works.* °

5. *Concerning obedience.* The first grade of humility is obedience without delay. This becomes those who, on account of

° Here follow seventy-two quotations from the Bible.

the holy service which they have professed, or on account of the
fear of hell or the glory of eternal life consider nothing dearer to
them than Christ: so that, so soon as anything is commanded by
their superior, they may not know how to suffer delay in doing it,
even as if it were a divine command. Concerning whom the Lord
said: *As soon as he heard of Me he obeyed Me.* And again He said
to the learned men: *He who heareth you heareth Me.* Therefore
let all such, straightway leaving their own affairs and giving up
their own will, with unoccupied hands and leaving incomplete
what they were doing—the foot of obedience being foremost,—
follow with their deeds the voice of him who orders. And, as it
were, in the same moment, let the aforesaid command of the
master and the perfected work of the disciple—both together in
the swiftness of the fear of God,—be called into being by those
who are possessed with a desire of advancing to eternal life. And
therefore let them seize the narrow way of which the Lord says:
Narrow is the way which leadeth unto life. Thus, not living
according to their own judgment nor obeying their own desires
and pleasures, but walking under another's judgment and
command, passing their time in monasteries, let them desire an
abbot to rule over them. Without doubt all such live up to that
precept of the Lord in which He says: *I am not come to do My
own will but the will of Him that sent Me. . . .*

6. *Concerning silence.* Let us do as the prophet says: *I said, I
will take heed to my ways that I sin not with my tongue, I have
kept my mouth with a bridle: I was dumb with silence, I held my
peace even from good; and my sorrow was stirred.* Here the
prophet shows that if one ought at times, for the sake of silence, to
refrain from good sayings; how much more, as a punishment for
sin, ought one to cease from evil words. . . . And therefore, if
anything is to be asked of the prior, let it be asked with all
humility and subjection of reverence; lest one seem to speak more
than is fitting. Scurrilities, however, or idle words and those
exciting laughter, we condemn in all places with a lasting
prohibition: nor do we permit a disciple to open his mouth for
such sayings.

7. *Concerning humility. . . .* The sixth grade of humility is, that
a monk be contented with all lowliness or extremity, and

consider himself, with regard to everything which is enjoined on him, as a poor and unworthy workman; saying to himself with the prophet: *I was reduced to nothing and was ignorant; I was made as the cattle before Thee, and I am always with Thee.* The seventh grade of humility is, not only that he, with his tongue, pronounce himself viler and more worthless than all; but that he also believe it in the innermost workings of his heart; humbling himself and saying with the prophet, etc. . . . The eighth degree of humility is that a monk do nothing except what the common rule of the monastery, or the example of his elders, urges him to do. The ninth degree of humility is that a monk restrain his tongue from speaking; and, keeping silence, do not speak until he is spoken to. The tenth grade of humility is that he be not ready, and easily inclined, to laugh. . . . The eleventh grade of humility is that a monk, when he speaks, speak slowly and without laughter, humbly with gravity, using few and reasonable words; and that he be not loud of voice. . . . The twelfth grade of humility is that a monk, shall not only with his heart but also with his body, always show humility to all who see him: that is, when at work, in the oratory, in the monastery, in the garden, on the road, in the fields. And everywhere, sitting or walking or standing, let him always be with head inclined, his looks fixed upon the ground; remembering every hour that he is guilty of his sins. Let him think that he is already being presented before the tremendous judgment of God, saying always to himself in his heart what that publican of the gospel, fixing his eyes on the earth, said: *Lord I am not worthy, I a sinner, so much as to lift up mine eyes unto Heaven.*

8. *Concerning the divine offices at night.* In the winter time, that is from the Calends of November until Easter, according to what is reasonable, they must rise at the eighth hour of the night, so that they rest a little more than half the night, and rise when they have already digested. But let the time that remains after vigils be kept for meditation by those brothers who are in any way behind hand with the psalter or lessons. From Easter, moreover, until the aforesaid Calends of November, let the hour of keeping vigils be so arranged that, a short interval being observed in which the brethren may go out for the necessities of nature, the matins, which are always to take place with the dawning light, may straightway follow.

9. *How many psalms are to be said at night.* In the winter first of all the verse shall be said: *Make haste oh God to deliver me; make haste to help me oh God.* Then, secondly, there shall be said three times: *Oh Lord open Thou my lips and my mouth shall show forth Thy praise.* To which is to be subjoined the third psalm and the *Gloria.* After this the ninety-fourth psalm is to be sung antiphonally or in unison. The Ambrosian chant shall then follow: then six psalms antiphonally. These having been said, the abbot shall, with the verse mentioned, give the blessing. And all being seated upon the benches, there shall be read in turn from the Scriptures—following out the analogy—three lessons; between which also three responses shall be sung. Two responses shall be said without the *Gloria;* but, after the third lesson, he who chants shall say the *Gloria.* And, when the Cantor begins to say this, all shall straightway rise from their seats out of honour and reverence for the holy Trinity. Books, moreover, of the Old as well as the New Testament of Divine authority shall be read at the Vigils; but also expositions of them which have been made by the most celebrated orthodox teachers and catholic Fathers. Moreover, after these three lessons with their responses, shall follow other six psalms to be sung with the Alleluia. After this a lesson of the Apostle shall follow, to be recited by heart; and verses and the supplication of the Litany, that is the *Kyrie eleison:* and thus shall end the nocturnal vigils.

10. *How in summer the nocturnal praise shall be carried on.* From Easter moreover until the Calends of November, the whole quantity of psalmody, as has been said above, shall be observed: except that the lessons from the Scripture, on account of the shortness of the nights, shall not be read at all. But in place of those three lessons, one from the Old Testament shall be said by memory, and a short response shall follow it. And everything else shall be carried out as has been said; that is, so that never less than the number of twelve psalms shall be said at nocturnal vigils; excepting the third and ninety-fourth psalms.

11. *How vigils shall be conducted on Sundays.* On Sundays they shall rise earlier for vigils. In which vigils let the following measure be observed; that is, after six psalms and a verse having been sung—as we arranged above,—all sitting down in their

places and in order upon the benches, there shall be read from Scripture, as we said above, four lessons with their responses. Only in the fourth response, however, shall the *Gloria* be said by the Cantor. When he begins this, straightway all shall rise with reverence. After which lessons shall follow other six psalms in order, antiphonally, like the former ones; and verses. After which, there shall again be read other four lessons with their responses, in the same order as above. After which there shall be said three canticles, which the abbot shall have chosen from the prophets: which canticles shall be sung with the Alleluia. Then after the verse has been said and the abbot has given his benediction, there shall be read other four lessons from the New Testament, in the same order as above. After the fourth response, moreover, the abbot shall begin the hymn: *We praise Thee O Lord.* This being finished the abbot shall read a lesson from the Gospel with honour and trembling, all standing. This being read through, all shall answer "Amen." And the abbot shall straightway cause the hymn: *It is a good thing to praise the Lord* to follow; and, the benediction being given, they shall begin matins. This order of vigils at all times of summer as well as winter shall be similarly observed on Sunday: unless by chance (may it not happen) they rise too late, and something from the lessons or responses must be shortened: as to which they must take the greatest care lest it occur. But if it happen, he through whose neglect it came about shall give proper satisfaction for it to God in the oratory°. . . .

16. *How Divine Service shall be held through the day.* As the prophet says: *Seven times in the day do I praise Thee.* Which sacred number of seven will thus be fulfilled by us if, at matins, at the first, third, sixth, ninth hours, at vesper time and at "completorium" we perform the duties of our service; for it is of these hours of the day that he said: *Seven times in the day do I praise Thee.* For, concerning nocturnal vigils, the same prophet says: *At midnight I arose to confess unto Thee.* Therefore, at these times, let us give thanks to our Creator concerning the judgments of His righteousness; that is, at matins, etc . . . , and at night we will rise and confess to Him.°. . .

°Long lists of psalms follow.

18. *In what order the psalms are to be said.* The order of the daily psalmody having been arranged, all the rest of the psalms that remain shall be equally divided among the vigils of the seven nights, separating, indeed, the psalms that are the longest among them; and twelve shall be appointed for each night. Laying great stress upon this fact, however, that if this distribution of psalms be not pleasing to any one, he shall arrange it otherwise if he think best; provided he sees to it under all circumstances that every week the entire psalter, to the number of 150 psalms, is said. And on Sunday at Vigils it shall always be begun anew. For those monks show a too scanty proof of their devotion, who, during the course of a week, sing less than the Psalter with its customary canticles: inasmuch as we read that our holy Fathers in one day rigidly fulfilled that, which would that we—lukewarm as we are—might perform in an entire week.

19. *Concerning the art of singing.* Whereas we believe that there is a divine presence, and that the eyes of the Lord look down everywhere upon the good and the evil: chiefly then, without any doubt, we may believe that this is the case when we are assisting at divine service. Therefore let us always be mindful of what the prophet says: *Serve the Lord in all fear;* and again, *Sing wisely;* and, *in the sight of the angels I will sing unto Thee.* Therefore let us consider how we ought to conduct ourselves before the face of the Divinity and His angels, and let us so stand and sing that our voice may accord with our intention.

20. *Concerning reverence for prayer.* If when to powerful men we wish to suggest anything, we do not presume to do it unless with reverence and humility: how much more should we supplicate with all humility, and devotion of purity, God who is the Lord of all. And let us know that we are heard, not for much speaking, but for purity of heart and compunction of tears. And, therefore, prayer ought to be brief and pure; unless perchance it be prolonged by the influence of the inspiration of the divine grace. When assembled together, then, let the prayer be altogether brief; and, the sign being given by the prior, let all rise together.

21. *Concerning the deans of the monastery.* If the congregation be a larger one, let there be elected from it brothers of good

standing and of holy character; and let them be made deans. And they shall be watchful over their decanates in all things, according to the mandates of God and the precepts of their abbot. And the deans elected shall be such that the abbot may safely share his burdens with them. And they shall not be elected according to order, but according to their merit of life and their advancement in wisdom. And, if any one of these deans be found perchance to be blameworthy, being puffed up by pride of something; and if, being warned once and again and a third time, he be unwilling to better himself,—let him be deposed; and let another, who is worthy, be chosen in his place. And we decree the like concerning the provost.

22. *How the monks shall sleep.* They shall sleep separately in separate beds. They shall receive positions for their beds, after the manner of their characters, according to the dispensation of their abbot. If it can be done, they shall all sleep in one place. If, however, their number do not permit it, they shall rest by tens or twenties, with elders who will concern themselves about them. A candle shall always be burning in that same cell until early in the morning. They shall sleep clothed, and girt with belts or with ropes; and they shall not have their knives at their sides while they sleep, lest perchance in a dream they should wound the sleepers. And let the monks be always on the alert; and, when the signal is given, rising without delay, let them hasten to mutually prepare themselves for the service of God—with all gravity and modesty, however. The younger brothers shall not have beds by themselves, but interspersed among those of the elder ones. And when they rise for the service of God, they shall exhort each other mutually with moderation, on account of the excuses that those who are sleepy are inclined to make.

23. *Concerning excommunication for faults.* If any one is found to be a scorner—being contumacious or disobedient, or a murmurer, or one acting in any way contrary to the holy Rule, and to the precepts of his elders: let such a one, according to the teaching of our Lord, be admonished once, and a second time, secretly, by his elders. If he do not amend his ways, he shall be rebuked publicly in the presence of all. But if, even then, he do not better himself—if he understands how great the penalty is—he shall be

subject to excommunication. But, if he is a wicked man, he shall be given over to corporal punishment.

24. *What ought to be the measure of the excommunication.* According to the amount of the fault the measure of the excommunication or of the discipline ought to be extended: which amount of the faults shall be determined by the judgment of the abbot. If any brother, however, be taken in lighter faults, he shall be prevented from participating at table. With regard to one deprived of participation at table, moreover, this shall be the regulation: that he shall not start a psalm or a chant in the oratory, or recite a lesson, until he has atoned. The refreshment of food, moreover, he shall take alone, after the refreshment of the brothers. So that if, for example, the brothers eat at the sixth hour, that brother shall do so at the ninth; if the brothers at the ninth, then he at Vespers; until by suitable satisfaction he gains pardon.

25. *Concerning graver faults.* That brother, moreover, who is held guilty of a graver fault shall be suspended at the same time from table and from the oratory. None of the brothers may in any way consort with him, or have speech with him. He shall be alone at the labour enjoined upon him, persisting in the struggle of penitence; knowing that terrible sentence of the Apostle who said that such a man was given over to the destruction of the flesh in order that his soul might be saved at the day of the Lord. The refection of food moreover he shall take alone, in the measure and at the time that the abbot shall appoint as suitable for him. Nor shall he be blessed by any one who passes by, nor shall any food be given him.

26. *Concerning those who, without being ordered by the abbot, associate with the excommunicated.* If any brother presume, without an order of the abbot, in any way to associate with an excommunicated brother, or to speak with him, or to give an order to him: he shall suffer the same penalty of excommunication.

27. *What care the abbot should exercise with regard to the excommunicated.* With all solicitude the abbot shall exercise care with regard to delinquent brothers: *They that be whole need not a physician, but they that are sick.* And therefore he ought to use every means, as a wise physician, to send in as it were secret

consolers—that is, wise elder brothers who, as it were secretly, shall console the wavering brother and lead him to the atonement of humility. And they shall comfort him lest he be swallowed up by overmuch sorrow. On the contrary, as the same apostle says, charity shall be confirmed in him, and he shall be prayed for by all. For the abbot should greatly exert his solicitude, and take care with all sagacity and industry, lest he lose any of the sheep entrusted to him. For he should know that he has undertaken the care of weak souls, not the tyranny over sound ones. And he shall fear the threat of the prophet through whom the Lord says: *Ye did take that which ye saw to be strong, and that which was weak ye did cast out.* And let him imitate the pious example of the good Shepherd, who, leaving the ninety and nine sheep upon the mountains, went out to seek the one sheep that had gone astray: and He had such compassion upon its infirmity, that He deigned to place it upon His sacred shoulders, and thus to carry it back to the flock.

28. *Concerning those who, being often rebuked, do not amend.* If any brother, having frequently been rebuked for any fault, do not amend even after he has been excommunicated, a more severe rebuke shall fall upon him;—that is, the punishment of the lash shall be inflicted upon him. But if he do not even then amend; or, if perchance—which God forbid,—swelled with pride he try even to defend his works: then the abbot shall act as a wise physician. If he have applied the fomentations, the ointments of exhortation, the medicaments of the Divine Scriptures; if he have proceeded to the last blasting of excommunication, or to blows with rods, and if he see that his efforts avail nothing: let him also— what is greater—call in the prayer of himself and all the brothers for him: that God who can do all things may work a cure upon an infirm brother. But if he be not healed even in this way, then at last the abbot may use the pruning knife, as the apostle says: *Remove evil from you,* etc.: lest one diseased sheep contaminate the whole flock.

29. *Whether brothers who leave the monastery ought again to be received.* A brother who goes out, or is cast out, of the monastery for his own fault, if he wish to return, shall first promise every amends for the fault on account of which he

departed; and thus he shall be received into the lowest degree—
so that thereby his humility may be proved. But if he again
depart, up to the third time he shall be received. Knowing that
after this every opportunity of return is denied to him.

30. *Concerning boys under age, how they shall be corrected.*
Every age or intelligence ought to have its proper bounds.
Therefore as often as boys or youths, or those who are less able
to understand how great is the punishment of excommunication:
as often as such persons offend, they shall either be afflicted with
excessive fasts, or coerced with severe blows, that they may be
healed.

31. *Concerning the cellarer of the monastery, what sort of a
person he shall be.* As cellarer of the monastery there shall be
elected from the congregation one who is wise, mature in
character, sober, not given to much eating, not proud, not
turbulent, not an upbraider, not tardy, not prodigal, but fearing
God: a father, as it were, to the whole congregation. He shall take
care of every thing, he shall do nothing without the order of the
abbot. He shall have charge of what things are ordered: he shall
not rebuff the brethren. If any brother by chance demand
anything unreasonably from him, he shall not, by spurning, rebuff
him; but reasonably, with humility, shall deny to him who
wrongly seeks.

Let him guard his soul, mindful always of that saying of the
apostle, that he who ministers well purchases to himself a good
degree. He shall care with all solicitude for the infirm and
youthful, for guests and for the poor; knowing without doubt that
he shall render account for all of these at the day of judgment. All
the utensils of the monastery, and all its substance, he shall look
upon as though they were the sacred vessels of the altar. He shall
deem nothing worthy of neglect; nor shall he give way to avarice;
nor shall he be prodigal or a squanderer of the substance of the
monastery; but he shall do everything with moderation and
according to the order of the abbot. He shall have humility above
all things: and when there is nothing substantial for him to give,
let a good word of reply be offered, as it is written: *a good word is
above the best gift.* Every thing which the abbot orders him to
have, let him have under his care; what he prohibits let him

refrain from. To the brethren he shall offer the fixed measure of food without any haughtiness or delay, in order that they be not offended; being mindful of the divine saying as to what he merits *who offends one of these little ones.* If the congregation is rather large, assistants shall be given him; by whose aid he himself, with a calm mind, shall fill the office committed to him. At suitable hours those things shall be given which are to be given, and those things shall be asked for which are to be asked for: so that no one may be disturbed or rebuffed in the house of God.

32. *Concerning the utensils or property of the monastery.* For the belongings of the monastery in utensils, or garments, or property of any kind, the abbot shall provide brothers of whose life and morals he is sure; and to them as he shall see fit he shall consign the different things to be taken care of and collected. Concerning which the abbot shall keep a list, so that when in turn the brothers succeed each other in the care of the things assigned, he may know what he gives or what he receives. If moreover any one have soiled or treated negligently the property of the monastery, he shall be rebuked; but if he do not amend, he shall be subjected to the discipline of the Rule.

33. *Whether the monks should have any thing of their own.* More than any thing else is this special vice to be cut off root and branch from the monastery, that one should presume to give or receive anything without the order of the abbot, or should have anything of his own. He should have absolutely not anything: neither a book, nor tablets, nor a pen—nothing at all.—For indeed it is not allowed to the monks to have their own bodies or wills in their own power. But all things necessary they must expect from the Father of the monastery; nor is it allowable to have anything which the abbot did not give or permit. All things shall be common to all, as it is written: *Let not any man presume or call anything his own.* But if any one shall have been discovered delighting in this most evil vice: being warned once and again, if he do not amend, let him be subjected to punishment.

34. *Whether all ought to receive necessaries equally.* As it is written: *It was divided among them singly, according as each had need:* whereby we do not say—far from it—that there should be an excepting of persons, but a consideration for infirmities.

Wherefore he who needs less, let him thank God and not be dismayed; but he who needs more, let him be humiliated on account of his infirmity, and not exalted on account of the mercy that is shown him. And thus all members will be in peace. Above all, let not the evil of murmuring appear, for any cause, through any word or sign whatever. But, if such a murmurer is discovered, he shall be subjected to stricter discipline.

35. *Concerning the weekly officers of the kitchen.* The brothers shall so serve each other in turn that no one shall be excused from the duty of cooking, unless either through sickness, or because he is occupied in some important work of utility. For, by this means, charity and a greater reward are acquired. Moreover assistants shall be provided for the weak, so that they may not do this as a burden, but may all have helpers according to the size of the congregation or the nature of the place. If the congregation is a large one the cellarer, or any who, as we have said, are occupied with matters of greater utility, shall be excused from cooking. The rest shall serve each other in turn with all charity. At the end of the week he (the weekly cook) shall, on Saturday, do the cleansing. He shall wash the towels with which the brothers wipe their hands or feet. Moreover as well he who enters into as well as he who goes out (of office) shall wash the feet of every body. He shall give back the vessels of his ministry clean and whole to the cellarer. And he, the cellarer, shall consign them thus to the one entering (into office), so that he shall know what he gives or what he receives. The weekly cooks moreover, one hour before the hour of refection, shall receive the measure of food previously fixed upon: the different drinking vessels, namely, and the bread; so that at the hour of refection, without murmuring and without heavy labour, they may serve their brothers. On solemn days moreover they shall fast until mass. The incoming and the outgoing weekly officers, moreover, shall, in the oratory, as soon as matins are finished on Sunday, prostrate themselves at the feet of all, begging to be prayed for. Furthermore he who has finished his week shall say this verse: *Blessed art Thou oh Lord God, who hast aided and consoled me.* This being said for the third time, he who retires shall receive the benediction. He who is entering shall follow and shall say: *O God come to my aid, O Lord hasten to*

help me. And this shall be repeated three times by all. And, receiving the benediction, he shall enter (upon his office).

36. *Concerning infirm brothers.* Before all, and above all, attention shall be paid to the care of the sick; so that they shall be served as if it were actually Christ. For He Himself said: *I was sick and ye visited Me.* And: *Inasmuch as ye have done it unto one of the least of these ye have done it unto Me.* But let the sick also consider that they are being served to the honour of God; and let them not offend by their abundance the brothers who serve them: which (offences) nevertheless are patiently to be borne, for, from such, a greater reward is acquired. Wherefore, let the abbot take the greatest care lest they suffer neglect. And for these infirm brothers a cell by itself shall be set apart, and a servitor, God-fearing, and diligent and careful. The use of baths shall be offered to the sick as often as it is necessary: to the healthy, and especially to youths, it shall not be so readily conceded. But also the eating of flesh shall be allowed to the sick, and altogether to the feeble, for their rehabilitation. But when they have grown better, they shall all, in the usual manner, abstain from flesh. The abbot, moreover, shall take the greatest care lest the sick are neglected by the cellarer or by the servitors: for whatever fault is committed by the disciples rebounds upon him.

37.

Although human nature itself is prone to have pity for these ages—that is, old age and infancy,—nevertheless the authority of the Rule also has regard for them. Their weakness shall always be considered, and in the matter of food, the strict tenor of the Rule shall by no means be observed, as far as they are concerned; but they shall be treated with pious consideration, and may anticipate the canonical hours.

38. *Concerning the weekly reader.* At the tables of the brothers when they eat the reading should not fail; nor may any one at random dare to take up the book and begin to read there; but he who is about to read for the whole week shall begin his duties on Sunday. And, entering upon his office after mass and communion, he shall ask all to pray for him, that God may avert from him the

spirit of elation. And this verse shall be said in the oratory three times by all, he however beginning it: "O Lord open Thou my lips and my mouth shall show forth Thy praise." And thus, having received the benediction, he shall enter upon his duties as reader. And there shall be the greatest silence at table, so that the muttering or the voice of no one shall be heard there, except that of the reader alone. But whatever things are necessary to those eating and drinking, the brothers shall so furnish them to each other in turn, that no one shall need to ask for anything. But if, nevertheless, something is wanted, it shall rather be sought by the employment of some sign than by the voice. Nor shall any one presume there to ask questions concerning the reading or anything else; nor shall an opportunity be given: unless perhaps the prior wishes to say something, briefly, for the purpose of edifying. Moreover the brother who reads for the week shall receive bread and wine before he begins to read, on account of the holy communion, and lest, perchance, it might be injurious for him to sustain a fast. Afterwards, moreover, he shall eat with the weekly cooks and the servitors. The brothers, moreover, shall read or sing not in rotation; but the ones shall do so who will edify their hearers.

39.

We believe, moreover, that, for the daily refection of the sixth as well as of the ninth hour, two cooked dishes, on account of the infirmities of the different ones, are enough for all tables: so that whoever, perchance, can not eat of one may partake of the other. Therefore let two cooked dishes suffice for all the brothers: and, if it is possible to obtain apples or growing vegetables, a third may be added. One full pound of bread shall suffice for a day, whether there be one refection, or a breakfast and a supper. But if they are going to have supper, the third part of that same pound shall be reserved by the cellarer, to be given back to those who are about to sup. But if, perchance, some greater labour shall have been performed, it shall be in the will and the power of the abbot, if it is expedient, to increase anything; surfeiting above all things being guarded against, so that indigestion may never seize a monk: for nothing is so contrary to every Christian as surfeiting, as our Lord says: *Take heed to yourselves, lest your hearts be overcharged with surfeiting.* But to younger boys the same quantity shall not be served, but less than that to the older ones; moderation being observed in all things. But the eating of the flesh of quadrupeds shall be abstained from altogether by every one, excepting alone the weak and the sick.

40. *Concerning the amount of drink.* Each one has his own gift from God, the one in this way, the other in that. Therefore it is with some hesitation that the amount of daily sustenance for others is fixed by us. Nevertheless, in view of the weakness of the infirm we believe that a hemina* of wine a day is enough for each one. Those moreover to whom God gives the ability of bearing abstinence shall know that they will have their own reward. But the prior shall judge if either the needs of the place, or labour or the heat of summer, requires more; considering in all things lest satiety or drunkenness creep in. Indeed we read that wine is not suitable for monks at all. But because, in our day, it is not possible to persuade the monks of this, let us agree at least as to the fact that we should not drink till we are sated, but sparingly. For wine can make even the wise to go astray. Where, moreover, the necessities of the place are such that the amount written above can not be found,—but much less or nothing at all,—those who live there shall bless God and shall not murmur. And we admonish them as to this above all: that they be without murmuring.

41. *At what hours the brothers ought to take their refection.* From the holy Easter time until Pentecost the brothers shall have their refection at the sixth hour; and at evening they shall sup. From Pentecost, moreover, through the whole summer,—if the monks do not have hard labour in the fields, or the extreme heat of the summer does not prevent them,—they shall fast on the fourth and sixth day until the ninth hour: but on the other days they shall have their repast at the sixth hour. Which sixth hour, if they have ordinary work in the fields, or if the heat of summer is not great, shall be kept to for the repast; and it shall be for the abbot to decide. And he shall so temper and arrange all things, that their souls may be saved on the one hand; and that, on the other, what the brothers do they shall do without any justifiable

*Not quite half a liter.—Ed.

murmuring. Moreover, from the Ides of September until the beginning of Lent, they shall always have their refection at the ninth hour. But in Lent, until Easter, they shall have their refection at Vesper time. And that same Vesper meal shall be so arranged that those who take their repast may not need the light of a lantern; but everything shall be consumed while it is still daylight. But indeed at all times, the hour, whether of supper or of refection, shall be so arranged, that everything may be done while it is still light.

42. *That after "completorium" no one shall speak.* At all times the monks ought to practise silence, but most of all in the nocturnal hours. And thus at all times, whether of fasting or of eating: if it be meal-time, as soon as they have risen from the table, all shall sit together and one shall read selections or lives of the Fathers, or indeed anything which will edify the hearers. But not the Pentateuch or Kings; for, to weak intellects, it will be of no use at that hour to hear this part of Scripture; but they shall be read at other times. But if the days are fast days, when Vespers have been said, after a short interval they shall come to the reading of the selections as we have said; and four or five pages, or as much as the hour permits having been read, they shall all congregate, upon the cessation of the reading. If, by chance, any one is occupied in a task assigned to him, he shall nevertheless approach. All therefore being gathered together, they shall say the completing prayer; and, going out from the "completorium," there shall be no further opportunity for any one to say anything. But if any one be found acting contrary to this rule of silence, he shall be subjected to a very severe punishment. Unless a necessity in the shape of guests should arise, or the abbot, by chance, should give some order. But even this, indeed, he shall do most seriously, with all gravity and moderation.

43. *Concerning those who come late to Divine Service or to table.* As soon as the signal for the hour of Divine Service has been heard, leaving everything that they had in hand they shall run with the greatest haste; with gravity, however, in order that scurrility may find no nourishment. Therefore let nothing be preferred to the service of God. But if any one should come to the nocturnal vigils after the *Gloria* of the ninety-fourth psalm—which on this account

we wish to have said quite lingeringly and with delay,—he shall not stand in his place in the choir, but shall stand last of all, or in a place which the abbot shall have set apart for such dilatory ones; that he may be seen by him or by all, until, the Divine Service being ended, he may show his repentance by giving public satisfaction. Moreover this is the reason why we have decreed that they ought to stand last or apart: that, being seen by all, even for very shame they may amend. For if they remain outside the oratory, there may be one perhaps who will either go back and go to sleep, or at any rate will sit down outside, or will give way to idle thoughts, and a chance will be given to the evil one. He shall rather enter within, that he lose not the whole, and that he amend for the time that remains. Moreover in the day time he who does not come to the Divine Service after the verse, and the *Gloria* of the first psalm which is said after the verse—according to the rule which we mentioned above,—shall stand last. Nor shall he presume to join the choir of singers until he render satisfaction; unless, indeed, the abbot allow him to do so by his permission, under condition that the guilty one shall afterwards render satisfaction. Moreover he who does not come to table before the verse, so that all together may say the verse and pray, and all as one may go to table: he who, through his negligence or fault, does not come, shall be rebuked for this up to the second time. If again he do not amend, he shall not be allowed to share in the common table; but, separated from the companionship of all, shall have his refection alone, his portion of wine being taken away from him until he render satisfaction and make amends. He, moreover, who is not present at that verse which is said after the meal shall suffer in like manner. Nor shall any one presume, before the hour fixed, or after it, to take any food or drink for himself. But if anything is offered to any one by the prior, and he refuse to accept it: at the hour when he desires that which he first refused, he shall not receive it or anything else at all, until he makes suitable amends.

44. *Concerning those who are excommunicated, how they shall render satisfaction.* He who, for graver faults, is excommunicated from the oratory and from table, shall, at the hour when the Divine Service is being celebrated in the oratory, lie prostrate before the gates of the oratory saying nothing, his head being placed not

otherwise than on the ground, lying headlong before the feet of all who go out from the oratory. And he shall continue doing this until the abbot shall judge that he have rendered satisfaction. And when he shall enter at the order of the abbot, he shall grovel at the feet of the abbot, and then of all, that they may pray for him. And then, if the abbot order it, he shall be received into the choir or into the grade which the abbot decrees: in such wise, nevertheless, that he may not presume to start a psalm, or a lesson, or anything else in the oratory, unless the abbot again order him to. And at all hours when the Divine Service reaches its end, he shall throw himself on the ground in the place where he stands: and shall render satisfaction in this way until the abbot orders him to desist at length from doing so. But those who, for light faults, are excommunicated from table alone, shall render satisfaction in the oratory: they shall do this until the abbot gives the order; until he blesses them and says, "it is enough."

45. *Concerning those who make mistakes in the oratory.* If any one, in saying a psalm, response, or antiphone or lesson, make a mistake: unless he humble himself there before all, giving satisfaction, he shall be subjected to greater punishment, as one who was unwilling to correct by humility that in which he had erred by neglect. But children, for such a fault, shall be whipped.

46. *Concerning those who err in any other matters.* If any one commit any fault while at any labour, in the kitchen, in the cellar, in the offices, in the bakery, while labouring at any art, or in any place; or shall break or lose anything, or commit any excess wherever he may be; and do not himself, coming before the abbot or the congregation, of his own accord give satisfaction and declare his error: if it become known through another, he shall be subjected to greater amends. But if the cause of his sin lie hidden in his soul, he may declare it to the abbot alone or to his spiritual elders; who may know how to cure his wounds, and not to uncover and make public those of another.

47. *Concerning the announcement of the hour of Divine Service.* The announcing of the hour of Divine Service, by night and by day, shall be the work of the abbot: either to announce it himself, or to enjoin this care on a brother so zealous that everything shall be fulfilled at the proper hours. And those who are

ordered to, shall, after the abbot, start the psalms or antiphones in their proper order. No one moreover shall presume to sing or to read unless he can fulfill this duty so that those hearing him shall be edified. And he whom the abbot orders to, shall do this with humility and gravity and trembling.

48. *Concerning the daily manual labour.* Idleness is the enemy of the soul. And therefore, at fixed times, the brothers ought to be occupied in manual labour; and again, at fixed times, in sacred reading. Therefore we believe that, according to this disposition, both seasons ought to be arranged; so that, from Easter until the Calends of October, going out early, from the first until the fourth hour they shall do what labour may be necessary. Moreover, from the fourth hour until about the sixth, they shall be free for reading. After the meal of the sixth hour, moreover, rising from table, they shall rest in their beds with all silence; or, perchance, he that wishes to read may so read to himself that he do not disturb another. And the *nona* (the second meal) shall be gone through with more moderately about the middle of the eighth hour; and again they shall work at what is to be done until Vespers. But, if the exigency or poverty of the place demands that they be occupied by themselves in picking fruits, they shall not be dismayed: for then they are truly monks if they live by the labours of their hands; as did also our fathers and the apostles. Let all things be done with moderation, however, on account of the fainthearted. From the Calends of October, moreover, until the beginning of Lent they shall be free for reading until the second full hour. At the second hour the *tertia* (morning service) shall be held, and all shall labour at the task which is enjoined upon them until the ninth. The first signal, moreover, of the ninth hour having been given, they shall each one leave off his work; and be ready when the second signal strikes. Moreover after the refection they shall be free for their readings or for psalms. But in the days of Lent, from dawn until the third full hour, they shall be free for their readings; and, until the tenth full hour, they shall do the labour that is enjoined on them. In which days of Lent they shall all receive separate books from the library; which they shall read entirely through in order. These books are to be given out on the first day of Lent. Above all there shall certainly be appointed one or two elders, who shall go round

the monastery at the hours in which the brothers are engaged in reading, and see to it that no troublesome brother chance to be found who is open to idleness and trifling, and is not intent on his reading; being not only of no use to himself, but also stirring up others. If such a one—may it not happen—be found, he shall be admonished once and a second time. If he do not amend, he shall be subject under the Rule to such punishment that the others may have fear. Nor shall brother join brother at unsuitable hours. Moreover on Sunday all shall engage in reading: excepting those who are deputed to various duties. But if anyone be so negligent and lazy that he will not or can not read, some task shall be imposed upon him which he can do; so that he be not idle. On feeble or delicate brothers such a labour or art is to be imposed, that they shall neither be idle, nor shall they be so oppressed by the violence of labour as to be driven to take flight. Their weakness is to be taken into consideration by the abbot.

49. Although at all times the life of the monk should be such as though Lent were being observed: nevertheless, since few have that virtue, we urge that, on those said days of Lent, he shall keep his life in all purity; and likewise wipe out, in those holy days, the negligencies of other times. This is then worthily done if we refrain from all vices, if we devote ourselves to prayer with weeping, to reading and compunction of heart, and to abstinence. Therefore, on these days, let us add of ourselves something to the ordinary amount of our service: special prayers, abstinence from food and drink;—so that each one, over and above the amount allotted to him, shall offer of his own will something to God with rejoicing of the Holy Spirit. That is, he shall restrict his body in food, drink, sleep, talkativeness, and merry-making; and, with the joy of a spiritual desire, shall await the holy Easter. The offering, moreover, that each one makes, he shall announce to his abbot; that it may be done with his prayers and by his will. For what is done without the permission of the spiritual Father, shall be put down to presumption and vain glory, and not to a monk's credit. Therefore all things are to be done according to the will of the abbot.

50. *Concerning brothers who labour far from the oratory, or who are on a journey.* Brothers who are at work very far off, and cannot betake themselves at the proper hour to the oratory, shall, if

the abbot deem this to be the case, celebrate the Divine Service there where they are at work; bending their knees in the fear of God. Likewise as to those who are sent on a journey: the established hours shall not escape them; but, according as they can, they shall perform of themselves, and not neglect to render, the rightful amount of service.

51. *Concerning brothers who do not journey very far.* A brother who is sent for any reply, and is expected to return to the monastery on the same day, shall not presume to eat outside, even if he be asked to by any one; unless perchance he be told to by his abbot. But if he do otherwise he shall be excommunicated.

52. *Concerning the oratory of the monastery.* The oratory shall be that which it is called; nor shall any thing else be done there or placed there. When the Divine Service is ended, let all go out with perfect silence and let reverence be paid to God: so that a brother who perchance especially desires to pray for himself, may not be impeded by the wickedness of another. But, if another wishes perchance to pray more secretly for himself, he shall simply enter and pray; not with a clamorous voice, but with tears, and inclining his heart. Therefore he who does not perform a similar act, shall not be permitted, when the Divine Service is ended, to remain in the oratory—as has been said—lest another suffer hindrance.

53. *Concerning the reception of guests.* All guests who come shall be received as though they were Christ: for He Himself said: *I was a stranger and ye took Me in.* And to all, fitting honour shall be shown; but, most of all, to servants of the faith and to pilgrims. When, therefore, a guest is announced, the prior or the brothers shall run to meet him, with every office of love. And first they shall pray together; and thus they shall be joined together in peace. Which kiss of peace shall not first be offered, unless a prayer have preceded; on account of the wiles of the devil. In the salutation itself, moreover, all humility shall be exhibited. In the case of all guests arriving or departing: with inclined head, or with prostrating of the whole body upon the ground, Christ, who is also received in them, shall be adored. The guests moreover, having been received, shall be conducted to prayer; and afterwards the prior, or one whom he himself orders, shall sit with them. The law of God shall be read before the guest that he may be edified; and,

after this, every kindness shall be exhibited. A fast may be broken by the prior on account of a guest; unless, perchance, it be a special day of fast which can not be violated. The brothers, moreover, shall continue their customary fasts. The abbot shall give water into the hands of his guests; and the abbot as well as the whole congregation shall wash the feet of all guests. This being done, they shall say this verse: "We have received, oh Lord, Thy loving-kindness in the midst of Thy temple." Chiefly in the reception of the poor and of pilgrims shall care be most anxiously exhibited: for in them Christ is received the more. For the very fear of the rich exacts honour for them. The kitchen of the abbot and the guests shall be by itself; so that guests coming at uncertain hours, as is always happening in a monastery, may not disturb the brothers. Into the control of which kitchen, two brothers, who can well fulfill that duty, shall enter yearly; and to them, according as they shall need it, help shall be administered; so that they may serve without murmuring. And again, when they are less occupied, they shall go out where they are commanded to, and labour. And not only in their case, but in all the offices of the monastery, such consideration shall be had, that, when they need it, help shall be given to them. And, when they are again at leisure, they shall obey orders. Likewise a brother, whose soul the fear of God possesses, shall have assigned to him the cell of the guests, where there shall be beds sufficiently strewn; and the house of God shall be administered wisely by the wise. Moreover he who has not been ordered to shall by no means join the guests or speak to them. But if he meet them or see them, saluting them humbly, as has been said, and seeking their blessing, he shall pass by, saying that he is not allowed to speak with a guest.

54. *Whether a monk should be allowed to receive letters or anything.* By no means shall it be allowed to a monk—either from his relatives, or from any man, or from one of his fellows—to receive or to give, without order of the abbot, letters, presents or any gift, however small. But even if, by his relatives, anything has been sent to him: he shall not presume to receive it, unless it have first been shown to the abbot. But if he order it to be received, it shall be in the power of the abbot to give it to whomever he may will. And the brother to whom it happened to

have been sent shall not be chagrined; that an opportunity be not given to the devil. Whoever, moreover, presumes otherwise, shall be subject to the discipline of the Rule.

55.

Vestments shall be given to the brothers according to the quality of the places where they dwell, or the temperature of the air. For in cold regions more is required; but in warm, less. This, therefore, is a matter for the abbot to decide. We nevertheless consider that for ordinary places there suffices for the monks a cowl and gown apiece—the cowl, in winter hairy, in summer plain or old,—and a working garment, on account of their labours. As clothing for the feet, shoes and boots. Concerning the colour and size of all of which things the monks shall not talk; but they shall be such as can be found in the province where they are or as can be bought the most cheaply. The abbot, moreover, shall provide, as to the measure, that those vestments be not short for those using them; but of suitable length. And, when new ones are received, they shall always straightway return the old ones, to be kept in the vestiary on account of the poor. It is enough, moreover, for a monk to have two gowns and two cowls; on account of the nights, and on account of washing the things themselves. Every thing, then, that is over this is superfluous, and ought to be removed. And the shoes, and whatever is old, they shall return when they receive something new. And those who are sent on a journey shall receive cloths for the loins from the vestiary; which on their return they shall restore, having washed them. And there shall be cowls and gowns some-what better than those which they have ordinarily: which, when they start on a journey, they shall receive from the vestiary, and, on returning, shall restore. As trappings for the beds, moreover, shall suffice a mat, a woollen covering, a woollen cloth under the pillow, and the pillow. And these beds are frequently to be searched by the abbot on account of private property; lest he find some. And, if any thing is found belonging to any one which he did not receive from the abbot, he shall be subjected to the most severe discipline. And, in order that this special vice may be cut off at the roots, there shall be given by the abbot all things which are necessary: that is, a cowl, a gown, shoes, boots, a binder for the loins, a knife, a pen, a needle, a handkerchief, tablets: so that all excuse of necessity shall be removed. By the same abbot, however, that sentence of the Acts of the Apostles shall always be regarded: *For there was given unto each man according unto his need.* Thus, therefore, the abbot also shall consider the infirmities of the needy, not the evil will of the envious. In all his judgments, nevertheless, he shall remember the retribution of God.

56. *Concerning the table of the abbot.* The table of the abbot shall always be with the guests and pilgrims. As often, however, as guests are lacking, it shall be in his power to summon those of the brothers whom he wishes. He shall see, nevertheless, that one or two elders are always left with the brothers, for the sake of discipline.

57. *Concerning the artificers of the monastery.* Artificers, if there are any in the monastery, shall practise with all humility their special arts, if the abbot permit it. But if any one of them becomes inflated with pride on account of knowledge of his art, to the extent that he seems to be conferring something on the monastery: such a one shall be plucked away from that art; and he shall not again return to it unless the abbot perchance again orders him to, he being humiliated. But, if anything from the works of the artificers is to be sold, they themselves shall take care through whose hands they (the works) are to pass, lest they (the intermediaries) presume to commit some fraud upon the monastery. They shall always remember Ananias and Sapphira; lest, perchance, the death that they suffered with regard to the body, these, or all those who have committed any fraud as to the property of the monastery, may suffer with regard to the soul. In the prices themselves, moreover, let not the evil of avarice crop out: but let the object always be given a little cheaper than it is given by other and secular persons; so that, in all things, God shall be glorified.

58. *Concerning the manner of receiving brothers.* When any new comer applies for conversion, an easy entrance shall not be granted him: but, as the apostle says, *Try the spirits if they be of God.* Therefore, if he who comes perseveres in knocking, and is seen after four or five days to patiently endure the insults inflicted upon him, and the difficulty of ingress, and to persist in his

demand: entrance shall be allowed him, and he shall remain for a few days in the cell of the guests. After this, moreover, he shall be in the cell of the novices, where he shall meditate and eat and sleep. And an elder shall be detailed off for him who shall be capable of saving souls, who shall altogether intently watch over him, and make it a care to see if he reverently seek God, if he be zealous in the service of God, in obedience, in suffering shame. And all the harshness and roughness of the means through which God is approached shall be told him in advance. If he promise perseverance in his steadfastness, after the lapse of two months this Rule shall be read to him in order, and it shall be said to him: Behold the law under which thou dost wish to serve; if thou canst observe it, enter; but if thou canst not, depart freely. If he have stood firm thus far, then he shall be led into the aforesaid cell of the novices; and again he shall be proven with all patience. And, after the lapse of six months, the Rule shall be read to him; that he may know upon what he is entering. And, if he stand firm thus far, after four months the same Rule shall again be re-read to him. And if, having deliberated with himself, he shall promise to keep everything, and to obey all the commands that are laid upon him: then he shall be received in the congregation; knowing that it is decreed, by the law of the Rule, that from that day he shall not be allowed to depart from the monastery, nor to shake free his neck from the yoke of the Rule, which, after such tardy deliberation, he was at liberty either to refuse or receive. He who is to be received, moreover, shall, in the oratory, in the presence of all, make promise concerning his steadfastness and the change in his manner of life and his obedience to God and to His saints; so that if, at any time, he act contrary, he shall know that he shall be condemned by Him Whom he mocks. Concerning which promise he shall make a petition in the name of the saints whose relics are there, and of the abbot who is present. Which petition he shall write with his own hand. Or, if he really be not learned in letters, another, being asked by him, shall write it. And that novice shall make his sign; and with his own hand shall place it (the petition) above the altar. And when he has placed it there, the novice shall straightway commence this verse: "Receive me oh Lord according to thy promise and I shall live, and do not cast me down from my hope." Which verse the whole congregation shall repeat three times, adding: "Glory be to the Father." Then that brother novice shall prostrate himself at the feet of each one, that they may pray for him. And, already, from that day, he shall be considered as in the congregation. If he have any property, he shall either first present it to the poor, or, making a solemn donation, shall confer it on the monastery, keeping nothing at all for himself: as one, forsooth, who from that day, shall know that he shall not have power even over his own body. Straightway, therefore in the oratory, he shall take off his own garments in which he was clad, and shall put on the garments of the monastery. Moreover those garments which he has taken off shall be placed in the vestiary to be preserved; so that if, at any time, the devil persuading him, he shall consent to go forth from the monastery—may it not happen,—then, taking off the garments of the monastery, he may be cast out. That petition of his, nevertheless, which the abbot took from above the altar, he shall not receive again; but it shall be preserved in the monastery.

59. *Concerning the sons of nobles or of poor men who are presented.* If by chance any one of the nobles offers his son to God in the monastery: if the boy himself is a minor in age, his parents shall make the petition which we spoke of above. And, with an oblation, they shall enwrap that petition and the hand of the boy in the linen cloth of the altar; and thus they shall offer him. Concerning their property, moreover, either they shall promise in the present petition, under an oath, that they will never, either through some chosen person, or in any way whatever, give him any thing at any time, or furnish him with the means of possessing it. Or, indeed, if they be not willing to do this, and wish to offer something as alms to the monastery for their salvation, they shall make a donation of the things which they wish to give to the monastery; retaining for themselves, if they wish, the usufruct. And let all things be so observed that no suspicion may remain with the boy; by which being deceived he might perish—which God forbid,—as we have learned by experience. The poorer ones shall also do likewise. Those, however, who have nothing at all shall simply make their petition; and, with an oblation, shall offer their son before witnesses.

60. *Concerning priests who may chance to wish to dwell in the monastery.* If anyone of the order of priests ask to be received in the monastery, assent, indeed, shall not too quickly be given him. Nevertheless, if he altogether persist in this supplication, he shall know that he must observe all the discipline of the Rule; nor shall anything be relaxed unto him, that it may be as it is written: *Friend, wherefore art thou come?* Nevertheless it shall be allowed to him to stand after the abbot, and to give the benediction, or to hold mass; if, however, the abbot order him to. But, otherwise, he shall by no means presume to do anything, knowing that he is subject to the discipline of the Rule, and that, all the more, he shall give an example of humility to all. And if he chance to be present in the monastery for the sake of an ordination or anything, he shall expect the position that he had when he entered the monastery; not that which has been conceded to him out of reverence for his priesthood. Moreover, if any one of the clergy desire similarly to be associated with the monastery, he shall have a medium position given him. And he, none the less, shall make promise concerning his observance of the Rule, and concerning his own steadfastness.

61. *Concerning pilgrim monks, how they shall be received.* If any pilgrim monk come from distant parts,—if he wish as a guest to dwell in the monastery, and will be content with the customs which he finds in the place, and do not perchance by his lavishness disturb the monastery, but is simply content with what he finds: he shall be received for as long a time as he desires. If, indeed, he find fault with anything, or expose it, reasonably, and with the humility of charity: the abbot shall discuss it prudently, lest perchance God had sent him for this very thing. But if, afterwards, he wish to establish himself lastingly, such a wish shall not be refused: and all the more, since, in the time of his sojourn as guest, his manner of life could have become known. But, if he have been found lavish or vicious in the time of his sojourn as guest,—not only ought he not to be joined to the body of the monastery, but also it shall be said to him, honestly, that he must depart; lest, by sympathy with him, others also become contaminated. But, if he be not such a one as to merit being cast out: not only if he ask it, shall he be received and associated with the congregation, but he shall also be urged to remain; that by his example others may be instructed. For in every

place one God is served, and one King is warred for. And if the abbot perceive him to be such a one, he may be allowed to place him in a somewhat higher position. For the abbot can place not only a monk, but also one from the above grades of priests or clergy, in a greater place than that in which he enters; if he perceive their life to be such a one as to demand it. Moreover the abbot must take care lest, at any time, he receive a monk to dwell (with him) from another known monastery, without the consent of his abbot or letters of commendation. For it is written: *Do not unto another what thou wilt not that one do unto thee.*

62.

If any abbot seek to ordain for himself a priest or deacon, he shall elect from among his fold one who is worthy to perform the office of a priest. He who is ordained, moreover, shall beware of elation or pride. Nor shall he presume to do anything at all unless what he is ordered to by the abbot; knowing that he is all the more subject to the Rule. Nor, by reason of the priesthood, shall he forget obedience and discipline; but he shall advance more and more towards God. But he shall always expect to hold that position which he had when he entered the monastery: except when performing the service of the altar, and if, perchance, the election of the congregation and the will of the abbot incline to promote him on account of his merit of life. He shall, nevertheless, know that he is to observe the rule constituted for him by the deans or provosts: and that, if he presume otherwise, he shall be considered not a priest but a rebel. And if, having often been admonished, he do not amend: even the bishop shall be called in in testimony. But if, even then, he do not amend, his faults being glaring, he shall be thrust forth from the monastery. That is, if his contumaciousness shall have been of such a kind, that he was not willing to be subject to or to obey the Rule.

63. *Concerning rank in the congregation.* They shall preserve their rank in the monastery according as the time of their conversion and the merit of their life decrees; and as the abbot ordains. And the abbot shall not perturb the flock committed to him; nor, using as it were an arbitrary power, shall he unjustly dispose

anything. But he shall always reflect that he is to render account to God for all his judgments and works. Therefore, according to the order which he has decreed, or which the brothers themselves have held: thus they shall go to the absolution, to the communion, to the singing of the psalm, to their place in the choir. And in all places, altogether, age does not decide the rank or affect it; for Samuel and Daniel, as boys, judged the priests. Therefore excepting those who, as we have said, the abbot has, for a higher reason, preferred, or, for certain causes, degraded: all the rest, as they are converted, so they remain. Thus, for example, he who comes to the monastery at the second hour of the day, may know that he is younger than he who came at the first hour of the day, of whatever age or dignity he be. And, in the case of boys, discipline shall be observed in all things by all. The juniors, therefore, shall honour their seniors; the seniors shall love their juniors. In the very calling of names, it shall be allowed to no one to call another simply by his name: but the seniors shall call their juniors by the name of brothers. The juniors, moreover, shall call their seniors "nonni," which indicates paternal reverence. The abbot, moreover, because he is believed to be Christ's representative, shall be called Master and Abbot; not by his assumption, but through honour and love for Christ. His thoughts moreover shall be such, and he shall show himself such, that he may be worthy of such honour. Moreover, wherever the brothers meet each other, the junior shall seek a blessing from the senior. When the greater one passes, the lesser one shall rise and give him a place to sit down. Nor shall the junior presume to sit unless his senior bid him; so that it shall be done as is written: *Vying with each other in honour.* Boys, little ones or youths, shall obtain their places in the oratory or at table with discipline as the end in view. Out of doors moreover, or wherever they are, they shall be guarded and disciplined; until they come to an intelligent age.

64. *Concerning the ordination of an abbot.* In ordaining an abbot this consideration shall always be observed: that such a one shall be put into office as the whole congregation, according to the fear of God, with one heart—or even a part, however small, of the congregation with more prudent counsel—shall have chosen. He who is to be ordained, moreover, shall be elected for merit of life and learnedness in wisdom; even though he be the lowest in rank

in the congregation. But even if the whole congregation with one consent shall have elected a person consenting to their vices—which God forbid;—and those vices shall in any way come clearly to the knowledge of the bishop to whose diocese that place pertains, or to the neighbouring abbots or Christians: the latter shall not allow the consent of the wicked to prevail, but shall set up a dispenser worthy of the house of God; knowing that they will receive a good reward for this, if they do it chastely and with zeal for God. Just so they shall know, on the contrary, that they have sinned if they neglect it. The abbot who is ordained, moreover, shall reflect always what a burden he is undertaking, and to whom he is to render account of his stewardship. He shall know that he ought rather to be of help than to command. He ought, therefore, to be learned in the divine law, that he may know how to give forth both the new and the old; chaste, sober, merciful. He shall always exalt mercy over judgment, that he may obtain the same. He shall hate vice, he shall love the brethren. In his blame itself he shall act prudently and do nothing excessive; lest, while he is too desirous of removing the rust, the vessel be broken. And he shall always suspect his own frailty; and shall remember that a bruised reed is not to be crushed. By which we do not say that he shall permit vice to be nourished; but prudently, and with charity, he shall remove it, according as he finds it to be expedient in the case of each one, as we have already said. And he shall strive rather to be loved than feared. He shall not be troubled and anxious; he also shall not be too obstinate; he shall not be jealous and too suspicious; for then he will have no rest. In his commands he shall be provident, and shall consider whether they be of God or of the world. He shall use discernment and moderation with regard to the labours which he enjoins, thinking of the discretion of St. James who said: *if I overdrive my flocks they will die all in one day.* Accepting therefore this and other testimony of discretion the mother of the virutes, he shall so temper all things that there may be both what the strong desire, and the weak do not flee. And, especially, he shall keep the present Rule in all things; so that, when he hath ministered well, he shall hear from the Lord what that good servant did who obtained meat for his fellow servants in his day: *Verily I say unto you*, he said, *That he shall make him ruler over all his goods.*

65. *Concerning the provost of the monastery.* Very often,
indeed, it happens that, through the ordination of a provost, grave
scandals arise in monasteries; since there are some who, inflated
with the evil spirit of pride, and thinking themselves to be second
abbots, taking upon themselves to rule, nourish scandals, and
make dissensions in the congregation; especially in those places
where the provost is ordained by the same priest, or the same
abbots, who ordain the abbot. How absurd this is, is easily seen;
for, commencing with the ordination itself, a reason is given him
for being proud, since it is suggested to him by his thoughts that
he is exempt from the authority of his abbot in as much as he has
been ordained by the same persons as the abbot. Hence arise
envy, quarrels, detractions, emulations, dissensions, disturbances.
And when the abbot and the provost differ mutually in their
opinions, their souls, on the one hand, must be endangered by this
dissension; and those who are under them, while they pay court to
different sides, go to perdition. The evil of which danger is to be
referred to those who have made themselves the causes of such
things through the ordination. Wherefore we foresee that it is
expedient, for the sake of maintaining peace and charity, that the
ordering of his monastery shall rest with the will of the abbot.
And, if it can be done, all the necessities of the monastery shall, as
the abbot disposes, be seen to by deans, as we arranged before; so
that, by committing them to many, one may not become proud.
But if either the place demands it, or the congregation seeks it, the
abbot shall, with the counsel of God-fearing brothers, reasonably
and with humility, himself ordain for himself, as provost,
whomever he shall choose. Which provost, nevertheless, shall do
with reverence that which is enjoined upon him by his abbot,
doing nothing contrary to the will or order of the abbot; for in as
much as he is raised above the others, so much the more carefully
should he observe the precepts of the Rule. Which provost, if he
be found vicious, or deceived by the elation of pride; or if he be
proved a despiser of the holy Rule; he shall be warned by words
up to the fourth time. If he do not then amend, the correction of
the discipline of the Rule shall be administered to him. But if he
do not, even then, amend, he shall be cast down from the rank of
a provost, and another who is worthy shall be called in his place.
But if, even in the congregation, he be not quiet and obedient, he

shall also be expelled from the monastery. Nevertheless the abbot shall reflect that he is to render account to God for all his judgments; lest perchance a flame of envy or jealousy may burn his soul.

66. *Concerning the doorkeepers of the monastery.* At the door of the monastery shall be placed a wise old man who shall know how to receive a reply and to return one; whose ripeness of age will not permit him to trifle. Which doorkeeper ought to have a cell next to the door; so that those arriving may always find one present from whom they may receive a reply. And straightway, when any one has knocked, or a poor man has called out, he shall answer, "Thanks be to God?" or shall give the blessing; and with all the gentleness of the fear of God he shall hastily give a reply with the fervour of charity. And if this doorkeeper need assistance he may receive a younger brother.

A monastery, moreover, if it can be done, ought so to be arranged that everything necessary,—that is, water, a mill, a garden, a bakery,—may be made use of, and different arts be carried on, within the monastery; so that there shall be no need for the monks to wander about outside. For this is not at all good for their souls. We wish, moreover, that this Rule be read very often in the congregation; lest any of the brothers excuse himself on account of ignorance.

67. *Concerning brothers sent upon a journey.* Brothers who are to be sent upon a journey shall commend themselves to the prayers of all the brethren and of the abbot. And always, at the last prayer of the Divine Service, there shall be a calling to mind of all the absent ones. Having returned, moreover, from the journey—on the very day on which they return,—at all the canonical hours when the Divine Service is being carried on, prostrated on the floor of the oratory, they shall seek the prayers of all, on account of their excesses: lest perchance the sight of some evil thing, or the hearing of some idle discourse, may have met or happened to them on the journey. Let not any one presume to tell another what he has seen or heard outside of the monastery; for, very often, it means ruin. And if any one presume to, he shall be subject to the punishment of the Rule. Even so he who presumes to go beyond the confines of the monastery, or to go anywhere, or to do anything however trivial without the order of the abbot.

68. *If impossibilities are enjoined on a brother.* If on any brother by chance any burdensome or impossible tasks are enjoined, he shall receive indeed the command of him who orders with all gentleness and obedience. But if he shall see that the weight of the burden altogether exceeds the measure of his strength, he shall patiently and in due season suggest to him who is in authority the causes of the impossibility, but not with pride, or resisting, or contradicting. But if, after his suggestion, the command of the superior continue according to his first opinion, the junior shall know that thus it is expedient for him; and in all love, trusting in the aid of God, he shall obey.

69. *That, in the monastery, one shall not presume to defend another.* It is to be especially guarded against lest, on any occasion, one monk presume to defend another in the monastery, or to protect him as it were: even though they be joined by some nearness of relationship. Nor in any way shall the monks presume to do this; for thence can arise most grave occasion for scandals. But if any one transgress these commands, he shall be most severely punished.

70. *That no one shall presume to strike promiscuously.*—Every ground for presumption shall be forbidden in the monastery. We decree that it shall be allowed to no one to excommunicate or to strike any of his brothers; unless he be one to whom power is given by his abbot. Sinners, moreover, shall be called to account in the presence of all: so that the others may have fear. The care of disciplining, and the custody of children up to fifteen years of age, however, shall belong to all. But this also with all moderation and reason. For he who presumes in any way against one of riper age, without precept of the abbot; or who, even against children, becomes violent without discretion,—shall be subject to the discipline of the Rule; for it is written: *Do not unto another what thou wilt not that one do unto thee.*

71. *That they shall be mutually obedient.*—The virtue of obedience is not only to be exhibited by all to the abbot, but also the brothers shall be thus mutually obedient to each other; knowing that they shall approach God through this way of obedience. The command therefore of the abbot, or of the provosts who are constituted by him, being given the preference—since we do not allow private commands to have more

weight than his,—for the rest, all juniors shall obey their superiors with all charity and solicitude. But if any one is found contentious, he shall be punished. If, moreover, any brother, for any slight cause, be in any way rebuked by the abbot or by any one who is his superior; or if he feel, even lightly, that the mind of some superior is angered or moved against him, however little:— straightway, without delay, he shall so long lie prostrate at his feet, atoning, until, with the benediction, that anger shall be appeased. But if any one scorn to do this, he shall either be subjected to corporal punishment; or, if he be contumacious, he shall be expelled from the monastery.

72. *Concerning the good zeal which the monks ought to have.*—As there is an evil zeal of bitterness, which separates from God and leads to Hell; so there is a good zeal, which separates from vice and leads to God and to eternal life. Let the monks therefore exercise this zeal with the most fervent love: that is, let them mutually surpass each other in honour. Let them most patiently tolerate their weaknesses, whether of body or character; let them vie with each other in showing obedience. Let no one pursue what he thinks useful for himself, but rather what he thinks useful for another. Let them love the brotherhood with a chaste love; let them fear God; let them love their abbot with a sincere and humble love; let them prefer nothing whatever to Christ, Who leads us alike to eternal life.

73. *Concerning the fact that not every just observance is decreed in this Rule.*—We have written out this Rule, indeed, that we may show those observing it in the monasteries how to have some honesty of character, or beginning of conversion. But for those who hasten to the perfection of living, there are the teachings of the holy Fathers: the observance of which leads a man to the heights of perfeciton. For what page, or what discourse, of Divine authority of the Old or the New Testament is not a most perfect rule for human life? Or what book of the holy Catholic Fathers does not trumpet forth how by the right path we shall come to our Creator? Also the reading aloud of the Fathers, and their decrees, and their lives; also the Rule of our holy Father Basil—what else are they except instruments of virtue for well-living and obedient monks? We, moreover, blush with confusion

for the idle, and the evilly living and the negligent. Thou, therefore, whoever doth hasten to the celestial fatherland, perform with Christ's aid this Rule written out as the least of beginnings: and then at length, under God's protection, thou wilt come to the greater things that we have mentioned; to the summits of learning and virtue.

4
Paul the Deacon

Poems in Honor of St. Benedict,[1]
translated by William Dudley Foulke

See the bibliography for a complete translation of the
Dialogues *of Gregory the Great, to which Foulke's notes to*
these poems refer. A convenient translation of Book II, on St.
Benedict, is Myra L. Uhlfelder's version (Indianapolis, New
York, 1967).
In Foulke's notes, the following abbreviations are used:
"Waitz" (n. 24, 34) indicates the edition of "Pauli Historia
Langobardorum" *in* Monumenta Germaniae, Scriptores
Rerum Langobardicarum, *from which this translation is*
made.
"Bethmann" (n. 62) refers to one of his articles contained in
the tenth volume of the Archiv der Gesellschaft für ältere
deutsche Geschichtkunde, (Hanover, 1849).

Where, holy Benedict, shall I begin the long tale of thy
    triumphs!
Countless thy virtues to tell; where shall thy bard begin!

Father and saint, all hail! Thy name proclaimeth thy virtue,[2]
Shining light of the world! father and saint all hail!

Nursia,[3] praise him well, by such son proudly exalted,
Bringing the stars to the world—Nursia abundantly praise!

---

[1] The second book of the *Dialogues* of Gregory the Great elucidates the
meaning of these distichs of which some would otherwise be incomprehensible.

[2] *Benedictus*, "blessed." St. Gregory calls him "Blessed by grace and by name"
(*Dialogues*, Book II, Introduction).

[3] The birthplace of St. Benedict in Umbria (id.).

O the decorum of boyhood![4] Transcending his years by his
virtues,
Passing the wisdom of age,[5] O the decorum of youth!

Flower of the garden of heaven, the blossoms of earth
despising,[6]
Prized not the riches of Rome,[7] flower of the garden of
heaven!

Sadly the governess bore the broken halves of the vessel;
Joyfully, when restored, bore the preceptress the sieve.[8]

He who is named from the city, 'mid rocks concealeth the
novice—
Treasures of piety bears—he who is named from the town.[9]

Praises resound from the caves, deep hid from the vision of
mortals;
Known, Christ, only to Thee, praises resound from the
caves.[10]

Frost and the tempest and snow three years thou unwearied
endurest;

[4] He was sent to Rome to study literature and science, but while yet a boy was
filled with loathing at the profligacy of his fellow-students (id.).

[5] St. Gregory says of him that he bore the heart of an old man from the very time
of his boyhood. St. Gregory also says, "Indeed, surpassing his age in his morals, he
gave his mind to no pleasure" (id.).

[6] This again comes from St. Gregory. "He already despised the world in its
bloom as if it were withered" (id.).

[7] He left Rome for a hermitage at a boyish age. As St. Gregory says, "He
withdrew therefore, knowingly ignorant and wisely unlearned" (id.).

[8] His nurse or governess, who had taught him and brought him up in infancy,
followed him from Rome and tended him. To prepare food for him she borrowed
from a neighbor an earthen sieve or vessel for cleaning wheat; she broke it and
was in great distress, not having the money to replace it. Benedict repaired it by a
miracle (Dialogues II, chapter 1). St. Gregory says, "But Benedict, the religious
and pious boy, when he saw his nurse weeping, filled with pity for her grief, took
away both parts of the broken sieve and tearfully betook himself to prayer. When
he arose from his prayer he found the vessel whole and sound at his side, so that no
trace of the fracture could be found in it, and presently, having kindly consoled
his nurse, he returned the sieve to her whole and sound which she had brought to
him broken" (id.).

[9] Benedict fled from his nurse and sought the solitude of waste places, whereupon the monk Romanus (whose name is derived from Rome which was pre-
eminently "the City") concealed him in a cave and ministered to his necessities
(Dialogues, II, ch. 1).

[10] Benedict remained three years in this cave at Sublacus (Subiaco) about forty
miles from Rome (id.).

Filled with God's love thou dost scorn frost and the tempest
    and snow.

Holy devices are pleasing; approved are the tricks of the
    pious,
Whereby the saint was sustained—holy devices delight.[11]

"Here is the feast of God's love," he signals; the spiteful one
    checks him;
None the less faith undismayed signals "The feast is at
    hand."[12]

Duly observes he the festivals who lendeth ear to Christ's
    teaching,
And when he breaketh his fast, duly observes he the feast.[13]

Eager the swineherds bear to the cave the food that is
    grateful,
Coming with willing hearts, pleasant the food they bear.[14]

Fire is by fire overcome, with sharp thorns tearing the body,
Flesh is by spirit subdued, fire is by fire overcome.[15]

[11] "This Romanus," says St. Gregory, "lived not far off in a monastery under the rule of father Adeodatus. But he piously stole away his hours from the presence of this same father of his, and carried to Benedict on certain days what bread he could purloin for him to eat. There was no way indeed to his cave from the cell of Romanus, because this cell stood high above the rocks. But Romanus was accustomed to let down the bread from that rock tied by a very long cord on which cord he put a little bell, so that the man of God at the sound of the bell might know when Romanus was offering him bread and go and get it" (id.).

[12] "But the ancient enemy," continues St. Gregory, "envying the charity of the one and the refreshment of the other, when upon a certain day he beheld Romanus letting down the bread, threw a stone and broke the little bell. Romanus, however, did not cease from providing for St. Benedict in appropriate ways" (id.).

[13] After the death of Romanus, God appeared to a certain priest who was making ready a meal for himself for the Easter festival and said, "You are preparing delicacies for yourself while my servant is tormented by hunger." So the priest sought St. Benedict and found him in his cave; and after prayer and holy conversation the priest said, "Rise, let us take food, for to-day is Easter." Since Benedict lived far from men he did not know that the Easter festival was on that day, but the priest again affirmed it, saying, "Truly to-day is the day of Easter, of the Resurrection of our Lord. It is not at all fitting for thee to fast and I have been sent for this purpose that we may partake together of the gifts of God Almighty." Then blessing God, they took food (id.).

[14] The neighboring shepherds (or swineherds), discover St. Benedict in his concealment and supply the meagre food required by the hermit (id.).

[15] St. Benedict when at Sublacus was tempted by an evil spirit (which came to him in the form of a blackbird) with the recollection of a beautiful woman,

Deadly the poison concealed, yet, perceived from afar by
the shrewd one,
Brooked not the sign of the cross—deadly the poison concealed.[16]

Gentle reproving of scourges steadies the wandering spirit,
Gently the blows of the scourge roaming destruction avert.[17]

Forth from the native rock, flows water in streams never
failing,
Waters the hearts that are dry—ever unfailing the stream.[18]

Steel from the handle torn, thou seekest the deepest abysses,
Steel, thou desertest the depths, seeking the surface again.[19]

whereupon he rushed from his cave and flung himself naked into a thicket of
briers and nettles. Thereupon the fiends left him and he was never again beset
with the same temptation. St. Gregory says, "Since he burned well without in his
penances, he extinguished what was burning unlawfully within" (id. ch. 2).

[16] While Benedict was at Sublacus, a neighboring society of monks sent to
request that he would place himself at their head. He yielded upon great
persuasion and by the strictness of his life and rule filled them with rage, until one
of them offered him poison in a cup of wine. Benedict blessed it with the sign of
the cross, and the glass vessel in which it was contained was broken as if by a
stone. Benedict then returned to his cave (id. ch. 3).

[17] In one of the monasteries in the neighborhood, one of the brothers had an
aversion to long prayers, and with a wandering disposition went out and busied
himself with earthly and transitory things. After he had been admonished by the
abbot he was brought to Benedict, who reproved him earnestly. For two days he
observed the injunctions of the man of God but on the third day he went back to
his old habit and began to wander at the time of prayer. Benedict came to the
monastery and noticed that a little black boy was pulling the monk by the border
of his garment. "Then he said secretly to Pompeianus the father of the monastery
and to Maurus the servant of God—'Do you not see who it is that is drawing the
monk outside?' And they answered and said, 'No.' And he said to them, 'We will
pray that you also may see whom that monk is following.' And when they had
prayed for two days the monk Maurus saw, but Pompeianus, the father of that
monastery, could not see. On another day then after prayers, the man of God went
forth from the monastery and found the monk standing outside and struck him
with a switch for the blindness of his heart and he from that day submitted to no
further persuasion from the black boy, but remained immovable in his assiduity in
prayer."

[18] Many came to Sublacus to serve God, drawn by the fame of Benedict's
sanctity and miracles. He directed them to construct twelve monasteries in each of
which he placed twelve disciples with a superior (ch. 3). On one occasion certain
monks came to complain to him that three of the monasteries were in want of
water. Benedict by his prayers procured a fountain which gushed forth and
flowed down the mountain side (ch. 5).

[19] At another time, says Gregory, a certain Goth, poor in spirit came for
conversion, whom Benedict the man of God received most willingly. On a certain
day indeed he ordered that an iron tool be given to him, which from its likeness to

Bearing the father's commands, he flees and lives on the waters,
Borne by the waters he runs, bearing the father's commands.

Prompt to his master's bidding, the waves to him offered a pathway,
While he in ignorance ran, offered the waters a path.

Little lad, thou too art seized by the waves, yet perishest never,
Truthful witness art thou, little lad ready at hand.[20]

Hearts that are faithless groan, spurred on by malignant incentives;
Flaming with torrents of hell, hearts that are faithless groan.[21]

Beareth the raven with talons obliging the food that is offered;
Bidden, the raven bears far off the terrible food.[22]

Holy the bosom that mourns for a foe overthrown by destruction;
Holy the bosom that mourns when his disciple exults.[23]

a sickle (*falx*) is called a brush-hook (*falcastrum*), in order to cut away the briers from a certain place so that a garden should be made there. But the place which the Goth had undertaken to clear lay above the shore of a lake. And when that Goth was cutting away the thicket of thorns with the exertion of all his strength, the iron, springing forth from the handle, fell into the lake where the depth of the water was so great that there was no hope of getting back the tool. ° ° ° Then Benedict the man of God hearing these things went to the lake. He took the handle from the hand of the Goth and cast it into the lake and presently the iron came back from the bottom and went into the handle, and straightway he returned the iron tool to the Goth saying, "See, work and do not grieve" (ch. 6).

[20] These three distichs refer to Maurus and Placidius, two boys who were brought by their fathers, Equitius and Tertulius, to Benedict to be instructed (ch. 3). They became the chief disciples of St. Benedict, and were afterwards canonized. Placidius, while yet a child, in going to draw water, fell into a lake. Benedict, who was praying in his cell, had a revelation of the danger, and sent Maurus in all haste to help him. Maurus rushed to his assistance, and without knowing it, trod the water as if it had been dry land (ch. 7). Benedict attributed this miracle to the obedience of Maurus, but Maurus disclaimed all merit. The boy Placidius as the "truthful witness" now appeared and declared that he had seen the garb of the saint above his head when he was drawn from the water (id.).

[21] The wicked priest Florentius, who was filled with jealousy and envy at the superior holiness of the saint, endeavored to blacken his reputation, and at last attempted his life by sending him a poisoned loaf (ch. 8).

[22] Benedict, when the poisoned loaf was given him, being aware of the treachery, threw it upon the ground and commanded a tame raven to carry it away and place it beyond the reach of any living creature, which was done (id.)

[23] After the attempt was made upon his life, the saint departed from Sublacus, but scarcely had he left the place when Maurus, his faithful disciple, sent a

Seeking the Liris' sweet places, full splendid the train that attends thee;
Prompted from heaven thou art, seeking the Liris' fair site.[24]

Serpent accursed! thou ravest, despoiled of thy grove and thy altars!
Banished the crowd that adored! Curst serpent, how dost thou rave![25]

Impious sitter! Depart! To the walls let marbles be given!
Thou art constrained by command! Impious sitter depart![26]

Greedy the fire that is seen arising in flashes deceitful;
Bright jewel! Not by thy eyes—fire that consumeth is seen.[27]

While they are building the wall, the flesh of a brother is mangled,

messenger to tell him that his enemy Florentius had been crushed by the fall of a gallery of his house. Benedict wept for Florentius, and imposed a penance on Maurus for an expression of triumph at the judgment which had overtaken their enemy (ch. 8).

[24] Benedict at last left Sublacus and proceeded to Monte Cassino, a delightful spot, where he afterwards established the parent Benedictine monastery of Italy. At the foot of Monte Cassino flowed the river Liris (ch. 8, Waitz). Paul tells us (I, 26) that two angels in the shape of young men came to Benedict at the crossroads and pointed out the way, also that he went thither by divine admonition.

[25] A temple to Apollo stood in a consecrated grove near the summit of Monte Cassino, where a nest of idolaters still worshiped the god, or, as he was then regarded, the demon. Benedict, who had heard of this abomination, came to the place, preached Christianity, converted the worshipers, broke the statue, threw down the altar, burned the consecrated grove, and built two chapels, one to St. John the Baptist and the other to St. Martin of Tours, on the spot where the god was worshiped. The "old enemy," as Gregory calls him, did not bear this in silence, but appeared before the blessed father very hideous and infuriated, and seemed to rave against him with flaming eyes, first calling him "Benedict" (blessed), and when he would not answer, "Maledict" (accursed) (ch. 8).

[26] While the monks were building their monastery, a stone lay in the midst of them which they determined to lift into the building, but it was so immovable that it seemed evident that the "old enemy" was sitting upon it. The "man of God" was sent for, and when he had come and prayed and given his benediction, it was "lifted with such speed as if it had no weight before" (ch. 9).

[27] In digging the foundations of Monte Cassino, a bronze idol was discovered, from which issued a supernatural fire that to the brothers seemed as if it would burn up the kitchen. They threw water on it and tried to put it out. When Benedict came, attracted by the tumult, he found that this fire existed only in the eyes of the monks, and was not visible to him. Whereupon he delivered them from the illusion of the fancied fire (ch. 10).

But his preserver is there, while they are building the wall.[28]

Things that were hid are revealed, the greedy exposed to the
  daylight;
Gifts that are secretly ta'en, quickly to him are revealed.[29]

Tyrant cruel and fell! the snares of thy fraud are defeated;[30]
Tyrant stern! thou receiv'st bridle and curb for thy life! [31]

Towering walls of Numa—never shall foe overthrow them;
Whirlwinds he says shall destroy Numa's towering walls.[32]

[28] One of the monks who was assisting in building the monastery was crushed,
and was brought to St. Benedict, who prayed earnestly, restored him, and sent
him back to his work safe and sound (ch. 11).

[29] It was the custom of the monastery that whenever the monks went out on any
business, they should not partake of food and drink away from the convent. One
day when they remained later than usual, they took refreshment at the house of a
nun, and when they returned and asked the blessing of the saint, he inquired,
"Where did you eat?" and they answered, "Nowhere," and he said to them, "Why
do you lie? Did you not enter the dwelling of such a woman? Did you not take this
and that food? Did you not drink so many goblets?" and when they saw he knew
all they fell trembling at his feet and confessed (ch. 12). Much the same thing
occurred to the brother of the monk Valentinian, who came fasting to Benedict,
but was tempted to eat on the way by a companion accompanying him to the
monastery (ch. 13). Also on one occasion St. Benedict sent one of his disciples to a
company of nuns to deliver an exhortation. The nuns begged the monk to accept
some handkerchiefs they had made, and he hid them in his blossom. On his return
to the monastery Benedict asked, "Why have you suffered iniquity to enter into
your bosom?" The monk could not tell what the saint referred to. Benedict added,
"Was I not with you when you received the handkerchiefs from the nuns and hid
them in your bosom?" The monk fell at the feet of the abbot, repented his foolish
act and threw away the handkerchiefs (ch. 19).

[30] Totila, king of the Goths, hearing that Benedict possessed the spirit of
prophecy, and desiring to prove him, attired Riggo, his armor-bearer, in the royal
garments and sent him with an escort to the monastery. Benedict seeing him
coming cried out, "Put off, my son, those borrowed trappings; they are not thine
own" (ch. 14).

[31] Totila thereupon went in person to visit the saint, who chided him for his evil
deeds, told him that he would enter Rome, that he would pass across the sea (to
Sicily), and would reign nine years, but would die upon the tenth, all of which
occurred (ch. 15). Totila was held by the Romans of the Eastern empire to be a
usurper, a cruel tyrant, etc. His actual character shines brightly in contrast with
that of Justinian, against whom his wars were waged.

[32] This prophecy by Benedict was: "Rome shall not be exterminated by the
heathen, but, worn out by tempests and whirlwinds and an earthquake, shall
decay of itself" (ch. 15). The prediction relates to Totila's project of capturing
Rome. Rome was in fact taken by Totila in 546, retaken by Belisarius in 547, taken
again by Totila in 549, and retaken by Narses in 552 (Gibbon, ch. 43). On the
occasion of its first capture by Totila he actually demolished, it is said, one-third of

Grievous the foe to chastise thee for offering gifts at the altar;
Gifts to the altars thou bring'st—grievous the foe to chastise.[33]

It was foreknown that the sheepfolds should be to the heathen delivered;
That same heathen race all of the sheepfolds restores.[34]

Servant, friend of deceit, thou art tempted by serpent alluring;
Not by the serpent entrapped, servant and friend of deceit.[35]

Hush! spirit swollen with pride! Be silent! carp not, for he sees thee!
All things are known to the seer. Hush! spirit swollen with pride![36]

Famine is driven away by nourishment coming from heaven;
Gloomy hunger of mind also is driven away.[37]

the walls, and issued a decree that Rome should be changed into a pasture for cattle, but on the remonstrance of Belisarius he spared the city. Gregory insists that Benedict's prophecy was fulfilled (ch. 15).

[33] A certain priest possessed of a devil was brought to St. Benedict and healed, but was warned never to exercise the duties of his holy office, or he would be again delivered into the power of the devil. After some years, he neglected the warning and undertook again his sacred functions, whereupon the devil again took possession of him, and did not cease to torment him (ch. 16).

[34] Benedict predicted that his convent should pass into the hands of the Arian Langobards, by whom (after they had become converted to the Catholic faith) Monte Cassino was restored and the whole Benedictine order was greatly favored (ch. 17, see Waitz's note).

[35] A man of high condition sent St. Benedict two flasks of wine but the servant who carried them stole one and hid it. When he delivered the other at the monastery the saint said to him "See, my son, that you don't drink out of the flask you have hidden, but turn it over carefully and you will find what it has inside." The man did so and a serpent came forth. The servant afterwards became brother "Exhilaratus" (ch. 18).

[36] Once when St. Benedict was at supper, a monk who held a lamp in front of the table began silently to reflect in a spirit of pride and to say to himself, "Who is this man whom I must attend while he eats and hold his lamp and render him service, and who am I that serve him?" And the saint turned to him at once and began to reproach him earnestly saying, "Cross your heart, brother! What is it you are saying? Cross your heart." And he called the brothers together and directed that the lamp should be taken from his hands and that he should withdraw from this service and sit down quietly. And when the man was asked what he had in his heart, he told them and it was clear to all that nothing could be hidden from St. Benedict (ch. 20).

[37] At another time there was a famine in Campania, and wheat was lacking in the monastery so that only five loaves of bread could be found. And when Benedict

Bodiless, seen by the spirit, all hearts are amazed at thy
    presence;
Counseling things thou discern'st—hearts with amazement
    are dumb.[38]

At the command of thy voice they scorn to bridle their
    gossip. Forth from the tombs they flee at the command
    of thy voice.[39]

They at command of thy voice from the sacred rites are
    forbidden;
Present they are at these rites at the command of thy voice.[40]

Earth from its open breast drives forth the sepulchered body;
Earth when commanded by thee, keeps in her bosom the
    corpse.[41]

saw that the monks were troubled, he strove by modest reproofs to remove their
weak fears and promised that on the following day they should have an abundance. And indeed on the next day two hundred measures of flour were found in
sacks at the gates of the monastery, sent from God Almighty by an unknown hand.
When the monks saw this, they gave thanks to the Lord and now learned that even
when in want they should not doubt of abundance (ch. 21).

[38] Benedict had been asked to build a monastery near the city of Tarracina, and
sending certain disciples of his thither, he appointed over them a father superior
and one second in authority, and promised them that on a certain day he would
come and show them in what place they should build the chapel, in what place the
refectory, etc. They made due preparation to receive him, and in the night
preceding the promised day, he appeared to the father superior and to his
superintendent in their dreams and told them minutely where they should build
everything. Still they looked for him to come, and when he did not, they went to
him to make inquiry. And he answered, "Did I not come as I promised?" And
they said, "When did you come?" and he replied, "Did I not come to each of you
in your dreams and point out to you each of the places? Go and build every
building as you heard in your vision." And hearing these things they wondered
greatly and built the dwellings as they had been taught in the dream (ch. 22).

[39] Two certain ladies of a religious sisterhood were given to scandalous talk, and
Benedict sent them word that if they did not keep guard over their tongues he
would excommunicate them. But they continued in their evil ways and died and
were buried in church. Afterwards when mass was celebrated, as the officiating
deacon uttered the usual words, "Let those who are excommunicated depart,"
they were seen to rise from their graves and go out of church (ch. 23).

[40] That is, they rose from their graves at every mass until St. Benedict offered a
sacrifice for them, after which they remained in the tomb (id.).

[41] A certain novice who loved his parents more than he ought, one day went
home from the monastery without a benediction and died, and when he was
buried on the following day, his body was found cast forth from the tomb, and he
was buried again. This occurred a second time, whereupon they besought St.
Benedict in tears that he would deign to bestow his grace upon the body. He gave

Faithless the heart of the dragon that lures the truant to
hasten,[42]
While the treacherous fiend stops his prohibited way.

Deadly the foul distemper that stripped the head of its honor;
At his command it departs—noisome and deadly disease! [43]

Gold has the holy man none, yet promises all to the needy,
Promises all and draws coins of bright metal from heav'n! [44]

Thou to be pitied! With skin by the gall of a serpent dis-
colored!
Wretched one! Sound and whole, quickly thy skin is restored.[45]

Glass is dashed on the rocks and yet they are powerless to
break it;
Kept by the rugged rocks, safely the glass is preserved.[46]

Cellarer, why dost thou fear to offer a drop from the oil flask?
Look! the great jars overflow! Cellarer, why dost thou fear?[47]

them the host and told them to place it upon the corpse. When this was done the
body remained in the tomb (ch. 24).

[42] A certain monk of restless spirit would not remain in the community, and St.
Benedict, annoyed and offended by his importunities, ordered him to depart.
When he went out of the monastery a dragon with open mouth stood in his way
and attempted to devour him, whereupon he called aloud to the monks to run to
his assistance. When they did so they could not see the dragon, but they led the
monk back to the monastery trembling with fear. He promised never to depart
again and kept his promise (ch. 25).

[43] A boy had been seized with a leprosy so that his hair fell off and his skin was
swollen and he could no longer conceal his diseased humors. He was brought by
his father to Benedict and speedily healed (ch. 26).

[44] A poor man owed twelve solidi which he was unable to pay and applied in his
distress to St. Benedict who said he had not so large a sum, but asked the man to
come again in two days. The man returned at the time appointed and thirteen
solidi were found on a box in the monastery which was full of grain. St. Benedict
gave the whole to the man for his debt and his present needs (ch. 27).

[45] Poison was given to a certain man by his enemy in a potion, and although he
did not die, his skin changed color so that he resembled a leper. He was brought to
St. Benedict who restored him and removed the discoloration (ch. 27).

[46] During a time of famine Agapitus, a sub-deacon of Monte Cassino, applied to
St. Benedict for oil. There was then in the monastery only a few dregs at the
bottom of a glass bottle. Benedict commanded the cellarer to give what there was,
but the latter did not obey the order. When St. Benedict heard this he ordered the
bottle thrown out of the window upon the rocks, but the bottle was not broken
nor the oil spilled (ch. 28).

[47] He then assembled the whole house in full chapter and reproved the cellarer
and when the chapter broke up a huge jar which had been empty began to
overflow with oil (ch. 29).

Where is the healing for thee, and why is no hope of salvation;
Thou who dost ever destroy, where is the healing for thee? [48]

Old man worthy of tears! thou fallest by blow of the foeman,
But by a blow thou reviv'st—ancient one worthy of tears! [49]

Barbarous thongs encircle the hands that are guiltless of evil,
Hands that escape of themselves, slipping from barbarous
thongs. [50]

That proud man on the horse crying with threatening clamor,
Stretched on the ground he lies, arrogant man on the horse! [51]

Borne on the neck of his sire was the corpse of a child that had
perished;
Living, the child was borne forth on the neck of his sire. [52]

[48] This probably refers to the "old enemy," whom St. Benedict met in the shape
of a mule doctor with his horns and triple footfetters (ch. 30).

[49] This evil spirit found an old man drawing water, attacked him, threw him
upon the ground and tormented him bitterly. When St. Benedict saw him thus
cruelly treated, he gave him merely a box on the ear, and straightway drove out
the evil spirit so that it did not dare to return to him (ch. 30).

[50] A certain Goth named Zalla cruelly tormented a peasant to extort money from
him. The peasant said he had given all he possessed to the keeping of St. Benedict,
whereupon the Goth bound him with strong cords and made him run in front of
his horse to the monastery. They found St. Benedict sitting alone reading, and the
Goth in a threatening tone cried out, "Up! up! I say, give this peasant the money
you took from him." St. Benedict glanced at the peasant, whereupon the cords
broke and left the man free, and the Goth threw himself at the feet of the saint,
besought his prayers, and troubled the peasant no more for the money (ch. 31).

[51] This appears to be the same miracle as the preceding distich.

[52] A certain peasant brought to the monastery the body of his dead child, and
when he found St. Benedict was absent he laid the corpse down at the gate of the
monastery and went to look for the saint and when he saw him he began to cry
out, "Restore my son! Restore my son!" The man of God paused upon this word
saying, "Did I take away your son from you?" and the other answered, "He is
dead. Come bring him to life." Benedict asked, "Why do you impose burdens
upon us which we cannot bear?" But the other, whom his great grief overcame,
persisted in his petition, swearing that he would not depart unless they restored his
son to life. Presently the servant of God asked him saying, "Where is he?" and he
answered him, "See, his body lies at the gate of the monastery." When the man of
God came with the brethren, he bent his knees and lay down over the body of the
child and lifting himself, held his hands to Heaven saying, "Lord, consider not my
sins but the faith of this man who asks that his son should be brought to life, and
do Thou resotre to this little body the soul which Thou hast withdrawn." Presently
he had finished the words of his prayer and the whole body of the child was
trembling, and under the eyes of all who were present it appeared to throb with a
wonderful tremor and shaking, and presently Benedict held the boy by the hand
and gave him, living and whole again, to his father (ch. 32).

Love conquers all. By a storm the sister prevails o'er her
   brother.[53]
Sleep from their eyes was driven—love ever conquereth all.

Lovely with innocent charm, the form of a dove flies upward,
Enters the kingdom of heav'n—lovely with innocent charm![54]

O thou well fitted for God! To thee the whole world is
   unfolded,
Hidden things then dost prove, O thou well fitted for God!

Flaming the sphere that encircles the just man soaring to
   heaven,
Flaming the sphere that contains him who with love is consumed.[55]

Thrice called, he is at hand, to be counted a witness of
   marvels;
Thrice called, he is at hand, dear in the love of the saint.[56]

Brave leader! warning of wars, thou confirmest our hearts by
   example,[57]
Rushing the first to arms! brave leader warning of wars!

[53] This refers to Benedict's sister Scholastica who had devoted herself to a
religious life. Benedict used to visit her once a year and on one occasion when they
had been conversing until late in the evening, his sister entreated him to remain till
morning, but he refused. Scholastica then prayed that heaven would interfere and
render it impossible for him to leave her. Immediately a furious tempest came on
and Benedict was obliged to delay his departure and they held holy conversation
through the night. Gregory explains that the sister's prayers were in this case of
greater power than the brother's will since she had the greater love. It was a last
meeting, as Scholastica died three days afterwards (ch. 33 and 34).

[54] As St. Scholastica died, Benedict was praying in his cell, when suddenly her
soul appeared to him ascending to heaven in the form of a dove (ch. 34).

[55] On the night that St. Germanus died, Benedict opened his casement to look at
the starry heavens, and beheld a brilliant light, brighter than at midday, and the
whole world collected, as it were, under a single ray of the sun, and the soul of St.
Germanus, bishop of Capua, borne by angels to heaven in a sphere of fire (ch. 35).

[56] Servandus, a deacon and abbot of a monastery in Campania, was visiting
Monte Cassino when Benedict saw the fiery sphere, and was in a room in the
tower of the monastery just below that occupied by the saint. When Benedict saw
the vision, he called Servandus three times loudly by name, so that the latter might
be a witness of the marvelous sight. Servandus came, but saw only a little part of
the great light. Benedict sent to Capua and found that Germanus had died at the
moment of the vision (ch. 35).

[57] Gregory, referring to the establishment by Benedict of the Rule of the
Benedictine Order, says that in this Rule may be found the model of his own life,
"because he could not teach otherwise than he lived" (ch. 36).

Suitable tokens he gave, life's fellowships gladly forsaking;
Hastening to life in heaven, suitable tokens he gave.[58]

Diligent chanter of psalms, to his lute gave he never a respite;
Died with a song on his lips, diligent chanter of psalms!

Held in the same tomb they whose minds were ever united,[59]
Equal the fame that preserves those whose spirits were one!

Splendid appeared the pathway and crowded with gleaming
    torches,
Whereon the holy one rose—splendid the path that was
    seen.[60]

Seeking the stony enclosures, it[61] found salvation from error,
Shunned all error and sin, seeking the cloisters of stone.

Suppliant for a reward, thy servant has given thee verses,
Powerless, an exile, weak, meagre the verses he gives.

May they be fitting I pray, O guide to the paths celestial.
Benedict, father! I pray, may they be fitting for thee.[62]

[58] He foretold his own death, and told the absent what sign he would give them when his soul should leave his body. On the day of his death he took the sacrament, and held by the monks, stood with hands lifted to heaven, and breathed his last in prayer (ch. 37).

[59] St. Benedict and St. Scholastica were both buried at Monte Cassino. St. Gregory says, "Their bodies were not separated in the sepulcher whose minds were always one in God" (ch. 34).

[60] On the day St. Benedict died, two of his disciples at different places saw the same vision, a path spread with draperies and bright with innumerable torches, which began at the cell of St. Benedict and terminated in heaven, and a venerable old man, all glorious, said to them, "By this pathway St. Benedict, beloved of God, ascends to heaven." They knew from the sign what had been predicted (ch. 37).

[61] I. e., the pathway.

[62] The versification of these so-called elegiac epanaleptical distichs requires that the words composing the first two dactyls and the following long syllable at the beginning of the first line (a dactylic hexameter) shall be repeated at the end of the second line (a dactylic pentameter), thus composing the last half of that line. I have not been able to reproduce this extremely artificial berse in every case, but have kept as near to it as possible. This form of versification appears to have been first used in jest by Martial in the 9th Book of his *Epigrams*, 98, in the verses beginning:

> Rumpitur invidia quidam, carissima Juli,
>   Quod me Roma legit, rumpitur invidia.

Bethmann (p. 278) remarks that it was afterwards employed by Pentadius, Sedulius, Bede and Alcuin, but still later it fell into disuse.

Ebert suggests (*Litteratur des Mittelalters*, II, 55, note 4) that perhaps the purpose of this poem was to impress upon the memory of the reader a list of the miracles of St. Benedict. A knowledge of each particular miracle seems to have been presupposed.

We have also composed in the following manner a hymn in
iambic Archilochian meter containing each of the miracles of the
same father:

> O brothers all, with eager hearts
> Come ye, with fitting melody,
> Let us enjoy the pure delights
> Of this most famous festival.[1]

> Now Father Benedict the guide
> Who pointed out the narrow way,
> To the bright realms of heaven rose,
> Winning rewards for all his toils.

> Like a new star he shone, and drove
> Away the gloomy clouds of earth.
> He from the very dawn of life
> Despised the pleasures of the world.

> Of mighty power in miracles,
> Inspired by breath of the Most High,
> He shone in marvels, and foretold
> The future happenings of his age.

> Since he to many food would bear,
> The small bread vessel he repairs;
> Sought for himself a narrow cell,
> And fires by fires he sternly quenched.

> The goblet which the poison bore
> He broke by holy sign of cross;
> The roaming spirit he constrained
> By gentle scourging of the flesh.

> The streams gush forth from out the rocks;
> The steel returns from out the depths,

---

[1] The festival of St. Benedict occurring March 21.

Coursing compliant through the waves;
The boy by the saint's garb shuns death.[2]

The hidden poison is revealed;
The bird fulfills the saint's commands;
Destruction overcomes his foe;
The roaring lion perforce departs.[3]

The stubborn mass is moved with ease;[4]
The fire fantastic disappears;
Unto the mangled, health returns;
Sin of the absent stands revealed.

O crafty ruler, thou art caught!
Wicked possessor, thou dost flee![5]
Deeds of the future, ye are known!
Heart, thou dost hide[6] no secret things!

The buildings are laid out in dreams;[7]
The earth casts forth the buried corpse;
The wand'rer is by dragon stayed;
The gold coins fall in rain from heaven.

The glass resists the rugged rocks;
The great jars overflow with oil;
Thy glance releases one in bonds;
Bodies of dead recover life.

The power of such a radiant light
By sister's prayer is overcome;

---

[2] When Placidus was saved from drowning in the lake he claimed that he had seen the *melote* (monk's garb of skins) of St. Benedict (*Dialogues* II, ch. 7; see Du Cange).

[3] This probably refers to the heathen worship suppressed by Benedict at Monte Cassino.

[4] This refers to the stone which the devil rendered immovable when the monks were building the monastery.

[5] Totila departed greatly alarmed at Benedict's prophecies (ch. 15).

[6] Read *contegis* for *contigis*.

[7] The monastery of Tarracina.

And who loves more can better sail
His bark than he who sees the pole.

A splendor through night's darkness gleamed
To former ages quite unknown,
Wherein a whole globe is beheld,
And upward drawn by flames, a saint.

Amid these wonders, fame he won
With the soft lute, like nectar sweet;
And for his followers he sketched
Fitly the line of holy life.[8]

To thy disciples, leader strong,
Be present now! we sigh for thee.
Shunning the serpent, we would grow
In virtues following thy steps!

---

[8] He promulgated the famous Rule of the Order, which became the general law of the monks of the Western Empire, and gave to monasticism its definite form (see ch. 36).

5
Jonas

Life of St. Columbanus

St. Columbanus (c.560–615), a contemporary of Gregory the Great, travelled from Ireland through Gaul and into Italy, where he founded a number of monasteries, the greatest being Bobbio in northern Italy. The independent and idiosyncratic Irish Christianity of the sixth century made much of both penitential pilgrimage out of Ireland and the conversion of pagans. Many such Irish monks came to Gaul, but the life of Columbanus by Jonas, derived from impressions of the saint's own companions, is the only complete one we possess.

6. Columban, who is also called Columba, was born on the island of Ireland. This is situated in the extreme ocean and, according to common report, is charming, productive of various nations, and free from the wars which trouble other nations. Here lives the race of the Scots, who, although they lack the laws of the other nations, flourish in the doctrine of Christian strength, and exceed in faith all the neighboring tribes. Columban was born amid the beginnings of that race's faith, in order that the religion, which that race cherished uncompromisingly, might be increased by his own fruitful toil and the protecting care of his associates.

But what happened before his birth, before he saw the light of this world, must not be passed over in silence. For when his mother, after having conceived, was bearing him in her womb, suddenly in a tempestuous night, while she was buried in sleep, she saw the sun rise from her bosom and issuing forth resplendent, furnish great light to the world. After she had arisen from sleep and Aurora rising had driven away the dark shadows from

the world, she began to think earnestly of these matters, joyfully
and wisely weighing the import of so great a vision; and she
sought an increase of consolation from such of her neighbors as
were learned, asking that with wise hearts they should examine
carefully the meaning of so great a vision. At length she was told
by those who had wisely considered the matter, that she was
carrying in her womb a man of remarkable genius, who would
provide what would be useful for her own salvation and for that
of her neighbors.

After the mother learned this she watched over him with so
great care that she would scarcely entrust him even to his nearest
relatives. So the life of the boy aspired to the cultivation of good
works under the leadership of Christ, without whom no good
work is done. Nor without reason had the mother seen the shining
sun proceed from her bosom, the sun which shines brightly in the
members of the Church, the mother of all, like a glowing
Phoebus. As the Lord says: "Then shall the righteous shine forth as
the sun in the kingdom of their Father." So Deborah, with the
voice of prayer, formerly spoke to the Lord, by the admonition of
the Holy Spirit, saying: "But let them that love Thee be as the sun
when he goeth forth in his might."

For the milky way in the heavens, although it is itself bright, is
rendered more beautiful by the presence of the other stars; just as
the daylight, increased by the splendor of Phoebus, shines more
benignantly upon the world. So the body of the Church, enriched
by the splendor of its Founder, is augmented by the hosts of saints
and is made resplendent by religion and learning, so that those
who come after draw profit from the concourse of the learned.
And just as the sun or moon and all the stars ennoble the day and
night by their refulgence, so the merits of the holy priests increase
the glory of the Church.

7. When Columban's childhood was over and he became
older, he began to devote himself enthusiastically to the pursuit of
grammar and the sciences, and studied with fruitful zeal all
through his boyhood and youth, until he became a man. But, as
his fine figure, his splendid color, and his noble manliness made
him beloved by all, the old enemy began finally to turn his deadly
weapons upon him, in order to catch in his nets this youth, whom

he saw growing so rapidly in grace. And he aroused against him the lust of lascivious maidens, especially of those whose fine figure and superficial beauty are wont to enkindle mad desires in the minds of wretched men.

But when that excellent soldier saw that he was surrounded on all sides by so deadly weapons, and perceived the cunning and shrewdness of the enemy who was fighting against him, and that by an act of human frailty, he might quickly fall over a precipice and be destroyed,—as Livy says, "No one is rendered so sacred by religion, no one is so guarded, that lust is unable to prevail against him,"—holding in his left hand the shield of the Gospel and bearing in his right hand the two-edged sword, he prepared to advance and attack the hostile lines threatening him. He feared lest, ensnared by the lusts of the world, he should in vain have spent so much labor on grammar, rhetoric, geometry and the Holy Scriptures. And in these perils he was strengthened by a particular aid.

8. When he was already meditating upon this purpose, he came to the dwelling of a holy and devout woman. He at first addressed her humbly, afterwards he began to exhort her, as far as lay in his power. As she saw the increasing strength of the youth she said: "I have gone forth to the strife as far as it lay in my power. Lo, twelve years have passed by, since I have been far from my home and have sought out this place of pilgrimage. With the aid of Christ, never since then have I engaged in secular matters; after putting my hand to the plough, I have not turned backward. And if the weakness of my sex had not prevented me, I would have crossed the sea and chosen a better place among strangers as my home. But you, glowing with the fire of youth, stay quietly on your native soil; out of weakness you lend your ear even against your own will, to the voice of the flesh, and think you can associate with the female sex without sin. But do you recall the wiles of Eve, Adam's fall, how Samson was deceived by Delilah, how David was led to injustice by the beauty of Bathsheba, how the wise Solomon was ensnared by the love of a woman? Away, O youth! away! flee from corruption, into which, as you know, many have fallen. Forsake the path which leads to the gates of hell."

The youth, trembling at these words, which were such as to terrify a youth, thanked her for her reproaches, took leave of his companions and set out. His mother in anguish begged him not to leave her. But he said: "Hast thou not heard, 'He that loveth father or mother more than Me is not worthy of Me?' " He begged his mother, who placed herself in his way and held the door, to let him go. Weeping and stretched upon the floor, she said she would not permit it. Then leaping over both threshold and mother he asked his mother not to give way to her grief; she would never see him again in this life, but wherever the way of salvation led him, there he would go.

9. When he left his birthplace, called by the inhabitants, Lagener-land,[1] he betook himself to a holy man named Sinell, who at this time was distinguished among his countrymen for his unusual piety and knowledge of the Holy Scriptures. And when the holy man saw that St. Columban had great ability, he instructed him in the knowledge of all the Holy Scriptures. Nevertheless, as was usual, the master attempted to draw out the pupils under false pretences, in order that he might learn their dispositions, either the glowing excess of the senses, or the torpor induced by slothfulness. He began to inquire into Columban's disposition by difficult questions. But the latter tremblingly, nevertheless wisely, in order not to appear disobedient, nor touched by the vice of the love of vainglory, obeyed his master, and explained in turn all the objections that were made, mindful of the saying of the Psalmist, "Open thy mouth wide and I will fill it." Thus Columban collected such treasures of holy wisdom in his breast that he could, even as a youth, expound the Psalter in fitting language and could make many other extracts worthy to be sung, and instructive to read.

Then he endeavored to enter a society of monks, and went to the monastery of Bangor.[2] The abbot, the holy Congall, renowned for his virtues, was a faithful father to his monks and was held in high esteem for the fervor of his faith and the order and discipline which he preserved. Here Columban gave himself entirely to fasting and prayer, to bearing the easy yoke of Christ, to mortifying the flesh,

[1] Leinster, in Ireland.
[2] In the County of Ulster, in Ireland.

to taking the cross upon himself and following Christ, in order that he who was to be a teacher of others might show the learning which he taught more fruitfully by his own example in mortifying his own body; and that he who was to instruct others might first instruct himself.

After he had been many years in the cloister he longed to go into strange lands, in obedience to the command which the Lord gave Abraham: "Get thee out of thy country, and from thy kindred, and from thy father's house, into a land that I will show thee." Accordingly he confessed to the venerable father, Congall, the burning desire of his heart and the longing enkindled by the fire of the Lord, concerning which the Lord says: "I am come to send fire on the earth; and what will I, if it be already kindled?"[3] But he did not receive the answer which he wished, for it was hard for Congall to bear the loss of so great a comfort. At length, however, the latter began to conquer himself and to think that he ought not to consider his own need more than the necessities of others. Nor was it done without the will of the Almighty, who had educated His novice for future strifes, in order that He might win glorious triumphs from his victory and secure joyful victories from the phalanxes of slaughtered enemies.

The abbot accordingly called St. Columban, and although sorrowful, he considered the good of others before his own good, and bestowed upon him the bond of peace, the strength of solace and companions who were known for their piety.

10. Having collected a band of brethren, St. Columban asked the prayers of all, that he might be assisted in his coming journey, and that he might have their pious aid. So he started out in the twentieth[4] year of his life, and under the guidance of Christ went to the seashore with twelve companions. Here they waited to see if the mercy of the Almighty would allow their purpose to succeed, and learned that the spirit of the all-merciful Judge was with them. So they embarked, and began the dangerous journey across the channel and sailed quickly with a smooth sea and favorable wind to the coast of Brittany. Here they rested for a while to recover

---

[3] Luke xii., 49. I have followed the King James version for the translation. The Vulgate, which is quoted here, reads *quem volo ut ardeat.*

[4] More probably, thirtieth. The manuscripts differ.

their strength and discussed their plans anxiously, until finally they decided to enter the land of Gaul. They wanted zealously and shrewdly to inquire into the disposition of the inhabitants in order to remain longer if they found they could sow the seeds of salvation; or in case they found the hearts of the people in darkness, go on to the nearest nations.

11. Accordingly, they left Brittany and proceeded into the Gallic lands. At that time, either because of the numerous enemies from without, or on account of the carelessness of the bishops, the Christian faith had almost departed from that country. The creed alone remained. But the saving grace of penance and the longing to root out the lusts of the flesh were to be found only in a few. Everywhere that he went the noble man preached the Gospel. And it pleased the people, because his teaching was adorned by eloquence and enforced by examples of virtue.

So great was his humility and that of his followers, that just as the children of this world seek honor and authority, so they on the contrary vied with one another in the practice of humility, mindful of that saying: "He that humbleth himself shall be exalted," and of the text in Isaiah: "But to this man will I look, even to him that is poor and of a contrite spirit, and trembleth at my word." Such piety and love dwelt in them all, that for them there was only one will and one renunciation.

Modesty and *moderation*, *meekness* and *mildness* adorned them all in equal measure. The evils of sloth and dissension were banished. Pride and haughtiness were expiated by severe punishments. Scorn and envy were driven out by faithful diligence. So great was the might of their patience, love and mildness that no one could doubt that the God of mercy dwelt among them. If they found that one among them was in error, they strove in common, with equal right, to restrain the sinner by their reproaches. They had everything in common. If anyone claimed anything as his own, he was shut out from association with the others and punished by penances. No one dared to return evil for evil, or to let fall a harsh word; so that people must have believed that an angelic life was being lived by mortal men. The holy man was reverenced with so great gratitude that where he remained for a time in a house, all hearts were resolved to practice the faith more strictly.

12. Finally, the reports about Columban spread to the court of King Sigibert, who at this time ruled with honor over the two Frankish kingdoms of Austrasia and Burgundy.[5] The name of the Franks was held in honor above that of any of the other inhabitants of Gaul. When the holy man with his companions appeared before the king, the greatness of his learning caused him to stand high in the favor of the king and court. Finally, the king begged him to remain in Gallic territory, not to go to other peoples and leave him; everything that he wished should be done. Then he replied to the king that he did not wish to be enriched with the treasures of others, but as far as he was not hindered by the weakness of the flesh to follow the command of the Gospel: "Whosoever will come after me, let him deny himself and take up his cross and follow me."

Then the king answered and said: "If you wish to take the cross of Christ upon you and follow Him, seek the quiet of a hermitage. Only be careful, for the increase of your own reward and for our spiritual good, to remain in our kingdom and not to go to the neighboring peoples." As the choice was left to him in this manner, he followed the king's advice and chose for himself a hermitage. At that time there was a great wilderness called *Vosagus*,[6] in which there was a castle, which had long been in ruins, and which had been called for ages, *Anagrates*.[7] When the holy man came to that place, he settled there with his followers, in spite of the entire loneliness, the wilderness and the rocks, mindful of the proverb that, "Man shall not live by bread alone," but shall have sufficient food from the bread of life and shall never hunger.

13. While the man of God was in that place with his companions, one of the brethren, either as a test or because of some sin, began to be chastised by a violent fever. Since they had no food except such as the barks and herbs furnished, they began with one mind to desire that all should give themselves up to prayer and fasting for the sake of the welfare of their sick brother. Having now fasted for three days and having nothing to refresh their wearied bodies, suddenly they saw a certain man standing before

---

[5] Sigibert died 575, and was king only of Austrasia.
[6] The Vosges.
[7] Anegray.

their gate with horses loaded with a supply of bread and condiments. He said that he had been led by a sudden impulse of his heart to bear aid from his own substance to those who were, for Christ's sake, suffering from so great poverty in the wilderness. Therefore, having presented to the man of God what he had brought, he began to ask earnestly that the holy man should pray to God in behalf of his wife, who for a whole year had been burning with so violent a fever that it now seemed impossible that she could be restored to health. As he made his request with a humble and contrite heart, the man of God was unwilling to deny him any comfort, and having called together the brethren he invoked the mercy of God in behalf of that woman. When he and his companions had completed their prayer, the woman who had been in such imminent peril of death, was immediately restored to her health. When her husband had received the benediction from the man of God and had returned home, he found his wife sitting there. He questioned her as to the time when the fever left her and learned that she had been healed at the very hour when the man of God had prayed to the Lord in her behalf.

14. Therefore, after a brief space of time in which they piously endeavored to propitiate Christ and to atone for their evil thoughts, through mortification of the flesh and extreme fasting, they mortified their members to the glory of God, and desired to preserve the inviolate state of their religion. By their extreme severities every lust of the flesh was expelled, so that the plunderer and robber of all virtues fled. Nine days had already passed in which the man of God and his companions had taken no other food than the bark of trees and the roots of herbs. But the compassion of the divine virtue tempered the bitterness of the food. A certain abbot, named Caramtoc, who ruled over a monastry of which the name was *Salicis*, was warned by a vision, that he should bear the necessities of life to God's servant Columban, dwelling in the wilderness. Therefore, Caramtoc rising called his cellarer, Marculf by name, and told him what had happened. The latter replied, "Do as you have been told." Caramtoc therefore ordered Marculf to go and prepare everything that he could, to carry to St. Columban. Marculf, accordingly, having loaded his wagons started out. But when the hour

of darkness came on, he sought in vain for a way to continue his
journey. Nevertheless, he thought that if the command was from
God, the power of the Commander would show the way to the
horses, if they were left to their own guidance. Wonderful
power! The horses, advancing, followed an unknown road and in
a direct course proceeded to Anegray to the doors of St. Columban. Marculf amazed followed the tracks of the horses, came to
the man of God and presented what he had brought. The latter
returned thanks to his Creator because He did not neglect to
prepare a table for His servants in the wilderness. Therefore,
having received a benediction from him, Marculf returned by the
path by which he had come and disclosed to all what had
happened. Then crowds of people and throngs of the infirm
began to crowd about St. Columban in order that they might
recover their health and in order to seek aid in all their infirmities.
When he was unable to rid himself of their importunities, obeying
the petitions and prayers of all, through his prayers and relying
upon the divine aid, he healed the infirmities of all who came to
him.

15. While the holy man was wandering through the dark
woods and was carrying on his shoulder a book of the Holy
Scripture, he happened to be meditating. And suddenly the
thought came into his mind, which he would prefer, to suffer
injuries from men or to be exposed to the rage of wild beasts.
While he thought earnestly, frequently signing his forehead with
the sign of the cross and praying, he decided that it was better to
suffer from the ferocity of wild beasts, without any sin on their
part, than from the madness of men who would lose their souls.
And while he was turning this over in his mind he perceived
twelve wolves approaching and standing on the right and on the
left, while he was in the middle. He stood still and said: "Oh, God,
come to my aid. Oh, Lord, hasten to aid me!" They came nearer
and seized his clothing. As he stood firm they left him unterrified
and wandered off into the woods. Having passed through this
temptation in safety, he continued his course through the woods.
And before he had gone far he heard the voices of many Suevi,
wandering in the hidden paths. At this time they were robbing in
those places. And so at length by his firmness, having dismissed

the temptation, he escaped the misfortune. But he did not know clearly whether this was some of the devil's deceit or whether it had actually happened.

At another time he withdrew from his cell and entering the wilderness by a longer road he found an immense cliff with precipitous sides and rocky paths difficult for men. There he perceived a hollow in the rock. Entering to explore its hidden recesses he found in the interior of the cave the home of a bear, and the bear itself. He ordered the beast to depart and not to return to that place again. The beast mercifully went, nor did she dare to return again. The place was distant from Anegray seven miles more or less.

16. At one time he was living alone in that hollow rock, separated from the society of others and, as was his custom, dwelling in hidden places or more remotely in the wilderness, so that when the feasts of the Lord or saints' days came, he might, with his mind wholly free from disquieting cares, devote himself to prayer, and might be ready for every religious thought. He was so attenuated by fasting that he scarcely seemed alive. Nor did he eat anything except a small measure of the herbs of the field, or of the little apples which that wilderness produces and which are commonly called *bolluca*. His drink was water. And as he was always occupied with other cares, he could not get this regularly; at least during the time when he was performing his vows.

A little boy named Domoalis was in his service. This boy went alone to tell the father when certain events happened at the monastery and to carry back his directions to the brethren. When this boy had remained for several days in the hollow of this lofty rock, which was difficult of approach from all directions, he began to complain because he could not get water quickly. It tired his knees to bring it with so great labor through the difficult mountain paths. Columban said to him: "My son, get to work; make a little hole in the back of the rock. Remember the Lord produced streams of water from a rock for the people of Israel." He obeyed and attempted to make a hole in the rock. The holy man immediately fell upon his knees and prayed to God that He would aid him in his need. At length his prayers were heard; great power came to him, piously praying. And soon the fountain of water began to flow regularly and it remains to this day.

And not undeservedly has the merciful Lord granted the prayers of His saints, who on account of His commands have crucified their own wills, and who have so great faith that they do not doubt that they will obtain what they demand from His mercy. Because He has promised: "If ye have faith as a grain of mustard seed, ye shall say unto this mountain, remove hence to yonder place; and it shall remove; and nothing shall be impossible unto you." And elsewhere: "What things soever ye desire, when ye pray, believe that ye will receive them, and ye shall have them."

17. As the number of monks increased greatly, he sought in the same wilderness a better location for a convent. He found a place formerly strongly fortified, which was situated about eight miles from the first abode, and which had formerly been called *Luxovium*.[8] Here were baths constructed with unusual skill. A great number of stone idols, which in the old heathen times had been worshiped with horrible rites, stood in the forest near at hand. Here then the excellent man began to build a monastery. At the news of this people streamed in from all directions in order to consecrate themselves to the practice of religion, so that the large number of monks scarcely had sufficient room. The children of the nobles from all directions strove to come thither; despising the spurned trappings of the world and the pomp of present wealth, they sought eternal rewards. Columban perceived that the people were rushing in from all directions to the remedy of penance, and that the walls of one monastery could with difficulty hold so great a throng of converts. Although they were of one purpose and heart, yet one monastery was insufficient for the abode of so great a number. Accordingly he sought out another spot especially remarkable for its bountiful supply of water and founded a second convent to which he gave the name of *Fontanas*.[9] In this he placed men whose piety could not be doubted. After he had settled the bands of monks in these places, he stayed alternately at

[8] Luxeuil in the department of Haute Saône.
[9] Fontaines.

the two convents, and full of the Holy Ghost, he established the rule which they were to follow. From this rule the prudent reader or listener may learn the extent and character of the holy man's learning.[10]

18. At that time a brother, named Autierin, asked to be allowed to make a pilgrimage into Ireland. Columban said, "Let us go into the wilderness and try to learn the will of God, whether you ought to go on the journey as you desire or remain in the assembly of the brethren." Accordingly they went forth and took with them a third youth, named Somarius, who is still alive. They went to the place in the wilderness that had been fixed upon, taking with them only a single loaf. When twelve days had passed, and nothing remained from the fragments of bread, and the time for breaking their fast was approaching, they were commanded by the father to go through the rocky cliffs and down to the bottom of the valleys and to bring back whatever they found that was suitable for food.

They went joyfully through the sloping valleys, down to the Moselle and found some fishes which had been caught previously by fishermen and were floating about on the water. Approaching, they found five large fishes, and taking three, which were alive, they carried them back to the father. But he said, "Why did you not bring five?" They replied, "We found two dead, so we left them." But he said, "You shall not eat of these until you bring those which you left." They, struck with wonder at the fullness of the divine grace, traversed again their dangerous path and chid themselves for leaving the manna which they had found. Afterwards they were ordered to cook the food. For, filled with the Holy Ghost, the father knew that the food had been prepared for himself by God.

19. At another time he was staying in the same wilderness, but not in the same place. Fifty days had already elapsed and only one of the brethren named Gall was with him. Columban commanded Gall to go to the Brusch and catch fish. The latter went, took his boat and went to the Loignon river. After he had gotten there, and had thrown his net into the water he saw a great

<hr>

[10] The rule can be found in Migne, *Patrologia*, vol. 80; cf. note, p. 36.

number of fishes coming. But they were not caught in the net, and went off again as if they had struck a wall. After working there all day and not being able to catch a fish, he returned and told the father that his labor had been in vain. The latter chid him for his disobedience in not going to the right place. Finally he said, "Go quickly to the place that you were ordered to try." Gall went accordingly, placed his net in the water, and it was filled with so great a number of fishes, that he could scarcely draw it.

20. At another time he was staying in the hollow of the rock mentioned above, from which he had expelled the bear, and for a long time he had been mortifying the flesh with prayer and fasting. By a revelation he learned that the brethren, who were near Luxeuil, were suffering from various diseases and only enough remained to care for the sick. Leaving his den, he went to Luxeuil. When he saw the afflicted, he commanded them all to rise and to thresh out the harvest on the threshing ground. Then those whose consciences were kindled by the fire of obedience arose and going to the threshing-place, attempted, full of faith to thresh out the grain on the ground. The father seeing that they were full of faith and the grace of obedience, said, "Cease and rest your limbs, weakened by sickness." They obeyed, wondering at their recovery, for no trace of the diseases remained; and they prepared the tables as he commanded, that all might be strengthened by a joyful banquet. Then Columban chid the disobedient, showed them the inadequacy of their faith and announced the long continuance of their illness. Wonderful revenge! For the disobedient were so ill for an entire year that they barely escaped death. They accomplished the full measure of penance, from the time when they were disobedient.

21. Meanwhile the time had come for gathering the crops into the storehouses, but the violent winds did not cease to pile up clouds; nevertheless it was urgently necessary to gather the crops so that the ears of grain should not rot upon the stalks. The man of God was at the monastery of Fontaines, where a new field had yielded a very rich crop. Violent blasts piled up the rain-clouds, and the heavens did not cease to pour down the rain upon the earth. The man of God considered anxiously what he ought to do. Faith strengthened his mind and taught him how to command

the fitting thing. He summoned all and ordered them to reap the crop. They wondered at the father's command and no one understood his purpose. All came with their reaping-hooks to cut the grain in the midst of the rain and watched to see what the father would do. He placed at the four corners of the field four very religious men, Comininus, Eunocus and Equanacus, who were Scots, and the fourth Gurganus, a Briton. Having arranged them, he himself with the others cut the grain in the middle. Wonderful virtue! The shower fled from the grain and the rain was scattered in every direction. The warm sun poured down upon those who were reaping in the middle and a strong warm wind blew as long as they heaped up the grain. Faith and prayer were of so great merit that the rain was driven off and they had sunshine in the midst of the storms.

22. At that time there was a duke named Waldelen, who ruled over the people between the Alps and the Jura. He had no children; in order that, as Juvencus says of Zachariah and Elizabeth, "the gift might be more welcome to those who had already given up hope." He with his wife Flavia, who was noble both by her family and by her disposition, came from the town of Besan on to St. Columban. Both of them begged of him that he would pray to the Lord on their behalf, for they had great wealth, but no son to whom they could leave it after their death. The holy man said to them: "If you will promise to consecrate His gift to the Lord and will give me the child so that I can raise him from the baptismal font, I will invoke the Lord's mercy for you that you may have not only the one whom you consecrate to the Lord, but as many more as you desire." Joyfully they promised what he wished, asking only that he would not cease to implore God to have mercy upon them. The man of God promised that they should soon have what they wished, only they must not desire to break the compact.

Wonderful to relate! hardly had they returned home when the wife felt that she had conceived. When she had borne a son, she brought him to the holy man and returned thanks to God, who had heard the prayers of His servants. Columban consecrated the child to the Lord, raised him from the font and, naming him Donatus, gave him back to his mother to be nursed. Later on, the child was educated in the monastery and taught wisdom. He became Bishop of Besançon, which he still is. Out of love for St. Columban he founded a monastery under Columban's rule. From an ancient structure there it was named *Palatium*. God fulfilled the promise made by His servant and gave to Waldelen a second son named Ramelen, distinguished for his nobility and wisdom. This son, after Waldelen's death, succeeded to his office, and although a layman he was truly filled with the fear of God. For he, too, out of love for the holy man, founded under his rule a monastery in the Jura Mountains on the *Movisana* River, and placed Siagrius there as abbot. The Lord added to His previous gifts two daughters, who were noble and perfect in the fear of Christ. After the death of her husband Flavia founded a nunnery in Besançon, gave it full protection and collected many nuns together. The grace of the man of God was so strong in them, that despising all the vain pomp of this life, they were zealous in the service of God.

23. If we try to include some things which may seem of little importance, the goodness of the Creator, who is equally merciful in very small matters and in great, who does not delay to turn His pitying ear to trifling details, just as in the very important matters He grants the desires of the suppliant, will be manifest to those who bawl envious detractions. For on a certain day when the excellent man of God had gone with the brethren to cut the harvest near Calmem, which is called *Baniaritia,* and they were cutting the crop, while the south wind blew, one of them, named Theudegisil, happened to cut his finger with a sickle, and the finger hung by only a small strip of skin. The man of God seeing Theudegisil standing apart, commanded him to continue the work with his companions. But the latter told the reason for his actions. Columban hastened to him, and with his own saliva restored the wounded finger to its former health. Then he ordered Theudegisil to make haste and put forth more strength. The latter who had grieved for a long time over his cut finger, joyfully began to work doubly hard and to press on before the others in cutting the grain. Theudegisil himself told us of this and showed his finger. A similar thing happened on another occasion at the monastery of Luxeuil.

24. For a parish priest, named Winnoc, the father of Babolen, who is now abbot of Bobbio, went to St. Columban. The latter

was in the forest with the brethren, getting a supply of wood. When Winnoc arrived, and was watching with wonder how they split the trunk of an oak so easily with their mallet and wedges, one of the latter flying from the trunk cut him in the middle of his forehead, so that great waves of blood ran from his veins. Columban, the man of God, seeing the blood flowing, and the bone uncovered, immediately fell on the ground in prayer, then rising healed the wound with his saliva, so that hardly a sign of a scar remained.

25.   On another occasion when St. Columban had come to dine at the monastery of Luxeuil, he laid his gloves, which the Gauls[11] call *wanti*, and which he was accustomed to wear when working, on a stone before the door of the refectory. Soon, in the quiet, a thievish raven flew up and carried off one of the gloves in its beak. After the meal, the man of God went out and looked for his gloves. When all were enquiring who had taken them, the holy man said, "There is no one who would venture to touch anything without permission, except the bird which was sent out by Noah and did not return to the ark." And, he added, the raven would not be able to feed its young if it did not quickly bring back the stolen object. While the brethren were looking, the raven flew into their midst and brought back in its beak the object which it had basely stolen. Nor did it attempt to fly away, but forgetful of its wild nature, humbly in the sight of all, awaited its punishment. The holy man commanded it to go. Oh, wonderful power of the eternal Judge who grants such power to His servants that they are glorified both by honors from men and by the obedience of birds![12]

26.   Another miracle was wrought by St. Columban and his cellarer, which I shall relate. When the meal-time came, and the latter was ready to serve out the beer (which is boiled down from the juice of corn or barley, and which is used in preference to other beverages by all the nations in the world—except the Scots and barbarous nations who inhabit the ocean—that is, in

---

[11] Should be Franks, i. e. Germans, who used this word.

[12] Grote says this miracle "is exactly in the character of the Homeric and Hesiodic age." See his interesting remarks in *History of Greece*, Vol. I. p. 473n. (New York, 1865).

Gaul, Britain, Ireland, Germany and the other nations who do not deviate from the customs of the above) he carried to the cellar a jar, called a *tybrum*, and placed it before the vat in which the beer was. Having drawn the plug, he permitted the beer to flow into the jar. Another brother called him suddenly by the father's command. He, burning with the fire of obedience, forgot to put in the plug, called a *daciculum*, and, carrying it in his hand, hastened to the blessed man. After he had done what the man of God wished, he returned quickly to the cellar, thinking that nothing would be left in the vat from which the beer was running. But he saw the beer had run into the jar and not the least drop had fallen outside, so that you would have believed that the jar had doubled in size. Great was the merit of Columban commanding, great the obedience of the cellarer, that the Lord thus wished to avert sadness from both of them, lest, if the zeal of either had diminished the substance of the brethren, both should go without needful food; so the just Judge hastened to wash away the faults of both, which had been committed by accident and with the Lord's permission, but which each would have asserted was due to his own remissness.

27. At that time the man of God, a lover of solitude, happened to be walking through the dense thickets of fruit-trees and found a bear ready to devour the body of a stag which wolves had killed, and the bear was licking up the blood. The man of God approached before it had eaten any of the flesh, and ordered it not to injure the hide which was needed for shoes. Then the beast, forgetting its ferocity, became gentle, and fawning and drooping its head left the body without a murmur, contrary to its custom. The man of God returning told this to the brethren, and ordered them to go and strip the hide from the body of the stag. When the brethren found the body they saw in the distance a great flock of birds of prey approaching, but these did not dare to touch the body, on account of Columban's command. The brethren waited at a distance for a long time to see whether any beast or bird would attempt to take the forbidden food. They saw them come, attracted by the smell, stop at a distance, and, turning as if it was something deadly and fatal, fly swiftly away.

28. While Columban on another occasion was staying at Lu-

xeuil, Winnoc, the priest whom we mentioned before, came to him and followed him wherever he went. They came to the storehouse in which the grain was kept. Winnoc, seeing and despising the smallness of the supply, said there was not enough to feed such a multitude, and chid him for his slothfulness in procuring food. St. Columban replied, "If men serve their Creator truly they will never feel need, for as the voice of the Psalmist makes known, 'I have not seen the righteous forsaken nor his seed begging their bread.' He, who satisfied five thousand men with five loaves, can very easily fill the storehouse with grain." While Winnoc stayed there that night, the storehouse was filled by the faith and prayers of the man of God. Winnoc, rising in the morning and passing by, unexpectedly saw the storehouse open and the custodian was standing before the door. He asked who had ordered this or what beasts of burden had brought this grain. The custodian replied, "It is not as you suppose. For see if the tracks of any animals are imprinted on the ground. The keys did not leave my person last night, but while the door was closed, the storehouse was filled with grain by the divine aid." Winnoc began to search carefully, with his eyes fixed on the ground, and to seek for traces of pack-animals. When he found nothing at all resembling these, he said, "The Lord is able to furnish a table for His servants in the wilderness."

A while after, Columban went to the monastery of Fontaines and found sixty brethren hoeing the ground and preparing the fields for the future crop. When he saw them breaking up the clods with great labor, he said, "May the Lord prepare for you a feast, my brethren." Hearing this the attendant said, "Father, believe me, we have only two loaves and a very little beer." Columban answered, "Go and bring those." The attendant went quickly and brought the two loaves and a little beer. Columban, raising his eyes to heaven, said, "Christ Jesus, only hope of the world, do Thou, who from five loaves satisfied five thousand men in the wilderness, multiply these loaves and this drink." Wonderful faith? All were satisfied and each one drank as much as he wished. The servant carried back twice as much in fragments and twice the amount of drink. And so he knew that faith is more deserving of the divine gifts than despair, which is wont to diminish even what one has.

29. When at one time the man of God was staying at Luxeuil, one of the brethren, who was also named Columban, was stricken with a fever and, lying at the point of death, was awaiting instantly a happy release. When he wanted to draw his last breath, confident of the eternal reward which he had sought in his long service, he saw a man clothed in light coming to him, and saying, "I am not able now to free you from your body, because I am hindered by the prayers and tears of your father Columban." When the sick man heard this, sorrowfully, as if he had awakened from sleep, he began to call his attendant Theudegisil, whom we mentioned above, and said, "Go quickly and summon our father Columban to me." The attendant went swiftly, and, finding Columban weeping in the church, asked him to hasten to the sick man. Columban came quickly and asked him what he wanted. The latter told him, saying, "Why do you detain me by your prayers in this sorrowful world? For those are present, who would lead me away if they were not hindered by your tears and prayers. I beseech you, remove the obstacles which retain me that the celestial kingdom may open for me." Columban, struck with fear, made a signal that all should come. His joy lessened his grief at the loss of his holy companion. He gave the dying man the body of Christ as a viaticum, and after the last kiss began the death-song. For they were of the same race and name and had left Ireland in the same company.

30. And do not wonder that the beasts and birds thus obeyed the command of the man of God. For we have learned from Chamnoald, royal chaplain at Laon, who was his attendant and disciple, that he has often seen Columban wandering about in the wilderness fasting and praying, and calling the wild beasts and birds. These came immediately at his command and he stroked them with his hand. The beasts and birds joyfully played, frisking about him, just as cats frisk about their mistresses. Chamnoald said he had often seen him call the little animal, which men commonly name a *squiruis*, from the tops of high trees and take it in his hand and put it on his neck and let it go into and come out from his bosom.

31. The fame of Columban had already penetrated into all parts of Gaul and Germany, and everyone was praising the venerable man. Theuderich too came often to him and humbly

begged his prayers. For Theuderich had succeeded to the kingdom in the following manner: Sigibert had been murdered in the royal estate of Vitry,[13] which is not far from Arras, at the instigation of his brother Chilperich, who was then living in Tournay and was being hunted to death by Sigibert. After the death of the latter, through the influence of his wife Brunhilda, the kingdom passed to his son Childebert (II). When the latter died in his youth,[14] he was succeeded by his two sons, Theudebert and Theuderich, who ruled together with their grandmother Brunhilda. Austrasia went to Theudebert, Burgundy to Theuderich, who thought that he was fortunate in having St. Columban in his kingdom.

As he very often visited Columban, the holy man began to reprove him because he sinned with concubines, and did not satisfy himself with the comforts of a lawful wife, in order to beget royal children from an honored queen, and not bastards by his concubines. After this reproof from Columban, the king promised to abstain from such sinful conduct. But the old serpent came to his grandmother Brunhilda, who was a second Jezebel, and aroused her pride against the holy man, because she saw that Theuderich was obedient to him. For she feared that her power and honor would be lessened if, after the expulsion of the concubines, a queen should rule the court.

32. St. Columban happened one day to go to Brunhilda, who was then on the estate of *Brocariaca*.[15] As she saw him enter the court, she led to him the illegitimate sons of Theuderich. When St. Columban saw her, he asked what she wanted of him. Brunhilda answered, "These are the king's sons; give them thy blessing." He replied, "Know that these boys will never bear the royal sceptre, for they were begotten in sin." Enraged, she told the boys to go. When after this Columban left the court, a loud cracking noise was heard, the whole house trembled and everyone shook with fear. But that did not avail to check the wrath of the wretched woman.

From that time she began to persecute the neighboring

---

[13] Vitry (between Arras and Tournay?)
[14] A. D. 596.
[15] Near Autun.

monasteries. She issued an order that none of the monks should be allowed to leave the lands of the monasteries, no one should receive them into other houses or give them any aid. When Columban saw that at the court all were arrayed against him, he hastened to *Spissia,* where the king was then staying, in order to subdue such defiance by his warnings. When he reached that place, about sunset, and it was announced to the king that Columban was there but would not enter the palace, Theuderich said it would be better with due reverence to offer the needful services to the man of God, than to arouse the wrath of the Lord, by insulting His servant. Accordingly he ordered suitable food to be prepared in the royal kitchen and sent to the servant of God.

When the attendants came to Columban and, in accordance with the king's command, offered him food and drink prepared with royal magnificence, he asked what they meant by it. When they told him that it was sent by the king, he pushed it from him and said: "It is written, 'The Most High is not pleased with the offerings of the wicked.' For it is not meet that the mouth of the servant of the Lord should be defiled by the food of him who shuts out the servant of God, not only from his own dwelling, but also from the dwellings of others." At these words all of the dishes broke into pieces, so that the wine and liquor ran out on the ground and the food was scattered here and there. Terrified, the servants announced this to the king. Full of anxiety, he, together with his grandmother, hastened to Columban early in the morning. Both begged him to forgive their past sins and promised amendment. With his fears quieted by this, Columban returned to his convent. But they failed to keep their promises, and very soon the persecutions were renewed with increased bitterness by the king, who continued in his former sinful course. Then Columban sent him a letter full of reproaches, and threatened him with the ban if he did not amend his conduct.

33. Now Brunhilda began again to incite the king against Columban in every way, urging all the nobles and others at court to do the same, and influenced the bishops to attack Columban's faith and to abolish his monastic rule. She succeeded so fully that the holy man was obliged to answer for his faith or leave the country. The king, incited by Brunhilda, went to Luxeuil and

accused Columban of violating the customs of the country and of not allowing all Christians to enter the interior of the monastery. To these accusations Columban answered, for he was unterrified and full of courage, that it was not his custom to allow laymen to enter the dwelling of the servant of God, but he had prepared a suitable place where all who came would be received. The king replied: "If you wish to enjoy any longer the gifts of our grace and favor, everyone in the future must be allowed free entrance everywhere." Columban answered: "If you dare to violate the monastic rule in any particular, I will not accept any gift or aid from you in the future. But if you come here to destroy the monasteries of the servant of God and to undermine their discipline and regulations, I tell you that your kingdom will be destroyed together with all your royal family." This the king afterward found to be true. In his audacity, he had already stepped into the refectory; terrified by these words, he withdrew hastily.

But when Columban attacked him with bitter insults, Theuderich said: "You want me to honor you with the crown of martyrdom; do not believe that I am foolish enough to commit such a crime. But I will follow a wiser and more useful plan. Since you depart from the common customs, I will send you back to the home from which you came." At the same time the members of the court resolved unanimously that they would not put up with anyone who was unwilling to associate with everyone. But Columban said that he would not leave his monastery unless he was dragged out by force.

34. The king now withdrew, but left behind a nobleman named Baudulf. The latter drove the holy man out of his monastery and carried him to Besançon into banishment, until the king had determined what further action to take. While there Columban heard that the prison was full of condemned men awaiting the death penalty. The man of God hastened to them and, having entered the gate without opposition, he preached the word of God to the condemned. They promised him that if they were liberated they would amend their lives and would do penance for the crimes which they had committed. After this Columban commanded his attendant, whom we have mentioned above [ch.

16], to take in his hand the iron to which their feet were fettered, and to pull it. When the boy took hold of it and pulled, it broke into bits like the rotten trunk of a tree. Columban ordered the condemned to leave the prison now that their feet were free and, after preaching the Gospel to them, he washed their feet and dried them with a linen towel. Then he commanded them to go to the church and do penance for the crimes they had committed and to wash away their faults by their tears. They hastened thither and found the doors of the church fastened.

When the captain of the soldiers saw the fetters of the condemned broken by Columban, through the power of God, and that only the empty prison remained, he started, although aroused from sleep, to follow the tracks of the condemned. The latter, seeing that the soldiers were coming after them and that the doors of the church were shut, hemmed in by the two-fold difficulty, reproached the man of God for having released them. But he, breathing anxiously, raised his face to heaven and prayed to the Lord that He would not permit those whom He had released from the iron by His strength, to be again delivered into the hands of the soldiers. Without delay, the goodness of the Creator opened the doors, which had been securely fastened, and disclosed a way of escape to those in peril. The condemned quickly entered the church. After their entrance the doors were shut without human hands, before the eyes of the soldiers, just as if a custodian with a key had quickly unlocked them and then locked them again. Columban arriving with his followers and the captain coming up at the same time with his soldiers, found the doors shut. They sought the janitor, Aspasius by name, to get the key. When he came with the key and tried to open the doors he said he had never found them more tightly closed. Nor did anyone, after that, dare to do any injury to the condemned, whom the divine grace had liberated.

35. As Columban now saw that he was not watched at all and that no one did him any injury, (for all saw that he was strong in the strength of the Lord and therefore all refrained from injuring him, in order not to be associated in guilt) one Sunday he climbed to the top of the mountain. For the city is so situated that the houses are clustered together on the side of a steep mountain.

Above, the lofty cliffs rise perpendicularly into the heavens. The mountain cut off on all sides by the river Dou, which surrounds it, leaves no path open for travelers. Columban waited till noon to see whether anyone would prevent his returning to his monastery. Then he took the road leading directly through the city. When they heard of this, Brunhilda and Theuderich were embittered still more. They again ordered a band of soldiers to carry off the man of God by violence and to take him again to his former place of exile. Accordingly the soldiers went with their captain and wandered through the precincts of the monastery, seeking the man of God. He was then in the vestibule of the church reading a book. They came repeatedly and passed near him, so that some struck against him with their feet and touched his garments with their garments, but did not see him because their eyes were blinded. And it was a most beautiful sight. He, exulting, perceived that he was sought and was not found. While he saw them, they did not see him sitting in the midst of them. The captain came and, looking through the window, saw the man of God sitting joyfully amid them and reading. Perceiving the power of God, he said: "Why do you go wandering about the vestibule of the church and do not find him? Your hearts are wholly filled with the madness of insanity; for you will not be able to find him whom the divine power conceals. Leave this undertaking and we will hasten to announce to the king that you could not find him." By this it was clearly shown that the captain of the soldiers had not come willingly to do injury to the man of God, and therefore had merited to see him.

36. They told the king. He, impelled by the madness of his wretched purpose, sent Count Bertarius, with the men of his guard, to seek more diligently for Columban, and at the same time Baudulf whom he had formerly sent. They finding the holy man in the church praying and singing psalms with all the brethren, said to him: "Oh man of God, we beg you to obey the king's orders and our own, and to return to the place whence you came to this land." But Columban answered, "I do not think it would be pleasing to my Creator if I should go back to the home which I left because of my love for Christ." When they saw that Columban would not obey them they withdrew. But they left behind several men of rough disposition and character.

Those who remained urged the man of God to have pity on them, since they had been perfidiously left behind to perform such a task, and to think of their peril. If they did not violently eject him they would be in danger of death. But he, as he had very often asserted, said he would not withdraw unless he was compelled to by violence. The men impelled by fear, since they were in imminent peril in either event, clung to the robe which he wore; others upon their knees besought him not to impute to them the guilt of so great a crime, since they were not following their own wishes, but obeying the commands of the king.

37. He finally decided to yield, in order not to imperil others, and departed amid universal sorrow and grief. Escorts were furnished him who were not to leave his side until they had conducted him to the boundary of the kingdom at Nantes. Ragamund was their leader. All the brethren followed, as if it was a funeral; for grief filled the hearts of all. The father in anxiety for the loss of so many members, raised his eyes to heaven, and said, "Oh Creator of the world, prepare for us a place where Thy people may worship Thee." Then he comforted the brethren, telling them to put their trust in the Lord and to give great praise to omnipotent God. This was not an injury to him or his followers, but an opportunity to increase the number of monks. Those who wished to follow him and had courage to bear all his sufferings might come. The others who wanted to remain in the monastery should do so, knowing that God would quickly avenge their injuries. But since the monks did not want to be deprived of the guardianship of their shepherd all resolved to go. But the king's servants declared that only those would be allowed to follow him who were his countrymen or who had come to him from Brittany; the others, by the king's command, were to remain in that place. When the father perceived that his followers were violently torn from him, his grief and that of his followers was increased. But he prayed to the Lord, the Comforter of all men, to take those into His own keeping, whom the king's violence tore from him. Among these was Eustasius, the scholar and servant of Columban, who was afterward abbot in this very convent, of which his uncle, Mietius, bishop of Langres, had charge.

38. So, twenty years after he had come to this place the holy man departed and went by the way of Besançon and Autun to the

fortress *Cavalo*. On the way the king's master of horse wanted to kill him with a lance. But the hand of God hindered it and lamed the man's hand, so that the lance fell on the ground at his feet and he himself seized by a supernatural power fell prone before Columban. The latter, however, cared for him till the next morning and then sent him home healed.

39. From *Cavalo* he went to the river *Chora*[16] where he stayed in the house of a noble and pious lady, named Theudemanda, and healed twelve demoniacs who came to him. On the same day he went to the village of *Chora* where he healed five mad men. In Auxerre, which he next went to, he said to his companion, Ragamund, "Know that within three years Chlotar, whom you now despise, will be your lord." But he answered, "Why do you tell me such things, my lord?" The latter replied, "You will see what I have announced if you are still alive."

40. Then leaving Auxerre, Columban saw a youth possessed by a demon running swiftly toward him. This youth had run twenty miles with all his might. Seeing him, Columban waited until the man, wounded by the devil's art, should come. The latter fell at the feet of the man of God and was immediately cured by his prayers and visibly restored to health. Then with guards preceding and following, Columban came to the city of Nevers in order to go in a boat on the Loire to the coast of Brittany. When they had reached this point and had gotten into the boat with difficulty, one of the guards, taking an oar, struck one of them, who was named Lua, a most holy and devout man.

The man of God, seeing that one of his followers was struck in his presence, said: "Why, cruel man, do you add to my grief? Is not the guilt of the crime which you have committed sufficient for your destruction? Why do you appear merciless against the merciful? Why do you strike a wearied member of Christ? Why do you vent your wrath on the gentle? Remember that you will be punished by God in this place, where in your rage you have struck a member of Christ." The vengeance, soon following, executed the penalty inflicted by that sentence. For as the man was returning again and came to the same place to cross the river, struck by the divine vengeance, he was drowned. Why was it that

[16]Probably the Cure, a branch of the Jonne (Abel).

the just Judge delayed the vengeance a little, unless it was that His saint might not be troubled by the sight of the man's punishment?

41. From that place they went to the city of Orleans, where sorrowfully they rested for a time on the banks of the Loire in tents, for, by order of the king, they were forbidden to enter the churches. When finally their provisions gave out, they sent two men into the city to get food. One of these was Potentinus, who later on founded a convent in Brittany, near the city of Coutances,[17] and who is still alive. When these men entered the city they found nothing, because the inhabitants, from fear of the king, did not dare to sell or give them anything, and they went back on the road by which they had entered the city. They met a Syrian woman in the street. When she saw them, she asked who they were. They explained the state of the case, and said that they were seeking food but had found nothing. She replied, "Come, my lords, to the house of your servant and take whatever you need. For I, too, am a stranger from the distant land of the Orient." They joyfully followed her to her house and sat down to rest until she brought what they sought. Her husband, who had long been blind, was sitting near them. When they asked him who he was, his wife replied, "My husband is from the same race of the Syrians that I am. As he is blind, I have led him about for many years." They said, "If he should go to Columban, the servant of Christ, he would receive his sight through the holy man's prayers." The man having faith in the promised gift, regained his courage, rose and, led by his wife, followed them. They told Columban of the hospitality given to pilgrims. They had not finished their story before the blind man came and prayed the man of God to restore his sight by prayer.

Columban, seeing the man's faith, asked all to pray for the blind man, and after lying for a long time prone on the ground, he rose, touched the man's eyes with his hand and made the sign of the cross. The man received his longed-for sight. He rejoiced in his recovered sight, because it was fitting that he, whose soul had been lighted internally by hospitality, should not lack the external vision.

After that a band of mad men, whom demons tortured with

[17] In the department of La Manche.

savage fury, hastened to the man of God to be cured. Health was granted them by the Lord; for all were healed by the man of God. The people of the city moved by these miracles supplied Columban with gifts secretly, because they did not dare to furnish anything openly on account of the guards, lest they should incur the wrath of the king. Thence Columban and his followers continued on their way.

42. And proceeding on the Loire, they came to the city of Tours. There the holy man begged the guards to stop and permit him to visit the grave of St. Martin. The guards refused, strove to go on quickly, urged the oarsmen to put forth their strength and pass swiftly by the harbor, and commanded the helmsman to keep the boat in mid-stream. St. Columban seeing this, raised his eyes sadly to heaven, grieving at being subjected to great sorrow, and that he was not permitted to see the graves of the saints. In spite of all their efforts the boat stopped as if anchored, as soon as it got opposite the harbor, and turned its bow to the landing-place. The guards seeing that they could not prevail, unwillingly allowed the boat to go where it would. In a wonderful manner it sped, as if winged, from mid-stream to the harbor, and entering this accomplished the wish of the man of God.

He, truly, gave thanks to the eternal King, who does not disdain to comply with the wishes of His servants. Landing, Columban went to the grave of St. Martin and spent the whole night there in prayer. In the morning he was invited by Leoparius, the bishop of the city, to break his fast. He accepted, especially for the sake of refreshing his brethren, and spent that day with the bishop. When he sat down at table with the bishop, at the hour of refection, and was asked why he was returning to his native land, he replied, "That dog Theuderich has driven me away from the brethren."

43. Then one of the guests, named Chrodowald, who was married to one of Theudebert's cousins, but who was a follower of Theuderich, replied in a humble voice to the man of God, "It is pleasanter to drink milk than wormwood," and declared that he would be faithful to King Theuderich, as he had sworn, so long as it was in his power. Columban said to him, "I know that you want to keep your oath of fidelity to King Theuderich, and you will be glad to take my message to your lord and friend, if you serve King

Theuderich. Announce, therefore, to Theuderich that he and his children will die within three years, and his entire family will be exterminated by the Lord." "Why," said the man, "do you announce such tidings, O servant of God?" "I dare not conceal what the Lord has ordered me to reveal." All the inhabitants of Gaul saw this fulfilled later, and this confirmed what had been announced previously to Ragamund.

44. After the repast, the man of God returned to the boat and found his companions very sorrowful. On enquiring what had happened, he learned that what they had in the boat had been stolen in the night, and also the gold which he had not given to the poor. Having heard this, he returned to the grave of the holy confessor and complained that he had not watched by the relics of the saint in order that the latter should allow him and his followers to suffer loss. Immediately he who had stolen the bag of gold began to be tormented and tortured, and cried out that he had concealed the pieces of gold in this place and that. All his associates rushed to return all that had been stolen and prayed the man of God to pardon the great crime. This miracle struck such terror into all, that those who heard of it did not dare to touch anything which belonged to the man of God, believing that all was consecrated. After supplying him with food Leoparius said farewell to St. Columban.

45. Joyfully then they went in the boat to the city of Nantes and there stopped for a short time. One day a beggar cried out before the door of the cell in which the man of God was meditating. Calling an attendant, Columban said: "Give the beggar some food." The attendant replied: "We have nothing except a very little meal." He asked: "How much have you?" The attendant replied that he thought he did not have more than a measure of meal. "Then give it all," he said, "and save nothing for the morrow." The servant obeyed and gave all to the beggar, reserving nothing for the common need.

Already the third day had dawned since they had been fasting, and had had scarcely anything except the grace of hope and faith, by which to refresh their exhausted limbs. Suddenly they heard the door open; when the doorkeeper asked why the ears of the brethren were troubled by the din, he who had opened the door said he had been sent by his mistress Procula. She said she had been divinely warned to send food to the man of God, Columban, and to his companions, who were staying near the city of Nantes. The man said the food would come immediately, and that he had been sent ahead to tell them to prepare receptacles to receive it. There were a hundred measures of wine, two hundred of grain, and a hundred of barley. The doorkeeper hastened to announce this to the father. But the latter said, very well, he knew it, and ordered that the brethren should come together to pray to the Lord in behalf of their benefactress, and at the same time to return thanks to their Creator who never fails to comfort His servants in every need; and after that they would receive the gifts.

Wonderful compassion of the Creator! He permits us to be in need, that He may show his mercy by giving to the needy. He permits us to be tempted, that by aiding us in our temptations He may turn the hearts of His servants more fully to Himself. He permits His followers to be cruelly tortured that they may delight more fully in restored health.

46. Another equally noble and pious woman, named Doda, sent two hundred measures of corn, and a hundred of mixed grain. This caused very great shame to the bishop of that city, named Suffronius, from whom nothing could be obtained as a gift or even by exchange. While Columban remained there, a certain woman tormented by a demon came to him, together with her daughter who was also suffering from a severe disease. When he saw them, he prayed to the Lord for them; after they had been healed, he commanded them to return home.

47. After this Suffronius, bishop of Nantes, and Count Theudebald made preparations to send St. Columban to Ireland, in accordance with the king's orders. But the man of God said: "If there is a ship here which is returning to Ireland, put my effects and my companions on it. In the meantime I will go in my skiff down the Loire to the ocean." They found a vessel which had brought Scottish wares and embarked all Columban's effects and companions. When with a favorable wind the oarsmen were now rowing the vessel down to the ocean, a huge wave came and drove the vessel on shore. It stuck fast on the land, and the water receding, remained quietly in the channel. The bark remained

high and dry for three days. Then the captain of the vessel understood that he was detained in this manner on account of the effects and companions of the man of God, that he had taken on board. He decided to disembark from the vessel all that belonged to Columban. Immediately a wave came and bore the vessel out to the ocean. Then all, filled with amazement, understood that God did not wish Columban to return home.

Accordingly he returned to the house in which he had formerly dwelt and no one opposed him; nay, rather, all aided the man of God with gifts and food, as far as lay in their power. Nor did he lack defence, because in all things he had the aid of the Creator, and He who keeps Israel under the shadow of His wings never slumbers. Thus truly He shows by granting all things to all men, that He wishes to be glorified by all in proportion to the greatness of His gifts.

48. Not long after this Columban went to Chlotar, Chilperich's son, who ruled in Neustria over the Franks who lived on the coast. Chlotar had already heard how the man of God had been persecuted by Brunhilda and Theuderich. He now received Columban as a veritable gift from heaven, and begged that he would remain in Neustria. Columban refused and said he did not wish to remain there, either for the sake of increasing the extent of his pilgrimage, or for the sake of avoiding enmities. But he remained some time with the king, and called his attention to several abuses, such as could hardly fail to exist at a king's court. Chlotar promised to correct everything according to Columban's command, for he zealously loved wisdom, and rejoiced in the blessing which he had secured.

In the meantime a strife arose between Theudebert and Theuderich over the boundaries of their kingdoms, and both sent to Chlotar to beg aid. The latter was disposed to aid one against the other, and asked Columban's advice. He, filled with the spirit of prophecy, answered that Chlotar ought not to unite with either, for within three years he would receive both kingdoms. Chlotar seeing that such things were prophesied by the man of God, aided neither, but full of faith awaited the promised time. Afterwards he triumphed victoriously.

49. Afterwards Columban asked Chlotar to aid him to go

through Theudebert's territory, if possible, and over the Alps to Italy. He received escorts who were to conduct him to Theudebert, and entering upon his journey went to the city of Paris. When he arrived there, he met at the gate a man having an unclean spirit, who was raving and rending his garments, while babbling. The latter addressed the man of God complainingly: "What are you doing in this place, O man of God?" From afar he had been crying out for a long time with his growling voice as he saw Columban, the man of God, approaching. When the latter saw him, he said: "Depart, evil one, depart! Do not dare to possess any longer the body washed by Christ. Yield to the power of God, and invoked by the name of Christ." But when the devil resisted for a long time with savage and cruel strength, the man of God placed his hand on the man's ear and struck the man's tongue and by the power of God commanded the devil to depart. Then rending the man with cruel violence so that bonds could scarcely restrain him, the devil, issuing forth amid great purging and vomiting made such a stench that those who stood by believed that they could endure the fumes of sulphur more easily.

50. Then Columban went to the city of Meaux. There he was received with great joy by a nobleman Hagneric, who was a friend of Theudebert, a wise man, and a counsellor grateful to the king, and was fortified by nobility and wisdom. The latter promised that he would take care of Columban until the latter reached the court of Theudebert, and said it was not necessary to have the other companions who were sent by the king. He declined the aid of the others in order to keep the man of God with himself as long as he could, and in order that his house might be ennobled by the learning of the latter. Columban blessed his house and consecrated to the Lord his daughter Burgundofara, who was still a child, and of whom we shall speak later.

Thence he proceeded to Eussy on the river Marne. There he was received by a man named Autharius, whose wife was named Aiga. They had sons under ten years of age, whom the mother brought to the man of God to be blessed. He, seeing the faith of the mother, consecrated the little children with his blessing. They later, when they grew up, were held in high esteem, first by King Chlotar, afterwards by Dagobert. After they had obtained great glory in the world, they made haste, lest in the glory of this world they should lose the eternal. The elder, Ado, withdrew of his own accord and founded, under the rule of St. Columban, a monastery near Mt. Jura.[18] The younger, Dado, founded, under the rule of the blessed man, a monastery near Brieg, on the little river Rébais.

So greatly did the man of God abound in faith, that whomsoever he consecrated, the last day found persevering in good works. And those whom he warned, rejoiced afterward that they had merited immunity. Nor did he, endued with so great strength, undeservedly obtain an increase of grace, who guided by his learning, was unwilling to deviate from the path of a just life.

51. From that place Columban proceeded to Theudebert, who received him joyfully. Many brethren had already come to him from Luxeuil, whom he received as if they had been snatched from the enemy. Now the king promised to seek out beautiful places, suitable for God's servants, where they could preach to the neighboring people. Columban declared, that if the king was in earnest and would actively support him, he would gladly remain there longer and try to sow the seeds of faith in the hearts of the neighboring peoples. Theudebert commissioned him to choose a suitable place, and, with the approval of all, he decided upon a long-ruined city, which was in the German land not far from the Rhine, and which was called *Brigantia*.[19] But what the man of God did, as he was ascending the Rhine in his boat, must not be passed over in silence.

52. As they journeyed, they came to the city which was formerly called Maguntiacum.[20] The oarsmen who had been sent by the king to aid the man of God, told him they had friends in the city who would supply needful food; for already they had long been fasting. The man of God told them to go; but they did not find any. They returned, and in reply to the questions of the man of God said they had been unable to obtain anything from their friends. Then he said: "Let me go for a short time to my friend." They wondered how he had a friend there, where he had

---

[18] The monastery Jouarre near Meaux.
[19] Bregenz.
[20] Mainz.

never been before. But he went to the church and, entering, threw himself on the pavement, and in a long prayer sought the protection of God, the source of all mercy. Immediately the bishop of the city went from his home to the church and, finding Columban, asked who he was. The latter said he was a pilgrim. The bishop answered: "If you need food, go to my house and take what you need." After thanking him and also the Creator who had inspired him, Columban hastened to the boat and directed that all the men, except one guard, should go and bring what they wished. But lest this should seem to anyone mere chance, that bishop was accustomed to protest that he had never before given food with so little thought. And he testified that he went to the church that day by divine admonition, on account of the merit of the blessed Columban.

53. At length they arrived at the place designated, which did not wholly please Columban; but he decided to remain, in order to spread the faith among the people, who were Swabians. Once, as he was going through this country, he discovered that the natives were going to make a heathen offering. They had a large cask that they called a *cupa*, and that held about twenty-six measures, filled with beer and set in their midst. On Columban's asking what they intended to do with it, they answered that they were making an offering to their God Wodan (whom others call Mercury). When he heard of this abomination, he breathed on the cask, and lo! it broke with a crash and fell in pieces so that all the beer ran out. Then it was clear that the devil had been concealed in the cask, and that through the earthly drink he had proposed to ensnare the souls of the participants. As the heathens saw that, they were amazed and said Columban had a strong breath, to split a wellbound cask in that manner. But he reproved them in the words of the Gospel, and commanded them to cease from such offerings and to go home. Many were converted then, by the preaching of the holy man, and turning to the learning and faith of Christ, were baptized by him. Others, who were already baptized but still lived in the heathenish unbelief, like a good shepherd, he again led by his words to the faith and into the bosom of the church.

54. At that time Theuderich and Brunhilda were venting their

wrath not only on Columban, but also on the holy Desiderius, bishop of Vienna. After they had driven the latter into banishment and had done him much evil, they crowned him at last with a glorious martyr's death. By his deeds, which have been narrated, and by his great adversities he deserved to have a glorious triumph near the Lord.

In the meantime Columban and his companions experienced a time of great need near the city of Bregenz. But although they were without food, they were bold and unterrified in their faith, so that they obtained food from the Lord. After their bodies had been exhausted by three days of fasting, they found so great an abundance of birds,—just as the quails formerly covered the camp of the children of Israel,—that the whole country near there was filled with birds. The man of God knew that this food had been scattered on the ground for his own safety and that of his brethren, and that the birds had come only because he was there. He ordered his followers first to render grateful praises to the Creator, and then to take the birds as food. And it was a wonderful and stupendous miracle; for the birds were seized according to the father's commands and did not attempt to fly away. The manna of birds remained for three days. On the fourth day, a priest from an adjacent city, warned by divine inspiration, sent a supply of grain to St. Columban. When the supply of grain arrived, the Omnipotent, who had furnished the winged food to those in want, immediately commanded the phalanxes of birds to depart. We learned this from Eustasius, who was present with the others, under the command of the servant of God. He said that no one of them remembered ever having seen birds of such a kind before; and the food was of so pleasant savor that it surpassed royal viands. Oh, wonderful gift of divine mercy! When earthly food was wanting to the servants of Christ, celestial was furnished; as was said of Israel: "He gave to them of the corn of heaven;" when earthly food was brought, the celestial which had been mercifully granted was taken away.

55. Then Columban was weakening his body by fasting, under a cliff in the wilderness, and he had no food except the apples of the country, which we have mentioned above. A fierce bear of great voracity came and began to lick off the necessary food and

carry the apples away in its mouth. When the meal-time came, Columban directed Chagnoald, his servant, to bring the usual quantity of apples. The latter went and saw the bear wandering about among the fruit-trees and bushes and licking off the apples. He returned hastily and told the father, who commanded him to go and set aside a part of the fruit-trees for food for the bear and order it to leave the others for himself. Chagnoald went in obedience to the command, and dividing with his staff the trees and bushes which bore the apples, he, in accordance with Columban's command, set aside the part that the bear should eat, and the other part that it should leave for the use of the man of God. Wonderful obedience of the bear! It did not venture at all to take food from the prohibited part but, as long as the man of God remained in that place, sought food only from the trees that had been assigned to it.

56. Once Columban thought of going to the land of the Wends, who are also called Slavs, in order to illuminate their darkened minds with the light of the Gospel, and to open the way of truth to those who had always wandered in error. When he proposed to make his vows, the angel of the Lord appeared to him in a vision, and showed him in a little circle the structure of the world, just as the circle of the universe is usually drawn with a pen in a book. "You perceive," the angel said, "how much remains set apart of the whole world. Go to the right or the left where you will, that you may enjoy the fruits of your labors." Therefore Columban remained where he was until the way to Italy opened before him.

57. In the meantime the compact of peace which Theuderich and Theudebert had made was broken, and each one, priding himself on the strength of his followers, endeavored to kill the other. Then Columban went to King Theudebert and demanded that he should resign his kingdom and enter a monastery, in order not to lose both earthly crown and everlasting life. The king and his companions laughed; they had never heard of a Merovingian on the throne, who had voluntarily given up everything and become a monk. But Columban said, if the king was not willing voluntarily to undertake the honor of the priestly office, he would soon be compelled to do it against his will. After these words the holy man returned to his cell; but his prophecy was soon verified by events. Theuderich immediately advanced against Theude-

bert, defeated him near Zülpich, and pursued him with a great army. Theudebert gathered new forces and a second battle was fought near Zülpich. Many fell on both sides, but Theudebert was finally defeated and fled.

At that time the man of God was staying in the wilderness, having only one attendant, Chagnoald. At the hour when the battle near Zülpich began, Columban was sitting on the trunk of a rotten oak, reading a book. Suddenly he was overcome by sleep and saw what was taking place between the two kings. Soon after he aroused, and calling his attendant, told him of the bloody battle, grieving at the loss of so much human blood. His attendant said with rash presumption: "My father, aid Theudebert with your prayers, so that he may defeat the common enemy, Theuderich." Columban answered: "Your advice is foolish and irreligious, for God, who commanded us to pray for our enemies, has not so willed. The just Judge has already determined what He wills concerning them." The attendant afterwards enquired and found that the battle had taken place on that day and at that hour, just as the man of God had revealed to him.

Theuderich pursued Theudebert, and the latter was captured by the treachery of his followers and sent to his grandmother, Brunhilda. She, in her fury, because she was on Theuderich's side, shut him up in a monastery, but after a few days she mercilessly had him murdered.

58. Not long after this Theuderich, struck by the hand of the Lord, perished in a conflagration in the city of Metz. Brunhilda then placed the crown on the head of his son Sigibert. But Chlotar thought of Columban's prophecy and gathered together an army to reconquer the land which belonged to him. Sigibert with his troops advanced to attack him, but was captured, together with his five brothers and great-grandmother Brunhilda, by Chlotar. The latter had the boys killed, one by one, but Brunhilda he had placed first on a camel in mockery and so exhibited to all her enemies round about; then she was bound to the tails of wild horses and thus perished wretchedly. As the whole family of Theuderich was now exterminated, Chlotar ruled alone over the three kingdoms,[21] and Columban's prophecy had been literally fulfilled. For one of the kings and his whole family had been

[21] Neustria, Austrasia and Burgundy.

entirely exterminated within three years; the second had been made a clerk by violence; the third was the possessor and ruler of all the kingdoms.

59. When Columban saw that Theudebert had been conquered by Theuderich, as we said above, he left Gaul and Germany and went to Italy. There he was received with honor by Agilulf, king of the Lombards. The latter granted him the privilege of settling in Italy wherever he pleased; and he did so, by God's direction. During his stay in Milan, he resolved to attack the errors of the heretics, that is, the Arian perfidy, which he wanted to cut out and exterminate with the cauterizing knife of the Scriptures. And he composed an excellent and learned work against them.

60. At that time a man named Jocundus appeared before the king and announced that he knew of a church of the holy Apostle Peter, in a lonely spot in the Apennines; the place had many advantages, it was unusually fertile, the water was full of fishes; it had long been called *Bobium*,[22] from the brook that flowed by it. There was another river in the neighborhood, by which Hannibal had once passed a winter and suffered the loss of a very great number of men, horses and elephants. Thither Columban now went, and with all diligence restored to its old beauty the church which was already half in ruins.

In this restoration the wonderful power of the Lord was visible. For, when beams of fir were cut amid the precipitous cliffs or in the dense woods, or those cut elsewhere, fell into such places by accident, so that beasts of burden could not approach, the man of God going with two or three companions, as many as the steep paths furnished footing for, placed, in a wonderful manner, on his own and his companions' shoulders beams of immense weight, which thirty or forty men could scarcely carry on level ground; and where they had hardly been able to walk before, on account of the steepness of the paths, and had moved as if weighed down with burdens, they now walked easily and joyfully, bearing their burden. The man of God, seeing that he was receiving so great aid, urged his companions to finish joyfully the work which they had begun, and to remain in the wilderness with renewed courage, affirming that this was God's will. Therefore he restored

[22]Bobbio.

the roof of the church and the ruined walls, and provided whatever else was necessary for a monastery.

61. During this time king Chlotar, when he saw that the words of Columban had been fulfilled, summoned Eustasius, who was then abbot of Luxeuil, and urged him to go with an escort of noblemen, whom Eustasius himself should select, to the holy Columban and beg the latter, wherever he might be, to come to Chlotar. Then the venerable disciple went to seek his master, and when he found the latter, he repeated Chlotar's words. But Columban declared, when he heard Chlotar's request, that he could not undertake the journey again. Eustasius he kept with himself for some time, warned him not to forget his own labors and work, to keep the band of brethren learned and obedient, to increase their numbers and educate them according to his own instructions.

To the king he sent a letter full of good advice, and begged him to extend his royal protection and aid to the brethren at Luxeuil. The king received the letter joyfully, as a most pleasing gift and as a pledge of his compact with the man of God. Nor did he forget the latter's request, but showed his favor in every way to the cloister, gave it yearly revenues, increased its territory in every direction, where the venerable Eustasius desired, and aided its inmates in every way that he could. After a single year in his monastery of Bobbio, Columban the man of God, ended his devout live on the XI. day before the Calends of December.[23] If anyone wishes to learn of his activity, let him seek it in the saint's writings.[24] His remains are buried there,[25] where they have proved their virtues, by the aid of Christ. To Him be glory for ever and ever, world without end. Amen.

[23]November 21st, probably 615.
[24]These are reprinted in Migne: *Patrologiae Latinae Cursus Completus*, Vol. 80.
[25]In Bobbio.

6
From *The Life of St. Gall*

The Driving Out of Demons

St. Gall, the companion of St. Columbanus, was equally revered, and the monastery bearing his name became one of the great centers of learning and artistic production in later centuries.

[St. Columban and St. Gall came, about the year 610, to a village near the Lake of Constance called Bregenz, where they had heard that there might be opportunity to serve God.] There the brethren's hands made ready a dwelling, and the holy Columban fervently prayed to Christ in behalf of that place. The superstitious pagans worshiped three idols of gilded metal, and believed in returning thanks to them rather than to the Creator of the world.

So Columban, the man of God, wished to destroy that superstition, and told Gall to talk to the people, since he himself excelled in Latin, but not in the language of that tribe. The people gathered at the temple for their wónted festival; but they were attracted by the sight of the strangers, not, however, by reverence for the divine religion. When they were assembled, Gall, the elect of God, fed their hearts with honeyed words, exhorting them to turn to their Creator, and to Jesus Christ the Son of God, who opened the gate of heaven for the human race, sunk in indifference and uncleanness.

Then before them all he broke in pieces with stones the enthroned idols, and cast them into the depths of the lake. Then part of the people confessed their sins and believed, but others were angry and enraged, and departed in wrath; and Columban, the man of God, blessed the water and sanctified the place, and remained there with his followers three years. . . .

Some time after, in the silence of the night, Gall, the elect of God, was laying nets in the water, and lo! he heard the demon of the mountain top calling to his fellow who dwelt in the depths of the lake. The demon of the lake answered, "I am here;" he of the mountain returned: "Arise, come to my aid! Behold the aliens come, and thrust me from my temple. Come, come! help me to drive them from our lands." The demon of the lake answered: "One of them is upon the lake, whom I could never harm. For I wished to break his nets, but see, I am vanquished and mourn. The sign of his prayer protects him always, and sleep never overcomes him."

Gall, the elect of God, heard this, and fortified himself on all sides with the sign of the cross, and said to them: "In the name of Jesus Christ, I command you, leave this place, and do not presume to harm any one here." And he hastened to return to the shore, and told his abbot what he had heard.

When Columban, the man of God, heard this, he called the brethren together in the church, and made the accustomed sign (the cross). Before the brethren could raise their voices, the voice of an unseen being was heard, and wailing and lamentation echoed from the mountain top. So the malicious demons departed with mourning, and the prayer of the brethren arose as they sent up their supplications to God.

III
Bishops: The World of Gregory of Tours

Edited and Translated by William C. McDermott

The office of bishop emerged as the most important institution in the early church, and when Christianity was first recognized as a legal religion early in the fourth century, and later the only official religion in the Roman Empire, the episcopal order acquired many of the technical marks of rank and status of the scale of the imperial civil service. Aristocratic bishops, whose office, costume, insignia and function reflected both ecclesiastical tradition and Roman administrative history, dominated the local churches of the fifth and sixth centuries. The episcopal office is one of the most complex administrative legacies surviving from the later western part of the Empire. Although bishops and monks were not necessarily mutually antagonistic, they present different points of view toward society and culture, and Gregory of Tours (c. 540–594) is one of the most eloquent representatives of this rank.

Introduction by William C. McDermott

Gaul in the sixth century was a strange mixture of relics of the ancient Greco-Roman culture, of new Frankish elements, and of the expanding influences of the church. Terror and violence existed in company with many of the elements of an orderly life. Disorder caused by the divisions of powerful Frankish kingdoms and the decentralization of power in this fragment of the Roman Empire was to some extent counterbalanced by the influence of the older, aristocratic Gallo-Roman families and by the sobering role of the church. In Gaul the conversion of the Franks under Clovis to orthodox Catholicism in 496 had stabilized ecclesiastical prestige and organization, which in turn helped maintain some order in those days of strife and lawlessness.

The mixture of disparate ingredients seemed at times to create chaos in which men "could endure neither their own vices nor the remedies for them."[1] However, in part because of the church, in part because of the resilience of the human mind, there was far more genuine optimism in the premier historian of this century than in Livy or in the modern Spenglers and Toynbees. It was significant that the historian Gregory was a member of an aristocratic Gallo-Roman family and a bishop of Tours.

Gregory's Family.[2] Georgius Florentius, who took the name Gregorius when he entered the church in honor of St. Gregory, his maternal great-grandfather, ordinarily spoke of himself with humility, but, when goaded by the insolent contempt of Riculf, stated that all but five of the bishops of Tours had been connected with his own family.[3] His father was Florentius, a senator, and there were notable names among his paternal ancestors: Vettius Epagathus, who was martyred at Lyons; Leocadius, a senator; St. Lusor; his grandfather Georgius, a senator; and his uncle St. Gallus, bishop of Clermont. His mother Armentaria also came from a distinguished family which included Florentinus, a senator; Duke Gundulf; St. Nicetius, bishop of Lyons; St. Gregory, at first count of Autun and then bishop of Langres; St. Tetricus, bishop of Langres; and Eufronius, bishop of Tours.[4]

Gregory was born at Clermont in Aquitania on November 30 in

---

[1] Livy, *Praef.*, 9: *donec ad haec tempora, quibus nec vitia nostra nec remedia pati possumus, perventum est.*

[2] The rest of this introduction is based partly on Gregory's text and partly on works listed in the bibliography: citations will be made only for specific points.

[3] *HF*, 5.49.

[4] Florentius (*VP*, 14.3); Epagathus (*VP*, 6.1); Leocadius (*HF*, 1.31); Lusor (*GC*, 90); Georgius (*VP*, 6.1); Gallus (*VP*, 6); Armentaria (*Mart.*, 1, *Praef.*); Florentinus (*VP*, 8.1); Gundulf (*HF*, 6.11); Nicetius (*VP*, 8); Gregory (*VP* 7); Tetricus (*VP*, 7.4); Eufronius (*HF*, 4.15). Cf. Dalton, 1, pp. 3–8; Leclercq, cols. 1711f.; Wieruszowski, pp. 53f.

538 or 539. This central section of Gaul was on the edge of the Frankish dominions and because of its wealth and fertility was a rich political prize. Gregory's father, who was moderately wealthy, suffered from ill health and died when his children were still young. An elder son, Peter, became deacon at Langres and was killed by a maternal cousin in 574 as the result of a quarrel involving many of the clergy of Langres.[5] A sister married Count Justinus and had two daughters, one of whom, Justina, became prioress of a convent.[6] When Gregory was about eight his education was entrusted to his paternal uncle Gallus, bishop of Clermont. After the death of St. Gallus he was the particular charge of Avitus, successor of Gallus in the bishopric in Gregory's native town.

His Education. Gregory in his prefaces often apologizes for his lack of rhetorical training and his faulty syntax, but actually his education was good in that he was brought up in an atmosphere of books and seems to have read widely. His acquaintance with secular authors is rather sketchy. The theory that his reading in them was confined to books of excerpts was adopted by Kurth, but probable exceptions have been pointed out by Krusch, Bonnet, and Manitius.[7] Roger's theory that his reading was confined in his youth to Christian doctrine and writings, and that he became familiar with pagan writers only later, is improbable.[8] Of all the pagan authors only Virgil made a real imprint on Gregory's mind,[9] but his reading in Christian poets and historians was wide and effective. Gregory's knowledge of law was fairly extensive and very practical.[10] There is little evidence that he was much affected by the great doctrinal writers of the third and fourth centuries.[11] To Gregory doctrine was a closed issue, as his

---

[5] *HF*, 5.5.

[6] Justinus (*GM*, 70; *Mart.*, 1.40; 2.2); Justina (*HF*, 10.15).

[7] Kurth, I, pp. 1–29. This longer essay, published in 1919, is an amplified version of an article in 1878. The later version answered the criticisms of Arndt, pp. 6f.; Krusch, p. 459; Bonnet, pp. 49–53; and Manitius, *NA*, 21 (1896), pp. 549–57. Laistner (p. 98) inclined toward Kurth's view.

[8] Pp. 103–10.

[9] In addition to the references in the two preceding notes cf. Leclercq, cols. 1720–22, and my notes below on *GM*, *Praef.*; *Mart.*, 1.9, 20, 40; *Curs.*, 13.

[10] Cf. Vinay, pp. 37–42.

[11] Cf. Laistner, pp. 99f.

profession of faith in the preface of the first book of his *History of the Franks* shows. In his writing he drew from his reading, but much of his material shows an even fuller use of oral source material—this is especially true in the section of his history which is contemporary, and in his collection of the stories of miraculous cures at the tombs of St. Martin at Tours and of St. Julian at Brioude. In summary, it is fair to say that Gregory's education was defective with respect to grammatical and literary technique; that his reading was wide but careless; and that his knowledge was extensive but at times inaccurate.

Gregory as Bishop. Gregory's ecclesiastical training and career were early crowned when he became bishop of Tours in 572 or 573 as successor to his mother's first cousin Eufronius. Despite his youth the people and clergy of Tours, as well as King Sigibert, were enthusiastic. This episcopal see was the premier bishopric of Gaul and needed a man of strong character, who would unite high birth with administrative ability and piety. The saintliness of a Martin might to some extent make up for humble birth, but in the eyes of the king and the people the important bishoprics were ordinarily better handled by men whose position had trained them in the exercise of power and influence. In the sixth century, the bishop stood beside the count as an administrator and, when secular nobles were brutal and greedy, as was frequently the case, the bishop was often the sole protection of the common people. An incompetent or venal bishop added to an unscrupulous count could wreak havoc in a community. Gregory's qualifications for the bishopric were high. This was doubly fortunate since Sigibert was assassinated in 575 and Gregory had to contend with King Chilperic, Queen Fredegundis, and Count Leduastes. It was a mark of Gregory's strength that he won many of his battles with them, had Leudastes deposed, and successfully resisted attempts at his own deposition. After Chilperic's assassination in 584 Gregory attained more freedom in his administration of the see of Tours.

Because of his aristocratic birth and his tenure of the episcopal office for·over twenty years, Gregory had many chances to become familiar with the important men of Gaul. His high office kept him from forming intimate friendships, but it greatly increased the number of his acquaintances. The importance of his bishopric and his determined character made his influence felt throughout the Frankish domains. His personal knowledge of high secular and ecclesiastical officials and his participation in national affairs give striking importance to his narrative of the events of the years from 575 to 591, which are included in the last six books of his history. During these years he was triply busy with the affairs of state, with religious duties and with writing, until his death in 593.[12] Arndt closed his admirable digest of the actions of Gregory from his elevation to the episcopal throne to his death with this eloquent statement:[13]

> The liberality and good will with which he acted as bishop are apparent from all of his books. He nourished those in want, he took to himself the infants and orphans, nor did he fail the church, whose resources he offered to buy peace for the citizens.[14] He cherished the saints with a burning love and zealously took care that their relics should be gathered together. And with these he enriched the churches under his control and granted health to the sick. Nor did he expend less zeal in building, as he could with justice write of himself in the epilogue of his "History of the Franks."[15]

His Literary Works. Gregory's writing was not separated from his ordinary activities. His personal life, his official career, and his literary endeavors were interwoven. From his writings we can reconstruct his life, since he continually refers to his family, his friends and his enemies, the political conditions of his see, his problems of administration, and his social and religious views. He

---

[12] The date of 594 is accepted by many scholars (e.g. Arndt, p. 11), but Krusch's arguments for 593 seem valid (pp. 453f.).

[13] Pp. 8–12: this summary is based largely on Gregory's own writings. The *vita Gregorii* attributed to Odo of Cluny, but actually composed by a cleric of Tours in the tenth century (cf. Monod, I, p. 25) adds little, since it was mainly based on a study of Gregory's works (it was printed by Bordier, IV, pp. 212–33). Monod (p. 105, note 1) gives a list of the chapters in *HF* which narrate events of which we are sure Gregory was an eye-witness.

[14] *HF*, 7.47.

[15] *HF*, 10.31. Kries (pp. 92–105) doubted the authenticity of this chapter, but Monod's refutation of this idea is complete (pp. 64–72).

was, despite his high position, a simple and modest man, and he reveals himself gentle but firm when attacked, lacking in guile, but not deceived more than once by the same intriguer. *His History.* Gregory never went far afield for material—he wrote on the history of his own country and on the great men of the church, particularly the church in Gaul. His best-known work is *The History of the Franks.* In the first book, after a brief introduction on universal history, he carried the story of Gaul down to the end of the fourth century and the death of St. Martin, his great predecessor in the see of Tours. The next three books cover the fifth century and the sixth to the death of Sigibert in 575. Much of the material is based on written sources which are now extant: St. Jerome, Orosius, Eusebius, Sulpicius Serverus. He also used the annalists and the lost histories of Renatus Profuturus Frigiredus and Sulpicius Alexander, among others.[16] He frequently used his sources carelessly, but in fairness to him it must be said that this seems to have been due to quoting from memory. This trait was very common in ancient and medieval times; only in recent days do we attempt to reproduce quotations verbatim, including faulty punctuation and bad grammar.

Gregory's good faith as a historian has frequently been impugned. He has been charged, with some justification, with excessive credulity and an intense ecclesiastical bias. Still it is doubtful whether in Merovingian Gaul of the sixth century Polybius himself could have avoided such faults. Gregory did believe stories of divine intervention which neither secular criticism nor ecclesiastical investigation would now accept, but credulity was the norm in his era.[17] Throughout all his works Gregory was thoroughly convinced that the cause of the church was just. This led him at times to strange conclusions, and to the justification of men whose morality and character were stained with foul crimes. The best-known instance is the case of Clovis. After Clovis had been baptized in the orthodox church Gregory said of him: "For God daily laid low his enemies under his hand

---

[16] The literature on Gregory's historiography and his use of source material is extensive and opinions of his accuracy vary widely. The most significant items are these: Kries, pp. 38–79; Monod, pp. 73–146; Wattenbach; Hellman; Kurth, II, pp. 117–206 and 207–71; Dalton, I, pp. 20–39; Krusch, *NA*, 49, (1930–32), pp. 457–69; Vinay, pp. 145–67, 193–244.

[17] Dill, pp. 324f.

and increased his kingdom, because he walked with an upright heart in His presence and did what was pleasing in His eyes."[18] No better comment on this can be found than Bonnet's note: "Ce n'est pas la faute de Grégoire si ces rois sont si peu vertueux."[19] A further charge that he favored the Gallo-Roman nobility in preference to the Franks is not confirmed by the evidence.

Gregory was continually concerned to discover the truth and to point the moral of the lessons of history, but he did not stand aside and weigh the evidence impartially. Even in his earlier chapters his feelings were deeply involved as he championed the church against those who would attack it. However, he did not distort the actual facts presented, and his narrative is composed in such a way that those who follow him can reinterpret the history of the times. The detailed narrative of the nineteen years covered in the last six books is an invaluable picture of Merovingian Gaul. No phase is left untouched: ecclesiastical and religious affairs are amply covered, political developments are outlined, and social and economic history come in for a share of attention. Without developing a conscious theory of history, he approached the modern idea that political action cannot be studied in a vacuum, even though he often failed to analyze the true interrelation of social and political events.

His Minor Works. Gregory often inserted into his history stories of the saints and the miracles worked by them. At the same time that he was writing his history he was also composing a series of hagiographic works. These works are by their very nature more monotonous and less significant than his history, but they are of great importance in filling out the picture of the times, and they contain much fascinating material. The translations in this volume are chosen from these works. In the epilogue of his history he enumerated most of his works:[20] "I have written ten books of the Histories, seven of Miracles, and one on the Lives of the Fathers; I also composed one book on the Psalter and one on Ecclesiastical Duties." Again in his preface to his work on the Confessors he lists eight works on miracles, including *The Lives of the Fathers*.

These eight books, which he groups together and apparently

18 *HF*, 2.40.
19 P. 6, note 2.
20 *HF*, 10.31.

considered the more important of his minor works, have the general title of *The Miracles (Miracula)*.[21] The prefaces of these books are included as the first part of this translation. The first book is *The Glory of the Blessed Martyrs (in gloria martyrum beatorum)* which devotes 106 chapters to martyrs and miraculous events associated with the martyrs. Prominence is given to those martyred in Gaul, although here more than in most of his works Gregory goes outside the boundaries of Gaul for his material. The second book is *The Passion and Miracles of St. Julian the Martyr (de passione et virtutibus sancti Iuliani martyris)*. Only the first chapter tells of the martyrdom of St. Julian at Brioude; the other forty-nine chapters concern the miracles connected with St. Julian. The next four books are *The Miracles of Blessed Martin the Bishop (de virtutibus beati Martini episcopi)*. Of the 207 chapters[22] of these four books only the first six go beyond the contemporary scene, the others fall within Gregory's own purview. The forty chapters of the first book form the second part of this translation and the introductory note sketches the background of the work. The seventh book is *The Lives of the Fathers (vita patrum)*. The twenty chapters of this book, which is largely biographical, wholly concern Gallic saints and churchmen. The accounts are quite lengthy. Two long chapters on St. Gallus of Clermont and St. Gregory of Langres are included as the third part of this translation. The eighth book is *The Glory of the Confessors (in gloria confessorum)*. The 110[23] chapters give rather brief accounts of notable figures of the church, mainly in Gaul, and include more biographical material than any of the first six books. The largest part of these eight books concerns the miracles wrought by the saints when alive, and those which occurred at their tombs, or by their intervention after their deaths, and it is obvious that oral tradition plays an important, often a vital, part in these accounts.

In addition to these, four other works are included in Krusch's edition. The first is *The Miracles of Blessed Andrew the Apostle (de miraculis beati Andreae apostoli)*, which was edited by Max

---

[21] The order followed here is that used by Krusch in his edition: it is surely the order in which Gregory himself arranged the books. The abbreviations used for the titles of Gregory's works are listed at the beginning of the bibliography.

[22] I.e. 40, 60, 60, 47.

[23] Chapters 105–7 are missing. They probably were never written by Gregory.

Bonnet, who argued convincingly that it is authentic, although Gregory did not include it in his own list of his works.[24] It has less interest than the other works since it is adapted from a single Latin source. The second is *The Passion of the Seven Sainted Martyrs Sleeping at Ephesus* (*passio sanctorum martyrum septem dormientium apud Ephesum*), which is included in full as the fourth part of this translation. The third is *The Course of the Stars* (*de cursu stellarum ratio*). The first half of this work is included as the fifth part of this translation and the whole work is discussed in the introductory note. Finally, Gregory composed *A Commentary on the Psalms* (*in Psalterii tractatum commentarius*) which is the only one of his works which is not preserved in full. Only the introduction, titles, and two fragments survive. Other works have been attributed to Gregory, but are not by his hand. Gregory's history and his minor works alike, which were frequently imitated and widely consulted, gained him a lasting fame. Manitius mentions the dependence on Gregory of the so-called Fredegarius, of the author of the anonymous *liber historiae Francorum*, of Paul the Deacon, Wahlafrid Strabo, Notker Balbulus, and others.[25]

Dates of Composition. It is questionable whether certain knowledge of the dates of the composition of the various works by Gregory would be of great value from the historical or linguistic point of view. As in the case of many ancient and medieval authors, we do not have enough external or internal data to determine with certainty the exact dates of composition or publication. The problem in Gregory is complicated because he never really finished a work. As Krusch says:[26] "A difficult problem exists in determining at what time Gregory composed individual books, since even up to the time of his death he used zealous care on all his works. . . . It is well known that Gregory revised all of his works rather often." Monod and Krusch discussed this problem, and on the basis of their discussion Bonnet drew up a comparative table of the dates assigned by them, and added his own dates with a justification for his changes.[27] Later

---

[24] Pp. 821-6 (preface), 826-46 (text).

[25] I, pp. 223-5, 228, 269, 306, 361, 584, 704, 710.

[26] Pp. 451, 456; cf. Bonnet, p. 11.

[27] Monod, I, pp. 41-9; Krusch, pp. 451-56, 662 (*ad VP, Praef.*), 748 (*ad GC, Praef.*), 855; Bonnet, p. 11-15. Cf. also Kries, pp. 34-7 and Arndt, pp. 14-20.

Krusch presented additional arguments for his list of dates,[28] and I am inclined to agree that it is as nearly correct as such a summary list can be. It follows: *History* (574–593); *Martin* 1–2 (574–581); *The Seven Sleepers* (after 575, before 582); *Julian* (581–587); *Martin* 3 (before 587); *Fathers* 12, 15, 16, 19 (before 587); *Confessors* (without the preface, 587); *Martyrs* (590); *Fathers* 8 (591 or 592); *Martin* 4 (591–593); *Fathers* (as a collection, 593); *Confessors* (preface, 593). In addition Bonnet dates the *Andrew* in 593.

Gregory's Language. One difficulty in reading Gregory's Latin is its lack of uniformity. That is natural, since the language, as well as the politics of the period, was in a state of flux. However Gregory's syntax and orthography are extraordinarily varied, since his wide but careless reading and his lack of grammatical instruction created in his writing a language which is *sui generis*. At times one is tempted to believe that Gregory was guilty of artificial naïveté in his constant references to his own lack of grammatical skill and in his reckless variety in the use of tenses. Fortunately the research of Krusch, as represented in his indices of the orthography, lexicography, and grammar of Gregory,[29] and that of Bonnet in his analysis of the language of Gregory, enable the student to steer clear of many pitfalls in Gregory's text. Of interest at this point are the two final sentences in Bonnet:[30] "Ces tendances et ces procédés sont ceux d'un autodidacte qui voudrait faire comme les écrivains du métier, mais qui sent son impuissance à les imiter: tour à tour il s'y applique et il y renonce. Il en résulte un étrange contraste entre des formes oratoires usées et une fraîche et rude originalité." It is interesting to note that Arndt, Krusch, and Bonnet are very conservative in assigning irregularity in the text of Gregory to the fault of the copyist.[31] In this they seem to me to have followed the proper course.

This seems to be an appropriate place to make some comments

[28] *NA*, 16 (1891), pp. 432f.
[29] Pp. 912–63.
[30] P. 752.
[31] An opposite point of view was expressed by C. U. Clark in *The American Journal of Philology*, 60 (1939), p. 138: "For years I have been urging a careful study of the rhetorical *cursus* in Gregory of Tours and other late writers; it seems incredible that a bishop who used this refinement could be guilty of the linguistic inaccuracies which abound in the MSS; I would assign these to the scribes."

about the text and the translation. The bibliography indicates the text which is followed and the notes show where the translator has departed from that text. Should the student care to turn to the text, the references given in the preceding paragraph will be of great help. In places where there is particular difficulty or where Bonnet is particularly helpful, references have been inserted in the notes. However, since students are likely to approach medieval Latin from the classical, a few examples of the ecclesiastical turn given to classical words which occur frequently in Gregory may be interesting: *sanctus* "Saint, sainted"; *virtus* "miracle, miraculous power"; *temptator* "the tempter," i.e., the Devil; *beatus* "blessed"; *templum* "church"; *puellae religiosae* "nuns"; *oratorium* "chapel"; *clerici* "clerks, clerics, clergy, monks"; *presbiter* "priest"; *saeculum* "this life, the world." Geographical names may appear strange at first, more so to the student of modern times than to the classicist. These have usually been given in modern form, although at times the Latin form in Gregory has been retained when the Merovingian form has currency. The works of Jacobs and Longnon as well as Krusch's index of proper names[32] are an invaluable aid here. Examples of this practice are: *Arverna urbs* "Clermont," i.e., Clermont-Ferrand, or Auvergne; *Agustidunensis urbs* "Autun"; *Biturigus* "Bourges"; *Lingones* "Langres"; *Turones* "Tours"; etc. Many of these names show almost endless variety in Gregory's text. The plurals *Galliae* and *Hispaniae*, which go back to classical usage in referring to the several provinces of an area, are given as "Gaul" and "Spain." In general, proper names have been Anglicized when an English form is current: *Gregorius* "Gregory"; *Iulianus* "Julian"; *Chlodovechus* "Clovis." This is especially true of biblical names: e.g., *Noe* "Noah." *Sidrach, Misach et Abdenago* might be unintelligible to those familiar only with the "Shadrach, Meshach, and Abed-nego" of the English versions. However, some less familiar names have been left in the form found in the text or have been changed to the ordinary Latin form. The translator could not bring himself to Anglicize *sanctus Gallus* as "St. Gall." Translators must compromise between a very literal version and an extremely free version. The former alternative is often poor English, the

[32] Pp. 884–911.

latter a poor representation of the original. In this translation I have made an attempt to steer a middle course. The grammatical errors and ungainly structure of many of the sentences could not be reproduced in intelligible English. Many changes had to be made, but an attempt has been made to reproduce the spirit, structure, and content of the original. In attempting this, I was aided more by reading the complete works in Latin than by consultation of grammars or lexica.

Gregory and the Bible. The tremendous influence of the Bible on Gregory's language is immediately obvious to the most casual reader. There are frequent quotations, especially in prefatory material, and in sections which involve speculation rather than narration. Again in Gregory, as in so many medieval writers, words used in the text of the Bible became so familiar that they were part of his ordinary vocabulary. Biblical phraseology permeates the whole text, although it is so much more frequent in the account of the seven martyrs of Ephesus than elsewhere, that in that passage it seems to be a reflection of the original which Gregory used.

The sources of the biblical passages quoted by Gregory are given in the notes. Casual allusions to biblical passages are not cited unless some special point is involved. Here the references are to the American revised version of the Bible except when the reference is to a book not included in that version (e.g., *Judith*). When the reference to the *versio Vulgata* is different (as in the case of Kings and Psalms) the reference to the Vulgate is included in parentheses. The present translation is in each case a translation of the passage in Gregory, even though Gregory's citation may vary from the text of the Vulgate. This occurs at times because of Gregory's faulty memory, possibly at times because of copyist's errors, frequently because Gregory was using a Latin translation other than St. Jerome's version.[33]

---

[33] For Gregory's use of the Bible cf. Bonnet, pp. 53-61. A good digest of our information concerning the Latin versions of the Bible is to be found in the essay by H. F. D. Sparks, "The Latin Bible" in H. W. Robinson, *The Bible in its Ancient and English Versions* (Oxford, 1940), pp. 100-27, 306f. The English and Latin texts used are noted at the beginning of the bibliography under *ARV* and *Vulg.*

7
Gregory's Prefaces

Introductory Note. Much material about Gregory is to be found in the five prefaces and the epilogue of *The History of the Franks*. In his general preface he mourned that there was little learning in Gaul and made excuses for his own temerity in writing in his own unlearned style. In the prefaces of the first and third books he gave his confession of faith, in that of the second book he mentioned sources, and in that of the fourth book he spoke eloquently of the ills of civil war. In all of these he made it plain that he did not aim to speak "without anger or special pleading"[1] but rather for the "edification of the church."[2] In the last chapter of the tenth book he sketched briefly the careers of the first eighteen bishops of Tours.[3] He was the nineteenth, and he listed his own accomplishments and works. Similarly in each of his eight books on the lives and miracles of the saints (*Miracula*)[4] he made some introductory remarks. The first preface is notable for Gregory's opposition to the secular learning which was based on Cicero, Virgil, and other pagan authors. This attitude was common from early Christian times, but never wholly drove the study of the pagan classics from the monastic schools. The third preface is appealing because of Gregory's modesty about his accomplishments in literature, and because of the touching story of his vision in which his mother Armentaria urged him to write of St. Martin.[5]

---

[1] *Sine ira et studio* (Tacitus, *Annales*, 1.1).

[2] *Ad eclesiae aedificationem* (*GM, Praef.*).

[3] I have followed the order and the names in *HF*, 10.31, although they differ somewhat from Gregory's earlier notices (*HF*, 2.14, 3.17): cf. Duchesne, *Fastes*, II, pp. 280–309 and Dalton, II, pp. 602f.

[4] The general title *Miracula* is sometimes found in citations (e.g., in Du Cange), but it is now customary to cite the individual works.

[5] In like manner the shade of the Elder Drusus urged the Elder Pliny in a dream to write an account of his (i.e., Drusus') exploits; Pliny, *Ep.*, 3.5.4.

In the eighth preface he shows a somewhat more confident air in defending his many pious works on the saints. Throughout these eight prefaces as well as those of his history, citations from the Bible occur, as might be expected, more frequently than in the body of his narratives. The order given below is that which is listed in the eighth preface.[6] Since Gregory mentions the eighth book in his seventh preface, the prefaces were apparently somewhat revised. Also the fourth book on the miracles of St. Martin seems to have been incomplete at Gregory's death, and certain items in the eighth book are later than the seventh. Consequently, we must assume that the writer felt free to go back and make additions to earlier books.[7]

1. Preface of
"The Glory of the Blessed Martyrs"[8]

The priest Hieronymus,[9] best teacher of the church after the apostle Paul, says that he was led before the judgment seat of the eternal Judge, and was bound and lashed severely as a punishment, because too often he read the clever arguments of Cicero and the false tales of Virgil; and that in the presence of the sacred angels he confessed to the Lord of All that he would never henceforth read or discuss anything except that which was judged worthy of God and useful for building the church.[10] But the apostle Paul also says:[11] "Let us follow the ways of peace and in turn let us guard that which pertains to instruction." And in another place:[12] "Let no evil speech proceed from your mouth, and if there be good speech let it be for instruction, that it may grant grace to its hearers." Therefore we ought to pursue, to

---

[6] Krusch's order: *GM; Iul.; Mart.*, 1–4; *VP; GC.* Dom Ruinart placed *GC* third: cf. *PL*, 71, col. 830. Bordier reversed *VP* and *GC.* The full titles of the books and the abbreviations used for them are found at the beginning of the bibliography.

[7] There is a discussion of the dates of composition of Gregory's works in my introduction.

[8] This was printed by Ruinart as the preface of the whole of the *Miracula* (*PL*, 71, cols. 705f.) by Krusch as the preface of *GM.*

[9] St. Jerome.

[10] *Epistulae*, 22.30. Gregory's recollection of the passage is inaccurate.

[11] *Romans*, 14.19.

[12] *Ephesians*, 4.29.

write, to speak, that which builds[13] the church of God and by sacred teaching enriches needy minds by the knowledge of perfect faith. For we ought not to recall the lying stories, or to follow the wisdom of the philosophers which is hostile to God, lest we fall under the judgment of eternal death by the decision of the Lord. Since I fear this, and I long to disclose some of the miracles of the saints which still lie hidden, I am eager not to be conquered or trapped by these snares. I do not recall in my work the flight of Saturn, the wrath of Juno, the adulteries of Jupiter, the wrongdoing of Neptune, the sceptre of Aeolus, the wars, shipwreck, and conquests of Aeneas. I am silent about the mission of Cupid, the cherishing of Ascanius, the marriage, tears, and savage death of Dido, the dreary antechamber of Pluto, the criminal seizure of Proserpina, the three-headed Cerberus. I will not repeat the speeches of Anchises, the ingenuity of the Ithacan, the shrewdness of Achilles, the deception of Sinon. I will not reveal the counsels of Laocoön, the strength of the son of Amphitryon, the battle, flight, and death of Cacus.[14] I will describe neither the appearance of the Eumenides and various monsters nor the other fabulous stories which this author mendaciously invented or depicted in heroic verse. Having glanced at all these events built on sand and soon to perish,[15] we return rather to divine and evangelical miracles. Whence John the Evangelist began by saying:[16] "In the beginning was the Word, and the Word was with God, and God was the Word. This was in the beginning with God. All things are done through Him and without Him nothing is done." And then he says:[17] "And the Word was made flesh and lived among us and we saw His glory, glory as of the

[13] Gregory used the word *aedificatio* twice in this passage and it occurs twice in the quotations from St. Paul. Since it has a double meaning (building, edification), the full sense does not survive translation.

[14] The references to mythological stories are to the *Aeneid* of Virgil and show knowledge of books 1, 2, 4, 6, and 8. The translation follows the greatly improved interpretation of H. W. Garrod, *Classical Review* 33 (1919), p. 28: cf. also McDermott, pp. 279f. notes 8, 10, 11. N. Tamassia's suggestion of Homeric reminiscences both in this passage and in the story of Clovis and the *urceus* of Soissons (*HF*, 2.27) seems untenable: "Gregorio di Tours e Omero," *Atti del R. Ist. Veneto*, 88.2 (1928–29), pp. 1209–36 (for this passage, p. 1229).

[15] *Matthew*, 7.26: a peculiarly inept quotation.

[16] *John*, 1.1–3.

[17] *John*, 1.14.

Only Begotten from the Father, full of grace and truth." And
because He was to be born in Bethlehem the prophet so speaks: [18]
"And you, Bethlehem Ephrathah, are not the least among the
thousands of Judah. From you a king will come forth who will
reign over my people Israel." Also Nathanael from Cana in
Galilee said this:[19] "Rabbi, you are the son of God, you are the
king of Israel." And He was also the salvation of the world
concerning Whom Simeon said:[20] "Now, Master, let your servant
go in peace, since my eyes have seen your salvation."

2. Preface of "The Passion and Miracles of St. Julian the Martyr"

In a certain way divine piety kindles in us a great fire to find
the path of justice, since it is said:[21] "The eyes of the Lord are
upon the just and His ears are open to their prayers." Thus it is
shown that he who has loved justice with his whole heart and has
prayed is heard by the Lord. May each one of us when he has
begun to sing these things spurn the temptations of the world,
scorn vain desires, leave evil paths, and attempt to traverse the
path of justice unhampered and without the burden of worldly
actions. For by this path Abel is counted just, Enoch is considered
blessed, Noah is set apart, Abraham is chosen, Isaac is consecrated, Jacob is amplified, Joseph is guarded, Moses is sanctified,
David is foreordained, Solomon is enriched, the three boys
prophesy amid the dewy flames,[22] and Daniel feeds amid harm-

---

[18] *Micah*, 5.2: *et tu, Bethlem Eufratha, non es minima in milibus Iuda. Ex te enim
prodiet rex, qui regat populum meum Israhel* (Gregory); *et tu, Bethlehem
Ephrata, parvulus es in millibus Juda; ex te mihi egredietur qui sit dominator in
Israel* (*Vulg.*); "But thou, Beth-lehem Ephrathah, . . . (*ARV*). Cf. *Matthew*, 2.6.
   [19] *John*, 1.49.
   [20] *Luke*, 2.29–30.
   [21] *Psalms*, 34.15 (*Ps.*, 33.16).
   [22] *Tres pueri inter incendia rorolenta vaticinantur.* The adjective *rorolentus*
occurs, as Bonnet noted, only in two other passages which refer to Shadrach,
Meshach, and Abed-nego: *HF*, 1.15: . . . *tres pueri in medium igneum roru-
lenti . . .*; *GM*, 9: . . . *illa misericordia, quae tres quondam Hebraeos pueros . . .
nube rorolenta resperserat.* On the basis of these passages Bonnet read *rorolenti* in
the present passage (p. 71, note 3) where it makes a smoother reading. However
Krusch's text is probably correct since the harshness of *inter incendia rorolenta* is
surely a reflection of a phrase in the Biblical account, *et fecit medium fornacis*

less beasts. By this path the apostles are directed, the blessed martyrs are glorified. You say, "How?" To be sure, when they care for the sick, raise up the dead, despise the present, long for the future, treat torturers with contempt and feel no punishment, they are hastening to the Heavenly Kingdom. Beyond doubt they would not obtain this by their own virtue were they not heard by the Lord as they walk most righteously on the path of justice.[23]

3. Preface of the First Book of "The Miracles of Blessed Martin the Bishop"[24]

The miracles which the Lord our God deigned to perform through his priest, the blessed Martin, in the flesh, he now deigns to confirm daily to strengthen the belief of the faithful. God who acted in him when he was in this world now endows his tomb with miraculous powers, and He who then sent him as a priest to the nations about to perish offers blessings to Christians through him. Therefore let no one doubt past miracles when he beholds the gift of the present signs given forth, since he sees the lame made straight, the blind given sight, demons put to flight, and other kinds of disease cured by his healing. Verily to increase faith in that account which was written by earlier men concerning his life, at the command of the Lord I will relate for posterity as many current miracles as I can recall. I would not presume to do this, had I not been warned twice and thrice in a vision. Nevertheless I call Almighty God to witness that by chance I saw in a dream at noon in the basilica of St. Martin many sick and oppressed by different diseases cured, and I saw these things while my mother was watching, who said to me: "Why are you slow in writing that which you see?" I answered: "You know that I am not learned in literature and being simple and unskilled

quasi ventum roris flantem: Dan., 3.50, (*Dan.*, 3.24–90 which was included in *Vulg.*, although it was not in the Hebrew version, is excluded from the *ARV*).
    [23]This passage was printed as a preface by Ruinart, but as the first half of *Iul.*, 1 by Krusch.
    [24]Ruinart printed this preface under the title *epistola in quatuor libros de virtutibus sancti Martini episcopi*. This revision of a translation already published (McDermott, pp. 281f.) is used by the kind permission of Professor M. S. Enslin, editor of *The Crozer Quarterly*.

would not dare describe such awe-inspiring miracles. Would that
Severus or Paulinus were alive, or indeed that Fortunatus were
present to describe these deeds! Since I am incompetent, I would
incur shame if I tried to do this." And she said to me: "Do you not
know that on account of the ignorance of our people the way you
can speak is considered more intelligible? So do not hesitate and
do not delay doing this since it will be a charge against you if you
pass over these deeds in silence." So I wish to do this but am
afflicted by double dread, equally by grief and fear; grief because
such great miracles done under our predecessors have not been
described, fear of approaching so excellent a work, since I am a
rustic. But led by the hope of divine favor I will approach what is
advised. For He, Who produced water from a dry rock in the
desert to quench the burning thirst of a people, is able, I believe,
to display these things through me though I lack eloquence.[25] It
will certainly be evident that He has again opened the mouth of
an ass if opening my unlearned lips He deems it worthy to
expound these deeds. But why do I fear my rusticity when the
Lord, our Redeemer and our God, chose for the destruction of the
vanity of worldly wisdom not orators but fishermen, not philosophers but rustics? And so I am confident because of your prayers
that even if my rude speech cannot decorate the page, the
glorious priest will make it gleam with his famous miracles.

4. Preface of the Second Book of "The Miracles of Blessed Martin the Bishop"

When we had written of the miracles of St. Martin, which we
have seen or which we have been able to find from the past
through faithful men, we burned with the thirst that there should
not be handed over to oblivion that which the Lord deigned to
perform for the praise of his priest. Indeed we wish to tell of
those things at which we marvel as being done in our own time,
and we leave little material for the more eloquent, since we
appropriate in our writings the mighty works of his miracles so

---

[25] *Per me elinguem*, Krusch, *App.* In *NA*, 19 (1894), p. 37 Krusch defended this
conjecture in place of the reading *per meae linguae* which he had originally
printed. Bonnet defended *linguae sterilitatem*, a reading of ms 14b: p. 527, note 2.

that what skill will not spread over our pages, the very accumulation of numerous miracles might grant.

5. Preface of the Third Book of "The Miracles of Blessed Martin the Bishop"

When, Christ disposing, we begin to write the third book on the miracles of the blessed Martin, we give thanks to Almighty God who has deigned to grant such a healer to us who might cure our infirmities, heal our wounds, and grant health-giving medicine. For at his blessed tomb the soul is humbled and prayer rises on high. If tears flow, if true remorse is present, if sighs rise from the depths of the heart, if wicked breasts are beaten, lamentation finds joy, the fault pardon, the grief of heart arrives at a remedy. For often the touch of the blessed tomb has ordered the flow of blood to stop, the blind to see, the paralyzed to rise, and also the bitterness of the breast to depart afar. Although I have often experienced this power, I think I am not worthy that amid the might of such great miracles I should also insert those which he deigned to perform for me. But again I am afraid that I shall appear guilty if like a thief I steal them away. I call to witness God and, believing that I am not deceived by His pity, I call to witness the hope which I place in His miraculous power that, as often as a headache attacks me, or a sharp pain beats my temples, or my sense of hearing grows faint in my ears, or a cloud suffuses the sight of my eyes, or pain besieges my limbs, straightway as soon as I have touched the aching part to the tomb or the drapery which hangs there, I recover my health. Because of that very touch, as I marvel silently, the pain recedes in its course.

6. Preface of the Fourth Book of "The Miracles of Blessed Martin the Bishop"

The prophet warns us with extremely salutary advice, when he says:[26] "O God, Your friends must be honored." Also in another

---

[26] *Honorandi sunt amici tui, Deus* (Gregory): *Mihi autem nimis honorificati sunt amici tui, Deus* (Vulg., *Ps.*, 138.17): "How precious also are thy thoughts unto me, O God!" (*ARV, Psalms*, 139.17).

psalm:[27] "He who exalts those who fear the Lord is joined with the blessedness of the eternal home." Therefore it is obvious to the human mind that not only those who are free from crime but also those who are given to the evil of guilty crime are warned that they should reverently grant respect to the friends of God. This action grants not only benefit in the present, but also offers consolation[28] in the future life. For often when we see the signs of miraculous power come forth from the tombs of the blessed, we are rightfully moved to pay reverent honor which is due them from whom we do not cease to beseech remedies for our illnesses. We do not doubt that remission of sins is gained by their prayers. Not only do we merit healing here, but also we are saved from the punishments of Hell by their intervention. For we are confident that, just as here they check all kinds of disease, so there they avert the savage torment of punishment; and just as here they ameliorate the heat of the body, so there they extinguish eternal heat;[29] and as here they cleanse the unclean sores of deadly leprosy, so there they obtain healing for the marks of crime by their intervention. And as here they bring back the dead to life, so there by placing their hands on those who have been buried in sin, they take them from the pools of Acheron and restore them to eternal life; wherefore each one rejoices in joy under the protection of his own patron, then more zealously pays the honor which is due his patron when he realizes that he has been cleansed by his patron's miraculous power of the weakness by which he was held. So now we in common with innumerable people have tried out the blessed priest Martin, the special patron for the whole world. And may our own worthless mind gain for him such veneration as befits a friend of God, who has so often restored us to health when we have been stricken by so many kinds of severe illness!

---

[27] *Qui timentes Dominum magnificat, beatitudine copulatur domus aeternae* (Gregory): *timentes autem Dominum glorificat* (*Vulg.*, *Ps.*, 14.4): "But honoreth them that fear Jehovah" (*ARV*, *Psalms*, 15.4).

[28] The double meaning of *refrigerium* "cooling, consolation" cannot be reproduced in English: cf. Bonnet, p. 243.

[29] *Febres* "fevers, heat" is used in a play on words in this sentence as *refrigerium* is used above. One copyist spoiled this play on words by changing *aeternas* (*sc. febres*) below to *flammas aeternas*: cf. Krusch, *App.*

7. Preface of "The Lives of the Fathers"

I had decided to write only of that which was done by divine power at the sepulchers of the blessed martyrs and confessors, but recently I have found material about those whom the merit of blessed conversation has borne to Heaven and whose path of life, known by definite accounts, in my opinion built the church. Under the pressure of this opportunity I will not delay saying something about them, since the life of the saints not only lays open their deeds, but also incites the minds of the hearers to imitation. And some ask whether we ought to say "The Life of the Saints" or "Lives." Aulus Gellius too and many of the grammarians[30] wished to say "lives."[31] For the author Pliny says in the third book of his *Art of Grammar*:[32] "the ancients spoke of the 'lives' (*vitas*) of each one of us, but the grammarians thought that 'life' (*vitam*) has no plural number." Whence it is obvious that it is better to say "The Life of the Fathers" than "Lives," because, although there is a diversity of merits and virtues, nevertheless one life of the body nourishes all in the world. I admit I have written in the following book of the confessors something on the life of certain ones who have performed fewer works in the body because, although they be counted great from the miraculous power of God, nonetheless there is but little to write about them. Although unskilled and unlearned, we presume to publish more lengthy accounts in this book, which we wish to call "The Life of the Saints." We pray to the Master that He deign to put the word in our mouth since he has often unlocked the lips of the dumb for

[30] *Philosophorum* "grammarians." Gregory often used such words as *philosophus* carelessly.

[31] Gellius has no comment on this point in his *Noctes Atticae*, but he does use the plural in two places (1.3.1; 13.2.1). It is unlikely that Gregory consulted Gellius or Pliny the Elder. I assume that he found this reference, including quotations from Gellius and Pliny, in a glossary. However it is often assumed that he used those authors directly: cf. Arndt, p. 7; Bonnet, pp. 52f.; Manitius, *NA*, 21 (1896), pp. 555f.

[32] Pliny refers to his own work on grammar in the preface of his "Natural History": (28) . . . *libellos, quos de grammatica edidi*, . . . This is obviously the same as the *dubii sermonis octo* (*libri*) which is listed by the younger Pliny in his catalogue of his uncle's works (*Ep.*, 3.5.5.): cf. J. W. Beck, *C. Plinii Secundi librorum dubii sermonis VIII reliquiae* (Leipzig, 1894), pp. XVIIIf., 42.

their original[33] use, and that He consider those deeds proclaimed in praise of Him which He orders written in the case of the saints.

8. Preface of "The Glory of the Confessors"

It is shameful for a foolish man, or a rascal, or an unskilled or lazy man, to attempt what he cannot fulfill. But what shall I do, since I will not allow concealment of the results which I have often seen of the miraculous powers of the blessed men, or which I have learned were accomplished through the testimony of good men of certain trustworthiness? But since I am ignorant of literature, rhetoric, and the art of grammar, I fear that when I shall have begun to write, men of education will say to me:

> Ignorant rustic, why do you judge that your name should be placed among writers? Do you think that this work will be accepted by the learned, although artistic genius does not abound in it, and no knowledge of literature aids it? You have no useful subject in literature; you do not know how to distinguish among nouns; very often you put the feminine for the masculine, the neuter for the feminine, and the masculine for the neuter; you do not put prepositions in the proper place which the authority of noble teachers sanctions.[34] For you put the accusative for the ablative and again the ablative for the accusative. Do you think it is fitting that the sluggish ox should play the games of the palaestra, or the slothful ass should run with quick flight amid the ranks of the ball players?[35] The crow will certainly not be able to cover its blackness by the feathers of the white doves, nor will the darkness of pitch be changed by the color of white milk.[36] To be sure, it is not possible that these things should happen, nor will you be counted among other writers.

[33] *Praestinos*, i.e. *pristinos*: cf. Bonnet, p. 493, note 1.

[34] *Dictatorum* "teachers": Krusch (*Index*, p. 943) defined *dictator* in this passage as *qui scribenda dictat;* cf. also Bonnet, p. 90, note 2.

[35] For *sphaeristae* cf. Sidonius, *Ep.*, 5.17.7, and H. J. Leon, "Ball Playing at Rome," *Classical Bulletin* 23 (1947), pp. 65-7.

[36] On Gregory's use of proverbs cf. Manitius, *NA*, 21 (1896), pp. 552f.

But nevertheless I shall reply to them and say:

> I do your work, and through my rusticity I shall offer to you material on which you may exercise your wisdom.[37] For in my opinion these writings will offer one benefit to you, to be sure so that, what we narrate briefly, crudely and in an obscure style, you may expand in more lengthy pages clearly and brilliantly in verse.

Therefore, in the first book we have inserted some of the miracles of the Lord, of the sainted apostles and of the rest of the martyrs, which so far have been hidden and which God deigns to increase daily to strengthen the faith of the faithful, because it were extremely harmful that they should be forgotten. In the second, we have placed the miracles of St. Julian. Four books on the miracles of St. Martin. The seventh on the lives of certain fortunate men.[38] We are now writing this eighth book on the miracles of the confessors. Since, as we have often testified before, artistic genius is not ours nor does eloquence in speaking aid us, we especially beg the reader to grant pardon freely for our rashness, since no worldly vanity causes us to write, but shame urges us to be silent while love and fear of Christ impel us to publish these works. And since I began the first book with the miracles of the Lord, I wish to make a beginning for this book with the miracles of the sainted angels.

---

[37] *Vestram prudentiam exercebo*: for the expansion in the translation cf. Bordier, and Bonnet, p. 79, note 6.

[38] *Feliciosorum*, Ruinart, Bordier, Krusch, and Morf. Bonnet follows the reading of ms 4 and prints *religiosorum* (p. 195, note 6; p. 238, note 7).

8
The Miracles of St. Martin

Introductory Note. This section consists of a translation of the whole of the first book of *The Miracles of Blessed Martin the Bishop.* The preface to this book is included in the preceding section. The book is comparatively short and is more typical of Gregory's hagiography than the other passages included. It may seem less interesting to the modern reader since there is constant repetition of somewhat similar stories. However, in a work like this, we can see more clearly even than in purely historical passages the difficulties and dangers endured by the common people of this period. Gregory's compassion led him to take great interest in stories of the humble as well as in stories of the great. A recent study clearly shows by reference to the works of Gregory, how Christianity had wrought a change in the attitude of society towards the lower class, and how the church became their patron. The general conclusion states effectively though with some exaggeration: "The sixth century in Gaul stands out preëminently, not only as a period of great spiritual renaissance in general, but also as one in which respect for poverty and for the poor, in whom Christ himself stood personified, operated as a strong social force and was the moving spirit of the age."[1]

Gregory's preoccupation with miracles at the shrines of the saints was not wholly a matter of personal feeling. He was interested in and fascinated by miraculous cures, and he had a burning desire to believe in them.[2] At times his enumeration of the proofs of their validity seems to be an attempt to prove them to himself. However, he always has in the back of his mind a

---

[1] Mac Gonagle, p. 105. Three sections of this dissertation are of especial interest here: "The Protection of the Poor" (pp. 22–35); "The Mystic Power of the Poor" (pp. 94-99); "St. Martin, Protector of the Poor" (pp. 90-94).

[2] Cf. Latouche, pp. 90f.

special purpose, *aedificatio ecclesiae*. Widening the power, effectiveness, and consolation of the church is a prime motive in most of the accounts of the saints and their miracles before, during, and after Gregory's day. Often the purpose of the story is to call the afflicted and the wretched back to the church. Many times the stories serve as warnings to the wicked or to heretics. Some passages warn the powerful nobles that they should neither encroach upon the prerogatives of the church nor seize church property.[3] The motives that influenced Gregory in his writing were powerful throughout the medieval period. The tremendous popularity of stories such as these can be shown by the almost endless works collected in the great *Acta Sanctorum* of the Bollandists.[4] Gregory's own work was important in the inspiration and spreading of the type, and the multiplication of the manuscripts of the *Miracula* attests their popularity.[5] Gregory's naïve enthusiasm and his unswerving, though at times ill-informed, orthodoxy contributed to his popularity. Of this phase of his work Professor Laistner said:[6]

> His insistence on the reality and frequency of miracles, not merely in the *History* but still more in his other works, made Gregory one of the most influential writers for the development of hagiography in the West. . . . Thus he gave to the Middle Ages some of the best examples of a type of literature at once edifying and readable, because it satisfied the common human love for a good story and at the same time took men's thoughts away for a spell from the violence and sordid reality of their mundane existence.

The use of the anecdotal story may reflect Gregory's style of preaching. Many passages seem to have been written to be delivered orally rather than read, and this may also reflect Gregory's method of collecting his materials. Naturally he used the available books, although he sometimes fails to follow his

[3] MacGonagle comments on the strength of the belief among all classes in the mystical power of the saints (pp. 67–72), and especially that of St. Martin (pp. 86–90).
[4] A note on this work is given under the abbreviation *AASS* in the bibliography.
[5] Krusch, pp. 462–75; *NA*, 19 (1894), pp. 25–45; *App.*, pp. 708–25.
[6] P. 102.

written sources punctiliously, but he seems to have acquired more vital portions of his material through extended conversations.[7] His use of oral source material adds to the vigor and value of his hagiographic works and the latter part of his *History of the Franks*. Another point of interest is his distrust of doctors and of medicine. This distrust was natural in a day when many doctors were ignorant or superstitious, but it was also to some extent due to the fact that inevitable conflict arose between those who believed in the miraculous healing power of the shrines of the saints and those who preferred the healing power of secular physicians.[8] Gregory's references to his personal experiences of the healing power of the tomb of St. Martin lead us to believe that he may have enjoyed mild hypochondria.[9]

St. Martin's place in the history of the church in France adds interest to these stories of his great shrine in the city of Tours. Martin combined in himself during his lifetime qualities which made him one of the most famous men in early Gallic history.[10]After his death the memory of his saintly character and the reputation of the miraculous power of his tomb at Tours com-

[7]Not only was he familiar with the works of Fortunatus, but he also included stories which he learned orally from him (*Mart.*, 1.13–16). Cf. Krusch, pp. 457–9, and Vinay, pp. 155–67 (for his use of oral sources in *HF*).

[8]*Mart.*, 1.27: cf. Dalton, I, pp. 418–24.

[9]E.g., *Mart.*, 1.32–33; 2.1; 3.1; 4.1–2.

[10]The source material on St. Martin is listed in the handbook edited by the Bollandists, *Bibliotheca hagiographica Latina*, II (Brussels, 1901), pp. 823–31; *supplementum* (Brussels, 1911), pp. 221f. All accounts of the life and early miracles of St. Martin go back to the account of Sulpicius Severus whose material on St. Martin has been elaborately treated by Paul Monceaux, who translated Sulpicius' works which deal with Martin (*vita Martini, dialogi*, three letters and two chapters from the *chronica*), and prefaced his translation with an elaborate account of the saint: *Saint Martin: récits de Sulpice Sévère*, translated into French with an introduction (Paris, 1926). Monceaux's work has been translated into English by Mary C. Watt: *St. Martin of Tours, the Chronicles of Sulpicius Severus*, (London, 1928). A translation of all of the works of Severus by Alexander Roberts is included in *Nicene and Post-Nicene Fathers*, 2nd. series, XI (New York, 1894), pp. 1–122 (*vita Martini*, pp. 3–17; *dialogi*, pp. 24–54). An authoritative and brilliant article by the late Bollandist, Father Hippolyte Delehaye, sheds light on Severus' account of St. Martin as well as many other questions: "Saint Martin et Sulpice Sévère," *Analecta Bollandiana*, 38 (1920), pp. 5–136. Material on St. Martin has not yet been included in the *Acta sanctorum* since the last volume goes only to November 10. Father Delehaye's article was part of the preliminary work on St. Martin for the volume including November 11. A brief account in English is

bined to make him the premier saint of Gaul.[11] This influence has fluctuated but has never really become negligible, even after the sack of the basilica by the Protestants in 1562, and its destruction by the revolutionaries in 1793. Bayet estimated that there were in France in his day 3,675 churches dedicated to St. Martin, and that 425 towns or villages were named for the saint.[12] So strong is the influence of St. Martin that his story is inextricably interwoven with the history of France. One recent proof of this lasting influence is a new biography of St. Martin in which Henri Ghéon with eloquent and pious fervor lauds his character and deeds.[13] It is perhaps typical of the devotion of the French that Ghéon with charming and rather naïve enthusiasm finds in St. Martin the typical French virtues. At one place he says:[14] "No man is more sensible than a saint. But the quality of sound sense is stronger, more in evidence, more steadily present in French saints."

Martin was born about 336[15] in Sabaria in Pannonia but passed

that of J. G. Cazenove in Smith and Wace, *Dictionary of Christian Biography, Literature, Sects, and Doctrines*, III (London, 1882), pp. 838–45, *s.v. Martinus (1)*; a simple and plain account is that of S. Baring-Gould, *Lives of the Saints*, (2nd. ed., Edinburgh, 1914), XIII, pp. 241–61. A sympathetic study from the point of view of the relationship of Martin and Sulpicius Severus is that of E. S. Duckett, *Latin Writers of the Fifth Century* (New York, 1930), pp. 182–95; T. R. Glover's earlier account is more penetrating and less sympathetic: *Life and Letters in the Fourth Century* (Cambridge, 1901), pp. 278–301.

[11] Cf. C. Bayet in Lavisse, *Histoire de France*, II, 1 (Paris, 1903), pp. 13–18.

[12] *Op. cit.*, p. 16, note 1.

[13] *St. Martin of Tours*, tr. by F. J. Sheed, New York, 1946: from *Saint Martin (Les grands coeurs)*, (Paris, 1941).

[14] *Op. cit.*, p. 88 (Fr. ed., p. 133).

[15] Gregory sets the death of St. Martin during the consulship of "Caesarius and Atticus" (*Mart.*, 1.3). Flavius Caesarius and Nonius Atticus Maximus were the consuls of A. D. 397 (W. Liebenam, *Fasti consulares imperii Romani*, Bonn, 1909, p. 40), but Krusch in his note on this passage argued that Gregory was confused both here and in *HF*, 10.31. Krusch's chronology is this: St. Martin was born in 336, was ordained bishop on July 4, 370, and died on November 11, 401. According to Krusch he lived to the age of 65 and was bishop for 31 years, 4 months and 7 days, although Gregory says that he died in his 81st year and was bishop 25 years, 4 months, and 10 days (*Mart.*, 1.3). I have followed Krusch with some reluctance. Father Delehaye has argued cogently for the great credibility of Gregory's dating (*Anal. Boll.*, 38, 1920, pp. 19–33) and concluded that Martin was born about 315 and died in 397. Monceaux considered three dates as certain: July 4, 371 (consecration as bishop), 385 (Martin at Trèves), Nov. 8 and 11, 397 (death and funeral)—French ed., pp. 19f., Eng. ed., pp. 7f. The conflict in dating is probably insoluble.

his childhood in Ticinum (Pavia) in Italy, where his father had been stationed. Although he had become a catechumen, i.e., had begun to receive instruction in the church, he followed his father's profession and became a soldier. While in service at Amiens in Gaul he performed his most famous act of self-abnegation. Cutting his military cloak in half with his sword, he shared it with a shivering beggar at the gate of Amiens. Though mocked for this action, he dreamt that the Master appeared to him in a dream in the half garment and said, "Martin, though a catechumen, hath clothed Me with this cloak." He was then baptized and was soon discharged from the army. A visit to St. Hilary of Poitiers, whose guest he was for a considerable time, had a determining effect on his career. Hilary wished to ordain him as a deacon, but Martin would accept only the position of exorcist. Soon, with Hilary's approval but with his urgent appeal to return later, he went to Pannonia to attempt the conversion of his parents. He was successful in the case of his mother, but the prevalence of the Arian heresy forced him to leave. Since Hilary had been exiled from Gaul, Martin went to Italy where he showed his bent for seclusion by retiring to the island of Gallinaria off the coast of the Riviera. About 360, after Hilary had returned to Gaul, Martin fulfilled his promise to return. He settled about five miles from Poitiers and applied himself to the rigorous and ascetic life of a hermit. Subsequently his love of poverty and seclusion, combined with a burning zeal and truly remarkable executive ability, led him to found the earliest monastery in Gaul at Locociagum, which is now Ligugé. Under the patronage of Hilary his influence became strong. When he yielded with extreme and genuine reluctance to the call to serve as bishop of Tours, and was ordained on July 4, 370, he conducted the episcopal office with efficiency and asceticism. While bishop, he founded the monastery at Marmoutier,[16] called *Maius Monasterium*, "the larger monastery," to distinguish it from Ligugé. He was also noted for his evangelical zeal in rooting out paganism, which still had a strong hold in the see of Tours. He had relations with the

---

[16] It was founded in 372 on the other side of the Loire (cf. Severus, *vita Martini*, 7.1). It later became a Benedictine monastery. Cf. Dalton, I, p. 352; II, p. 602; Longnon, pp. 276f.; Krusch, *Index*, p. 900 (seven references to it in Gregory).

Emperors Valentinian and Maximus, and visited each in turn at the city of Tréves. His latter years and his relations with the emperors and other bishops were embittered by his innocent involvement in the quarrel over the Priscillianist heresy. Although bitterly opposed to the heresy, Martin as bitterly opposed the harsh measures adopted against Priscillian and his adherents, and in his latter years avoided the court at Tréves and communication with the other bishops of Gaul. Before his call to Tours he had already established a reputation for saintliness, ascetic life, and miraculous power which vied with the reputations of the eastern hermit-saints of his day. As bishop, his reputation as a worker of miracles increased, and after his death the fame of the miraculous power of his tomb spread far and wide. His remarkable career ended with his death on November 11, 401.

Our Christian Achilles did not lack his Homer. He early became acquainted with Sulpicius Severus. Martin's rough personality had a remarkable effect upon Severus. This cultivated scholar, who had already shown the inclination to retire from the world, now became a monk, and devoted himself to the saint. His *Life of Martin* and his *Dialogues* which concern the miracles of St. Martin were written in a smooth and perspicuous style and gained wide popularity. In the latter part of the fifth century Paulinus of Périgueux composed a long poem on Martin. The first five books are a versification of the material in the two works of Severus.[17] The sixth book concerns miracles which occurred after the publication of the two works of Severus. Venantius Fortunatus,[18] the greatest of the Latin poets of the sixth century, also turned to Severus for material for his metrical life of St. Martin. It

---

[17] Cf. A. H. Chase, "The Metrical Lives of St. Martin of Tours by Paulinus and Fortunatus and the Prose Life by Sulpicius Severus," *Harvard Studies in Classical Philology*, 43 (1932), pp. 51-76. Chase (pp. 58-61) summarizes the use made of Severus by Paulinus and Fortunatus.

[18] Fortunatus' poetry contains both Christian and secular elements: F. J. E. Raby, *A History of Christian-Latin Poetry from the Beginnings to the Close of the Middle Ages* (Oxford, 1927), pp. 86-95; *A History of Secular Latin Poetry in the Middle Ages*, I (Oxford, 1934), pp. 127-42. A brief but excellent appreciation of Fortunatus is to be found in E. S. Duckett, *The Gateway to the Middle Ages* (New York, 1938), pp. 284-311. Cf. also Manitius, I, pp. 170-81. The standard edition of his works is *MGH, AA*, IV, I (*opera poetica*, ed. F. Leo, Berlin, 1881), IV, II (*opera pedestria*, ed. B. Krusch, Berlin, 1885).

is in four books[19] and was dedicated to his friends, Agnes and Radegunda. It is preceded by a letter in prose addressed to Gregory of Tours in which Gregory's own works on the miracles of St. Martin are mentioned.[20] Fortunatus announced his intention of turning that narrative into verse, an intention which he never carried out. Gregory's reference to Fortunatus' work on Martin is a further indication that Gregory never really finished a work, but kept it at hand and felt free to insert material later. The friendship of Gregory and Fortunatus is better attested in the poems of the latter than in the prose of the former.[21] In addition to many poems addressed to Gregory, one is addressed also to Armentaria, Gregory's mother.[22]

Gregory not only devoted four books to the miracles performed at the tomb of St. Martin, but also referred to him frequently in his *History of the Franks*.[23] He had been devoted to St. Martin in his earlier years, and his elevation to the see of Tours gave him added enthusiasm and opportunity for the collection of materials on the miraculous powers of the saint.

The First Book of "The Miracles of Blessed Martin the Bishop"

1. Indeed there are many who have written of the miracles of St. Martin in verse or in prose. Among these the first is the famous Severus Sulpicius, who had such a burning love for the saint of God that even during his lifetime he wrote one book on the remarkable events of Martin's life, and then after the passing of that blessed man he wrote two books called *Dialogues*.[24] In these books he included, at the suggestion of Postumianus,[25] some of

---

[19] Books 1-2 follow Severus' *vita Martini;* books 3-4 his *dialogi,* 1 (2)-2(3): cf. Chase, *loc. cit.,* pp. 58-61.

[20] *Cum iusseritis ut, opus illud Christo praestante intercessionibus domini Martini, quod de suis virtutibus explicuistis versibus debeat digeri, id agite ut mihi ipsum relatum iubeatis transmitti* (p. 293.11-13 Leo).

[21] *Carmina,* 5.4-5; 8-17; 8.11-21; 9.6-7; 10.12.

[22] *Ibid.,* 10.15.

[23] Krusch, *Index,* pp. 900f.

[24] Both of these prose works were edited by C. Halm, *CSEL,* I (Vienna, 1866), pp. 109-37 (*vita Martini*), 152-216 (*dialogi*).

[25] *Dial.,* 1.1-2. Postumianus is an interlocutor in the *Dialogi.*

the miracles of the hermits and anchorites. However, in no case was he able to find our Martin inferior. He likened him to the apostles and the earlier saints so that he said: "Happy indeed was Greece which was worthy to hear the preaching of the apostles, but Gaul was not wholly forsaken by Christ since He gave it Martin."[26]

2. The blessed Paulinus, bishop of Nola, wrote in verse[27] in five books those miracles which Severus had included and in the sixth book of his work he added those which occurred after the death of Severus.[28] He said:

> When men possessed by demons were whirled through the air over the balustrades of the basilica, and ten were thrown into a well by the influence of the demon, they were pulled out and taken up again unharmed.[29]

And we too have seen this done in our times.

> Also another demon entered the body of a man and drove him headlong to a stream as if about to drown the prey which he had taken. But the aid of the blessed confessor did not fail the man in mortal danger. For he entered the river and sought the farther bank, and emerged unharmed with even his clothing dry. And when he had come to Marmoutier he appeared cleansed.

Paulinus even gives witness that this man was accustomed to pour forth many voices and to speak very frequently in the tongues of unknown nations and to prophesy[30] the future and confess crimes.

[26] *Dial.*, 2(3).17.6. As frequently happens, Gregory's citation is inexact: *nec* for *nequaquam* and *donavit* for *donaverit* represent careless citation rather than a different text or the errors of a copyist.

[27] *Versu*, Krusch, *App.*; cf. Bonnet, p. 755 (*add.* to p. 284).

[28] This poem was not by the famous Paulinus of Nola, but by the more obscure Paulinus of Périgueux (*Petricordia*). This error in assignment of the poem was common, it occurs again in Gregory (*GC*, 108). Paulinus' poems were edited by M. Petschenig in *Poetae Christiani minores, CSEL*, XVI, 1 (Vienna, 1888), pp. 1–190. Gregory's summaries are brief and somewhat inaccurate digests of the passages in the sixth book of the poem.

[29] 6.39–70.

[30] *Fari*, a reading approved by Bonnet (p. 258, note 2); Krusch preferred *fateri* (as the equivalent of *fari*) in *NA*, 19 (1894), p. 37.

But, as we have said, as soon as he touched the sacred threshold, he departed whole.[31] When Egidius was besieged by the enemy and his troops were in disorder and all aid was cut off, he was attacked, but was freed after his enemies had been put to flight by prayer to the blessed man.[32] And a man possessed by a demon at the very hour that this occurred prophesied in the midst of the basilica that relief had been granted by the power of St. Martin.[33]

A certain girl, ill with a paralyzing disease, and, what is worse, entangled in the error of a fanatic cult, sought the tomb of the blessed one, and after celebrating a vigil there, was returned to health. Called back again to the vomit of her idolatry, she incurred again the weakness from which she had been freed by the power of the priest.[34]

A certain Hun, driven impetuously by the inspiration of a demon, violently seized the crown of the sepulcher which declared the merits of the saint. Soon deprived of sight, he was forced by the pain to restore his booty and he recovered his sight.[35]

When a certain man at the impulse of the Tempter attempted to strike another with drawn sword, his wrath was turned straightway back on himself. For by the judgment of God which followed swiftly, he pierced himself with that very sword.[36]

Finally, when the rejoicing populace wished to bring columns to ornament the blessed church, a certain envious man was opposed to this work and threatened his wife severely because she gave them permission when they sought wagons.[37] And when that proud man spurred his horse headlong into a small stream, he

---

[31] 6.71-105.

[32] Afranius Syagrius Aegidius, who was appointed *comes et magister utriusque militiae* by Majorianus in 457, was besieged by the Visigoths in Arles in 459. He died in 464 and was succeeded by his son Syagrius. Cf. *HF*, 2.11, 12, 18 and Seeck in *RE*, I, cols. 476f., *s.v. Aegidius*.

[33] 6.111-151.

[34] 6.165-214.

[35] 6.218-249.

[36] 6.250-264.

[37] I have followed in part the conjectual additions of Petschenig (p. 149): . . . *multa <in uxorem> minabatur, proeoquod solatium aliquod ad plaustra <vehenda> petentibus praeberet*. The addition of *vehenda* is unnecessary: it is omitted in the translation.

perished in the bosom of the waters suffocated by the blows of the flood.[38] Then following his funeral cortege they carried the columns to the blessed church.[39]

As often as oil was placed near the blessed sepulcher, they report that they saw it increase.

Truly St. Perpetuus,[40] the bishop, worthily called the disciple of the blessed man, carried a jar of oil to the sacred tomb so that the miraculous power of that just man might infuse and sanctify it. And the oil, scraped from the marble by which the sacred members are covered, with dust intermixed overflowed in such a quantity of oil that oily water, gleaming with the odor of nectar, poured over the garments of the priest. And many sick found healing in this.[41] And tempests too were often kept from fields purified by this liquid.

Then a certain devout man, when full of faith he had approached the sacred church and had thirsted for the grace of the saint, was reflecting on what he should take for protection from the blessed chapel. Approaching the sepulcher, he asked the attendant that he grant him a little wax from the tomb. When he received this, he departed joyfully and confidently placed it in a field in which he sowed a crop. When a very savage storm arose, such as had often laid waste the neighborhood in preceding years, it was kept from the field by the blessing, nor did it do the customary harm in that place.[42]

In truth, at the approach of a magnificent and long-anticipated Easter festival, the people devotedly went to the cell of the blessed man in which he often had lingered in converse with angels. They licked each place with their kisses, or wet with their tears each place where the blessed man[43] had sat, or had prayed, or where he had taken food, or where he had granted sleep to his

[38] *In sinu aquarum gurgitis ictibus suis suffocatus interiit.* Krusch interpreted this as meaning that he suffocated in shallow water in the sand which follows Severus, 6.278–80. Later in his appendix he adopted *sine,* a reading of a new ms, for *in sinu.*
[39] *Funere* is a conjecture by Petschenig for *iuvene* (*populo* is a variant). For the whole paragraph, Severus, 6.265–290.
[40] Sixth bishop of Tours: *HF,* 10.31, cf. Dalton, II, pp. 602f.
[41] 6.298–319.
[42] 6.325–336.
[43] *Aut,* Krusch, *App.* (replacing *ante*).

body after many labors. Then in a fleet of boats already prepared they made ready to cross the river, so that they might approach the blessed sepulcher, might pray with tears for forgiveness, and might prostrate themselves before the confessor. When they were sailing and a wind arose at the impulse of the Tempter, the ship was sinking in the depths and men and women were being snatched by the stream. And when they were being whirled amid the violence of the waves and all hope of escape had vanished, all with one voice shouted and said: "Compassionate Martin, snatch your servants from present death!" At these words, lo! a placid breath of wind raised up unharmed the limbs of those submerged by the waves, and restored them all to the shore that they longed for, and even the waters aided. Not one perished, but all were preserved and performed a festal Easter service with great exultation. For that miracle was not lacking, which parted the Jordan and led the people between the masses of water on a dry path, when Joshua consecrated on the farther bank twelve stones, taken from the bed of the river, and bearing the apostolic insignia,[44] or that which rescued Peter when, perishing, he held the Master's right hand lest he perish,[45] or that which drew forth from the depths of the sea a sailor, who was about to sink, and called upon the Master of Martin for aid.[46]

A certain man eager to take something as a blessing from the sacred chapel received wax from the holy sepulcher and placed in within the inner part of his home as a heavenly treasure. However, it happened that a fire, started by the envy of the Tempter, was kindled[47] with greedy flame around the house and, spreading over the dry boards, was consuming everything. In the meantime, he raised a shout to heaven and begged the aid of the blessed Martin. Then he remembered the particle of wax brought from the church of the saint. When he found it and threw it on the

---

[44]Cf. *Joshua*, 4.20. Gregory's phrase, *signa apostolica gestientes*, gives an allegorical interpretation not explicit in *Joshua*. Bordier printed the same text, but translated so as to keep the biblical meaning: ". . . qui devaient marquer comme un signe la mission d'Israël."

[45]Cf. *Matthew*, 14.31.

[46]6.351–460.

[47]*Circumdaretur*, Krusch, *App.*: *circumureretur* (Ruinart) was supported by Bonnet (p. 194, note 8).

flame, straightway the whole fire died down, and by a new miracle wax, which was accustomed to nourish fire, repressed the violence of fire by the force of holiness.[48] These things Paulinus wrote in verse in the sixth book of his work, having used as his authority for these events St. Perpetuus the bishop. Indeed when the manuscript of his authority had come to him, his grandson was seriously ill. But he trusted the miraculous power of the saint and said: "If it please you, blessed Martin, that I write something in praise of you, let it appear from this sick boy." When he had placed the manuscript on the boy's breast, the fever immediately died down and he was healed who had been sick.[49] Also, the bishop Fortunatus composed a whole work on his life in four books in verse.

3. Though unskilled, nonetheless, I am induced by these writers to try to weave together for remembrance some of those miracles of the most blessed Martin which happened after his death. I shall be zealous in writing to find as much as I can which is not included in the works of Severus or Paulinus. The glorious master Martin, brilliant and shining in the whole world, a new sun arising when the universe was declining, born at Sabaria in Pannonia, as an earlier history tells, was sent for the salvation of Gaul by the aid of God.[50] Lighting it with his miracles and signs, unwillingly at the insistence of the people, he undertook the duties of the bishopric at the city of Tours. In this office he passed a glorious and almost inimitable life for five quinquennia, twice two months and ten days, and in the eighty-first year of his life, during the consulship of Caesareus and Atticus,[51] died peacefully in the middle of the night. It is most manifest that his death on the Lord's Day was glorious and worthy of praise throughout the whole world, and we prove this in the following account by definite witnesses. It is thought that it is a sign of no small merit, that the Lord lifted him up to Paradise on that day on which the same Redeemer and Master rose a victor from the dead, and that,

[48] 6.467-499.
[49] The story is told by Paulinus in a short poem *de visitatione nepotuli sui* (Petschenig, pp. 161-64). For a discussion of the relation of St. Perpetuus and Paulinus cf. Chase, *loc. cit.*, pp. 52-7.
[50] Severus, *vita Martini*, 2.
[51] See p. 27, note 15 above.

as he had always celebrated the festivals of the Lord without pollution, so after the cares of the world he should be placed at rest on the Lord's Day.

4. Indeed the blessed Severinus, bishop of the city of Cologne,[52] a man of honorable life and praiseworthy in all ways, was traversing the sacred places, according to custom, with his clergy on the Lord's Day. At the hour in which the blessed man died he heard a chorus of those singing on high. And when he had called his archdeacon, he asked him if the voices, to which he was attentively listening, were reaching his ears. He replied: "Not at all." Then he said: "Listen carefully." The archdeacon then began to stretch his neck upward, and to prick up his ears, and to stand on tiptoe with the aid of his staff. But I believe that he was not of great enough merit that he might be worthy to hear these things. Then he and the blessed bishop both prostrated themselves on the ground and prayed to the Master that divine love might grant that he hear this. When they stood erect the old man again asked: "What do you hear?" He said: "I hear the voices of those singing as if in Heaven, but I do not know what else there is." The bishop replied to him: "I will tell you what is happening. My master, Bishop Martin, has gone from the world, and now the angels are carrying him on high with song. And when there was a delay for a little time, and these things might be heard, the Devil was trying to keep him with the wicked angels. When he found nothing of his in that man, he departed in confusion. What then will be our lot, sinners as we are, if the evil side wishes to harm such a great priest?" When the priest spoke such things, the archdeacon quickly sent to Tours a man to inquire diligently about these things. And when he came, he learned that the blessed man had died on that day and at that hour at which St. Severinus had heard the chorus of singers. But if we go back to the history of Severus, he wrote that at that very hour St. Martin had appeared to him with a book containing his own life.[53]

5. For at that time the blessed Ambrose, whose flowers of

---

[52] This is the original source for the story of this vision. The account in the *vita et translatio Sancti Severini* is copied from Gregory. This *vita* is printed in *AASS*, 23 *Octobris*, X (Brussels, 1862), pp. 56–64 (the specific passage is 1.8 on p. 58.)

[53] Severus, *Epist.*, 2 (Halm, pp. 142–5).

eloquence shed fragrance through the whole church, was bishop in charge of the city of Milan.[54] He followed this custom in his celebration of the rites of the Lord's Day. When the reader came with the book he did not presume to read before the saint had given him the order by a nod. However, it happened on that Lord's Day, after the lesson from the prophet had been read, and the man was standing before the altar to deliver the lesson from the blessed Paul, that the most blessed priest Ambrose was asleep above the sacred altar. Many saw this and at first nobody presumed to wake him; then, after a period of about two or three hours, they aroused him saying: "Now the hour passes. Let the master order the reader to read the lesson, for the people are watching and are extremely wearied." The blessed Ambrose in reply said: "Be not disturbed. I profited greatly in my sleep since the Lord deigned to show me a great miracle. You will learn that my brother Martin the priest has departed from his body and that I performed the funeral service, and after the completion of the service I had not finished the full chapter of the reading when you aroused me." Then they were stupefied and likewise in wonder noted the day and the time, and made careful inquiry. They found out that it was the very time and day on which the blessed confessor had said that he performed his funeral rites. O blessed man, at whose passing a number of the saints sang, a chorus of angels exulted, an army of all the heavenly virtues met together. The Devil is confounded in his presumption, the Church is strengthened by his virtue, priests are glorified by revelation. Michael took him up with the angels, Mary raised him up with choruses of virgins, Paradise with its saints holds him in joy. But why do we vie in his praise which we cannot sufficiently fulfill? He himself is praise of Him whose praise was never absent from his mouth. May we be able at least to unravel the plain story!

6. It will be worth our while to insert in our account how his sacred body was transferred, with the assent of an angel, to the place where it is now worshipped. In the sixty-fourth year after the passing of the glorious master Martin, the blessed Perpetuus

---

[54]"Since Ambrose was already dead at Easter 397, he never witnessed the death of Martin who died Nov. 11, 401" (Krusch).

was allotted the seat of power in the see of Tours.[55] And when he had gained this pinnacle with a great unanimity of votes, he decided to place over the blessed limbs the foundations of a larger church than there had been before. Pursuing this project with wisdom and zeal, he completed it with marvelous results. There is much which we might say about this building, but because it is still in existence we think it better to be silent concerning it. Therefore when the time, long desired by the priest, arrived for its dedication, and for the transfer of the sacred body from the place where it had been buried, the blessed Perpetuus called together for this holiday the neighboring priests and no small crowd of abbots and diverse monks. He wished to do this on the first of July. After a night of vigil, at the coming of morning they took up shovels and began to dig up the earth which was above the sacred tomb. When it had been uncovered, they placed their hands on the coffin to move it, and there the whole multitude labored but accomplished nothing further during the whole day. Finally after another night of vigil, they made an attempt on the next morning, but again were unable to accomplish anything. Then they were disturbed and terrified and did not know what they should do. One of the monks said: "You know that in three days it has been the custom to celebrate the anniversary of the founding of this bishopric, and perchance this occurrence warns you that the dedication should be postponed to that day." Then they applied themselves continuously to fasts, and prayers, and singing in harmony day and night, and so passed that three-day period. On the fourth day, after approaching and placing their hands upon the sepulcher, they were unable to move it. When all were terrified and were on the point of hiding with earth the vessel which they had uncovered, a venerable, white-haired old man,[56] gleaming like snow, appeared to them and said that he was an abbot. And he said to them: "Wherefore are you disturbed and slow? Do you not see your master Martin stands prepared to aid you if you but lay on your hands?" Then casting

---

[55] Perpetuus became bishop of Tours in Sept. 458, i.e. 57 years after Martin's death (Krusch).

[56] *Canitie senes*, Krusch, *App.* (*senes* a variant of the nominative *senex*). Krusch's earlier text was *canities senis* (genitive). Bonnet preferred *canities senes* (genitive): p. 344, note 2.

aside the cloak which he was wearing, he put his hand to the sarcophagus with the rest of the priests. Crosses were prepared and wax candles, and after a prayer had been chanted, all sang and raised their voices on high. Then at the attempt of the old man straightway the sarcophagus was easily moved and taken to the place where it is now worshipped in accordance with the will of the Lord. When this had been done as the priest wished, and masses had been said, they came to a banquet and carefully inquired for the old man but found him nowhere. But there was no man who had seen him go out of the church. I believe that some angel had been there who announced that he had seen the blessed man and then disappeared. In this place from that day many miracles occur which through negligence have not been recorded. We cannot pass over in silence such great events which we have seen happen, or which we know certainly have happened.

7. A certain man named Theodomundus, whose organs of speech and hearing were blocked, came to the sacred basilica and came back every day to bow himself in prayer. But he only moved his lips, for he was unable to produce a word of sense, since he was bereft of the use of his voice. He was seen to pray so fervently that often men saw him weep amid his unspoken words. If anyone for the sake of profit had given him alms, he immediately passed them on to beggars like himself, and asking by a nod for coins from others, he gave the money to the needy. And when he had stayed in this holy place for a space of three years with such devotion, on a certain day he was warned by divine piety and came before the sacred altar. As he stood with his eyes and hands raised to Heaven there burst from his mouth a stream of blood and corruption. And spewing on the ground, he began to groan heavily and to cough up matter mixed with blood in such a way that it might be thought that somebody was cutting his throat with a knife.[57] The corruption hung from his mouth like a bloody thread. Then with the bonds of his ears and his jaws broken, he raised himself up, and again lifting up his eyes and hands to Heaven, he poured forth from his bloody mouth these first words:

[57] *Guttur eius*, a conjecture which Bonnet defender without enthusiasm (pp. 348f.): *gutture* may be taken as accusative.

"I return great thanks to you, blessed master Martin, because opening my mouth you have caused me after so long a time to offer words in your praise." Then all the people in wonder and amazement at such a great miracle asked him if he had recovered his hearing likewise. He replied before all the people that he heard everything freely. Therefore so returned to health, he was taken in by Queen Clotild,[58] out of reverence for the miracle of St. Martin, and placed in the school where he committed to memory all of the Psalms. So God, having made him a complete monk, allowed him to stay for many years thereafter in service to the church.

8. A certain woman by name Chainemunda was bereft of the light of her eyes, and knew not how to travel by means of sight except when another guided her. Since she was devout and full of faith, she came to the venerable shrine of the blessed priest Martin. However, not only was she blind, as we have said, but also her whole body was full of sores. For this corruption had covered all of her limbs with pustules, and she was of a pitiable appearance and such a horrible sight that she was thought by the people to be leprous. And every day by feeling her way she kept coming to the chapel of the glorious protector. After almost three years, as she was standing before his sepulcher, her eyes were opened so that she saw everything clearly. And when all the feebleness of her limbs was removed, and when the liquid which flowed from her body was dried up, new skin grew back, and she so recovered her former health that no sign of her affliction remained on her body. She lived for many years thereafter and continually gave thanks to Almighty God, because He had restored her unharmed through His blessed confessor.

9. I will not omit a story which shows how invocation of his name quieted a stormy sea. When the blessed Baudenus,[59] bishop

---

[58] When Clovis died in 511, his widow Clotild went to Tours "and there, serving at the basilica of the blessed Martin, lived in that place with the greatest chastity and good-will all the rest of the days of her life, and rarely visited Paris" (*HF*, 2.43). She died at Tours in 544 (*HF*, 4.1). Her name is given at this point in the text as *Chrodegilde*, but the spelling varies: ten variants are listed by Krusch (*Index*, p. 890).

[59] Sixteenth bishop of Tours (*ca.* 546–5520. He had been King Lothar's *domesticus* (*HF*, 4.3).

of the city of Tours, was carried in a ship while crossing to his villa, a very terrible and violent windstorm arose suddenly. The placid sea is moved by the blast of the wind, the ship is battered by the mass of the waves. At first its prow is raised in the waves, then it slopes down amid the parting of the waters. Now they hang on the top of a watery mountain, now as the waves open they look down into the depths.[60] But the yard of the sail does not collapse since it bore the sign of the blessed cross. When their limbs were faint with fear, and all were prepared to die without hope of life, the elder man with tears prostrated himself in prayer, and raising his two hands to the stars[61] prayed for the aid of the blessed Martin, and was crying out that he should deign to aid them swiftly.[62] However, one of the treacherous men said: "That Martin whom you call has deserted you and aids you not in this peril." Truly I believe that these words came from the waylayer that he might disturb the blessed priest in his prayer. But he repelled this javelin with the breastplate of faith, and more and more besought the aid of the saint, while he at the same time urged all to pray. When this had been done, a very sweet odor like balsam suddenly came upon the ship, and the odor of frankincense spread as though an incense burner were being carried around. When this odor appeared, the savage force of the winds ceased, the great masses of overhanging waters were shattered, and there is restored a calm sea. All who had given themselves up to death marvel at the peace of the waves, and straightway are returned to shore since clear weather had been granted. But no one doubts that this tempest had been stilled by the arrival of the blessed man. Then all in common give thanks to the Lord, because he deigned to free them from this peril through the invocation of his priest.

10. At this time a certain man from Camara sought relics of the blessed Martin. When he had received these relics on the evening,

---

[60] *Scena* "top" (as Bordier "sommet"): cf. Bonnet, p. 213, note 1. This passage is very similar to Virgil, *Aen.*, 1.106-7, but Gregory seems to have misunderstood the second line. The whole account of the storm was influenced by *Aen.* 1.88-123.

[61] *Tunc resolutis timore membris, . . . et geminas tendens palmas ad astra, . . .* (Gregory): *extemplo Aeneae solvuntur frigore membra;/ingemit, et duplices tendens ad sidera palmas . . .* (Virgil, *Aen.*, 1.92-3.)

[62] Krusch's punctuation is incorrect (Bonnet, p. 719, note 1).

when he set out singing, and it became late while he was crossing the Liger river, the sky was darkened, and lo! lightning and thunder descended. During his journey, two boys with spears, torches emitting flames, offered light for him as he journeyed. The gleaming spears were advancing, revealing a miracle as well as comfort to the travelers, and showing the miraculous power of the blessed priest.

11. The unfruitful tongue falters in its desire to tell of such great miracles. The son of a certain Chararicus, king of Galicia, was seriously ill.[63] He had fallen into an illness so severe that he moved only in breathing. However, his father and the inhabitants of that place had joined themselves to the filthy Arian sect. But that region more than other provinces was also foul with leprosy. The king, when he saw that his son was beset with utmost danger, said to his man: "Tell me, I ask, what was the religious faith of Martin who they say gleams in Gaul with many miracles?" They said to him: "While alive he governed a people of the Catholic faith with pastoral care and asserted that the Son was venerated with substance and omnipotence equal to the Father and the Holy Ghost; but now he is placed in the seat of heaven and does not cease to provide his own people with continual benefits." He said: "If this be true which you report, let faithful friends hurry even to his church carrying many gifts; and if they obtain medicine for my little boy, I will believe what he believed after an inquiry into the Catholic faith." Therefore gold and silver were weighed out to the weight of his son, and this he sent to the venerable place of the sepulcher. Transported thither they prayed for the sick boy at the blessed tomb after offering the gifts. But since that heresy yet clung to the heart of the father, he did not immediately merit complete cure. However, the messengers returned and told the king that they had seen many miracles at the tomb of the blessed one, and said: "We do not know why your son has not become well." But he realized that his son could not be cured before he believed that Christ was equal with the Father. Hence he built for the honor of the blessed Martin a church of remarkable workmanship, and when it was finished, he proclaimed: "If I am deemed worthy to receive relics of that just man, I will believe

[63] The story of Chararicus occurs only in Gregory.

whatever the priests have preached." And so he sent his own men again with a greater gift. They came to the blessed place and asked for relics. And when according to custom relics were offered to them, they said: "We will not take them on these conditions, but, we ask, let permission be granted us to place objects here which we may take up again later." Then they placed upon the blessed sepulcher part of a silken cloak that had been weighed, for they said: "If we have found grace in the presence of the patron we seek, what we have placed here will weigh more later, and we will have in blessing what is sought through faith." Therefore they kept vigil for one night and at the coming of morning they weighed what they had placed. So much grace of that blessed man was poured into it that it raised the bronze bar as far as the scale had space to let it go up. And when the relics had been lifted up, they heard voices of those singing who had been thrown into jail in the city. The jailers wondered at the sweetness of the sound and asked what it was. They said: "The relics of lord Martin are being carried to Galicia, and hence we sing." Then they called with tears upon St. Martin to free them by his presence. When the jailers were terrified and fled and the bars of their prison cells were loosed, they rose free from chains and so came even to the sacred pledges in the sight of the people. Weeping and kissing the blessed relics, they gave thanks at the same time to the blessed Martin for their freedom, since he had deigned to save them by his pity. Then when the charges against them had been canceled by the judge through the intercession of the bishop of Tours, they were dismissed without harm. When those who carried the relics saw this, they rejoiced exceedingly and said: "Now we know that the blessed priest deigns to offer himself propitious to us though we be sinners." So they gave thanks, and on a prosperous voyage, under the guardianship of their patron, with smooth waves, with tempered breezes, with hanging sail, on a tranquil sea, they swiftly came to the port of Galicia. Then advised by God, blessed Martin[64] came from a

---

[64] This Martin was also born in Pannonia. He went to the Spanish peninsula where he became bishop of Dume and Braga. His death in 580 is mentioned by Gregory (*HF*, 5.37). A major part in the conversion of the Visigoths from the Arian heresy in 560 is attributed to him (Ruinart). Fortunatus was acquainted with him (*Carm.*, 5.1–2). For his life and literary work cf. Manitius, I, pp. 109–13.

distant region and he is now priest in that same place. But I do not believe that divine providence was lacking that he should leave his native land on the same day on which the blessed relics were raised up in this place. And so he entered the port of Galicia together with these pledges, which were received with the greatest veneration and which strengthened faith by miracles. For the son of the king was relieved of his illness and hastened to meet them. The blessed Martin then received the chief place in sacerdotal grace. The king confessed the unity of the Father, Son, and Holy Ghost and was anointed with his whole household. The vileness of leprosy was driven from the people, and that disease has never up to the present time appeared there on anyone. The Lord, at the arrival of the pledges of the blessed patron, granted such grace that it would take a long time to tell of the miracles which were performed there on that day. For that people is now so manifest in the love of Christ that all would most freely undergo martyrdom if a time of persecution should be at hand.

12. Queen Ultrogotho[65] also devoutly sought to gaze upon this after she heard of the miracles which occurred at the place where the sacred members rested, as if to hear the wisdom of Solomon.[66] Therefore, when she had abstained from food and sleep, and had given most generous alms, she came to the holy place. She entered the basilica, in fear and trembling without daring to approach the sepulcher, and proclaimed that she was unworthy, and that she could not approach that same place because her sins stood in the way. Nevertheless, when she had passed a night in watching and prayers and with flowing tears, she offered many gifts in the morning and sought that mass be celebrated in honor of the blessed confessor. While it was being celebrated, suddenly three blind men, who this long time were sitting at the feet of the blessed priest deprived of sight, were surrounded by great brilliance, and received their sight which they had formerly lost. After this had been done, the shout of those glorifying God was carried to heaven. The queen approached to see this miracle, the people gathered too, and all marveled at the woman's faith, and

---

[65] Ultrogotho (variant spelling, Ultrogotha) was driven into exile by Clothar after the death of her husband Childebert I in 558 (*HF*, 4.20; cf. Dalton, II, p. 522).

[66] *I Kings*, 10.1 (*III Reg.*, 10.1).

at the confessor's glory. But above all things our God is praised, Who manifests such miraculous power to His saints that He deems it worthy that such things be done through them, granting, amid the rest of the luminaries for this universe, a great star in the person of the blessed Martin, through whom these shadows might gleam with light who truly, like the fruitful olive,[67] might offer fruit each day to the Master by the conversion of the wretched.

13. But I will not pass over an event which I remember from the narration of my fellow servant, the venerable bishop Fortunatus.[68] A certain man in Italy, while pervaded by the poison of sores, was so afflicted in his danger that he despaired of life and asked some men if anyone had been at the church of the blessed Martin. Then a certain one of those who were standing near him said that he had been. The sick man asked what he had taken thence for a blessing. He said that he had not taken anything. He asked him a second time with what garment he had been dressed when he had come to the sacred church. He replied: those which he was wearing at that very time. Then, in faith, he cut a particle of the garment and placed it on the sore. As soon as it touched the limbs of the sick man, the wound of the sore lost the force of the poison. It offered such healing and miraculous power of the saint that it made the sick man well. He said that among the Italians this remedy flourished to such an extent that if anyone were stricken with sores, refuge was had in the neighboring chapel of the blessed Martin, and whatever first was taken from the curtain of the door, or from the draperies which hung from the wall, and was placed on and clung to the sick man, would be healing. This remedy had freed his fleshly father from death by the sores, and he asserted this as a witness for his Father.[69]

---

[67] *Psalms*, 52.8 (*Ps.*, 51.10).

[68] The material in paragraphs 13–16 is based on conversations with his friend Fortunatus. The direct quotation in 14 is a quotation from conversation. Only the story in 15 is found in the extant works of Fortunatus (*vita sancti Martini*, 4.665). This story is told in greater detail by Paul the Deacon in a chapter which gives valuable material on the life of the poet and includes Paul's own epitaph on Fortunatus (*Hist. Lang.*, 2.13). The English translation of Paul's history is an earlier volume of "The Translations and Reprints": *The History of the Langobards by Paul the Deacon*, translated by William D. Foulke, (Philadelphia, 1907).

[69] *Haec medella genitorem suum carnalem* (the father of Fortunatus) *ab interitu pusulae, ut ipse patris sui*, (the Heavenly Father) *testis adserit, liberavit.* Bordier

14. The same man told this story in these words:

In the upper part of a castle which is in that region of Italy which is called the third, a chapel of the blessed Martin was founded. And there during an invasion of the barbarians, when the enemy approached a neighboring tower treacherously with a nocturnal attack, a certain one of the guards in the tower had a lance, sword, knife, or dagger, which had been taken from the arsenal. For almost the space of an hour such a light shone from the whole sword that it seemed as if that iron weapon were turned to wax. Soon the guards, warned by this sign, were more intent on watching and drove off the hidden enemy with stones. Correctly we judge that this was done by the aid of St. Martin, who in his own vicinity offered to the people devoted to him careful and present guardianship.

And this miracle we learned from the aforesaid Fortunatus.

15. He likewise confessed that eyesight had returned[70] to him and to Felix, his fellow scholar in the school of rhetoric at Ravenna, when they touched their eyes with the oil which was burning in a lamp under an image of the blessed Martin.

16. Similarly in the aforesaid city, Placidus the procurator was given up by the doctors, and fled to the chapel of a neighboring nunnery and was lying in the courtyard. The blessed Martin came at night in a dream to the abbess and asked what she was doing.[71] She said that she was asleep. The saint said to her: "I must return now to Gaul, but I proclaim that I have remained here on account of that man who is lying in the courtyard." Then the abbess rose, related her vision, and promised the man that he would gain freedom from peril as he certainly deserved to do. But as the aforesaid priest asserts, it is much more desirable that Martin be revered in Italian localities than, if we may say so, where the pious limbs of the man lie buried. There it is desirable that the

does not contrast *genitor* and *pater*, but translates: ". . . son père selon la chair, dont il se porte garant en cette circonstance."

[70]*Redisse,* Krusch, *App.;* Bonnet, p. 554, note (where there is a comment on the striking anacoluthon: *sibi . . . socii sui Felicis . . . lumen redisse confessus est*).

[71]*Requiret quod,* Krusch, *App.*

frequent miracles performed there should be collected in a book, since such endless wonders are not recorded on paper.[72]

17. By the gate of Amiens, near which the blessed man once cut up his own cloak and clad a freezing poor man, a chapel was built by the faithful in which nuns now serve who have few resources because of the honor they pay the sainted priest, except that often the devotion of the faithful gives them support. Nevertheless, at a certain time they had a few beehives.[73] When an envious man saw these, he said to himself: "Perhaps I might be able to take away some of these hives." On the following night, instigated by a demon, he loaded a boat with three stolen hives so that he might more easily lay claim to what he had stolen after he crossed the river. But I believe that this theft trapped him, as was clearly shown afterward. When men hastened at the rising of the sun to the river port to cross they saw a boat, and the bees rising in a swarm from the hives and man lying below on his back. But as they had learned of the theft from the nuns, they thought he was held fast in sleep. As quickly as possible they hastened to bind him, but on approaching they found him dead. Immediately they informed the nuns and restored the stolen property to the sanctuary, since they marveled that so swift a sentence of divine vengeance had been visited upon the man.

18. So also at the chapel of Sireuil,[74] whose altar the fostering hand of the sacred confessor sanctified, many obtained the

---

[72] Krusch prints the following text: *in tantum (tantũ : : : : : :ut 3) ut frequentia miracula nec sparsa colligantur in verbis nec tam infinita recondantur in paginis.* The suggestion in ms 3 (cf. Krusch, p. 464) of a *lacuna* between *tantum* and *ut* leads me to believe that words such as *desiderabile est* have fallen out of the sentence, and my translation supplies them.

[73] *Civitas Ambianensium.* The chapel was later called *oratorium S. Martini ad Gemellos* (Saint-Martin aux Jumeaux); in Ruinart's time there was a column in it on which an inscription told the story of St. Martin and the beggar: cf. Ruinart, and Longnon, pp. 419f. Severus narrated this famous story with an appropriate reference to *Matthew*, 25.40 (*vita Martini*, 3.1–4).

[74] *Apud Siroialensim oratorium* (the spelling of the mss and editions varies). Ruinart stated without preference two identifications of the modern site—i.e. Ciran-la-Latte (Indre-et-Loire) and Saint-Cyran du Jambot (Indre): cf. Longnon, pp. 554f. Jacobs (pp. 112,132) accepted the former (equating it with Latta, *HF*, 4.48). Longnon showed definitely that both of these identifications were incorrect and that this place should be identified with one of two places now called Sireuil, probably that in Charente.

benefits they sought. A certain paralytic came and watched all night while holding a wax candle as high as he could. When morning came and light was returned to the world, his feet were loosed and in the sight of the people he leapt forth cured.

19. And I will not pass over in silence what he did for the blindness of a devoted woman, who had sought his aid at the blessed sepulcher. A certain woman, Bella by name, from the territory of Tours, lost the sight of her eyes and was seriously ill. And when she was pressed night and day by unceasing pain, she said to her family: "Had I been led to the basilica of lord Martin, I should have regained my health immediately. For I am confident that he is able to pour light on my eyes, since he was able to heal the leprosy of a poor man by implanting a kiss."[75] Then with an attendant leading her, she came to the holy place and, after she had devoted herself to fasts and frequent prayers, she recovered the sight which she had lost. And she was healed so completely that in her blindness she had come by another's guidance but she returned as an effective guide for the blind. Afterwards she married and bore children and, since she was in good health, paid thanks to him who healed her.

20. And because two or three times we have told of miracles performed and perils relieved by the mere invocation of the glorious name, I will tell how the blessed priest was called upon in the very precipice of death, and offered support to a certain man who was perishing. A certain Ammonius, agent of the sacred basilica, when he was returning home from dinner damp with wine, was dashed by an enemy from a cliff which was close by the road. The height of this place was about two hundred feet. And when he was whirling from the height of this precipice and was flying down without support of wings,[76] each second of his descent he kept calling on the aid of St. Martin. Then, as if struck from his animal by the hands of others, he was hurled upon the

---

[75] Severus, *vita Martini*, 18.3–5.

[76] *Sine alarum remigio.* This vivid metaphorical phrase *remigio alarum* ("on the oars of wings") is found in Virgil *Aen.* 1.301; also *remigium alarum*, *Aen.* 6.19; cf. Lucretius, 6.743; Quintilian, 8.6.18; Ovid, *Ars amatoria*, 245; *Met.*, 8.228; Apuleius, *Met.*, 6.15: the usage goes back to Aeschylus, *Agamemnon*, 52). Gregory found the phrase in the first book of Virgil's *Aeneid*. This mock-heroic passage is one of the few places in Gregory with a humorous tinge.

trees which were in the valley. And so, falling little by little from branch to branch, he came to the ground without peril of death. Nevertheless, lest the attempted trap of his ambusher might seem altogether fruitless, he lightly injured one foot. But when he came to the church of the glorious master, and knelt in prayer, he was relieved of all pain.

21. I believe it will not be considered superfluous if there be inserted in this account a tale of how the invocation of his name granted life to one who was on the point of death. In a certain place after a man had been arrested for theft, he was severely lashed and led to the gallows that he might be executed by hanging. And when he had come to such danger and death was now approaching, he sought a period for prayer. Then, with his hands lashed behind his back, he hurled himself flat on the ground and began with tears to call on the name of the blessed Martin, and begged that, even if he would not aid him in this dire necessity, he might pardon him of his sins hereafter. And after his prayer had been completed, he was hanged and the soliders left that place. However, the man himself with his mouth half open, moved his lips a little and kept on struggling to implore the aid of St. Martin. When they had departed, his hands and feet were immediately loosed. And when he had hung for a period of two days, it was revealed to a certain nun that she should release him. She came and found him still living. Then with the aid of the blessed Martin she took him down from the gallows and led him unharmed to the church. And there those who saw him gaped at him and marveling said: "How is he alive?" And they asked him how he had been freed. Then he said: "The blessed Martin freed me from present death and led me hither." Truly my opinion is that this miracle is not inferior to the raising of the dead. So the blessed confessor restored him to life, so to speak, after the power of death had been broken, and he had been snatched from its jaws. Even to this day he continues to live in this age as a testimony of the miraculous power of the blessed man.

22. Indeed I will not pass by what was done in the diocese of Candes.[77] For that place is illustrious with many miracles, since

---

[77] *Condatensis diocesis*, cf. Longnon, p. 271.

the blessed man, after he cast down the burden of the flesh, went from this place to the Master.[78] Therefore a man named Leomeris, the slave of a certain Andicavinus, stricken with apoplexy[79] grew stiff, and his hand was drawn together, and his tongue was tied. For a long time he was held by this weakness, and he did not do any work for himself or for his master.[80] When warned by faith, he had watched at the basilica of the blessed man, and his hand was straightened and his tongue was freed from all hindrance; he bore witness of the miracle of the blessed Martin to the people and said: "Behold! prove by my witness what the saint of God has done this night." Then having returned to his master, he told him everything which had been done. But he had little belief in the miraculous power of the glorious priest and put him back at his accustomed work. When he had begun to work, he fell again into this weakness. His master then realized that this was God's mysterious work and sent him again to the holy place to which he had gone before. In this place he spent the night with the greatest devotion, and when day came was renewed in that health which he had formerly gained.

23. I thought it proper also that I should not omit in my narrative what I heard the priest Wiliacharius tell.[81] At the time when he had hurried to king Clothar on account of the treachery of Chramnus,[82] he fled to the basilica of St. Martin. There he was placed in chains and guarded, but because of the miraculous power of the blessed priest the chains were broken in pieces and could not hold him. By some dangerous carelessness he was caught outside the courtyard. They led him, laden with iron and with his hands bound behind his back to the king. But he began to call out in a loud voice, and to pray that the blessed Martin should have pity upon him, and should not allow him to go away captive since in his devotion he had sought his church. And immediately

---

[78] Severus, *Epist.*, 3.6 (Halm, p. 147).

[79] Ruinart's interpretation of *a sanguine percussus*.

[80] *Neque <sibi neque> domino*, Bonnet's conjecture (p. 311, note 3).

[81] Wiliacharius is mentioned twice in the history (*HF*, 4.17, 20; cf. Dalton, II, pp. 521-3). In *HF*, 4.17 he should be identified as the priest in *HF*, 4.20 and the man mentioned here. His daughter Theoda was healed at the basilica of St. Martin (*Mart.*, 3.13).

[82] A. D. 558 (cf. *HF*, 4.20).

at these words, while the blessed bishop Eufronius was praying on the wall of the city opposite the basilica, his hands were freed, and all the links of the chains were broken and fell. However, he was led to the king a second time and was bound in leg irons and chains. But when the name of his oft-addressed patron was invoked, all the iron upon him was so shattered that you would have thought it like pottery. For just so long he was not released from his bonds, namely, until he had called upon that most sacred name; when it had been invoked, all were loosed. When the king with keen insight recognized the miraculous power of St. Martin at work there, he freed him from the load of his chains and restored him to his old freedom. From the mouth of the priest Wiliacharius himself I learned that this took place in the presence of many witnesses. Would that the blessed confessor would deign to manifest himself to me with such miraculous power that he might release the bonds of my sins as he wore away the vast weight of chains upon him.

24. Also Alpinus, count of the city of Tours, when he was severely afflicted for a whole year with pain in one foot, had no rest day or night, but amidst his torture continually begged the aid of the blessed Martin. The blessed confessor appeared to him in a vision at night,[83] smiling with happy countenance and bearing his accustomed insignia, and he placed the blessed sign of the sacred cross upon his afflicted foot. Soon all pain was put to flight, and he rose from his bed cured.

25. When these things had been experienced, Charigisilus, secretary of king Clothar,[84] whose hands and feet had been crippled by a humor, came to the sacred basilica, and gave himself to prayer for two or three months. He was visited by the blessed priest and received healing for his weakened limbs. Afterwards he was steward[85] of the aforesaid king and gave many benefits to the people of Tours and those who served the blessed basilica.

---

[83] Or a "vision of the night" if *nocte* is taken as a genitive (Bonnet, p. 341, note 4).

[84] *Referendarius* "secretary, director of the royal chancery." "Vorsteher der koeniglichen Kanzlei (in der merowingischer Zeit)" (Habel). Cf. Du Cange (V, p. 651, *s.v. referendarii: cui commissa erat annuli regii cura, quique regia diplomata subscribebat*) and Dalton, I, p. 200.

[85] *Domesticus* "steward, manager of the crown-lands," "Verwalter der koeniglichen Domaenen (zur der Merowinger)" (Habel). Cf. Dalton, II, p. 516.

26. I will tell also how the insane art of the Devil is bared at his basilica. A certain man named Aquilinus was practising hunting with his father in the woods of France. He incurred a very severe trembling when the Enemy[86] trapped him. He had a palpitation of the heart, and was seen at times to be out of his senses. In truth his parents realized that he was being punished by the entrance of a devil. As is the custom of the rustics, they obtained bandages for him and potions from the fortune-tellers and soothsayers. But when, as is customary, these things had no power, forced by grief they readily sought the aid of St. Martin and said: "He can lay bare this ambush[87] of evil since we have heard he exposed that wraith, worshipped with the false name of religion." They took him from that region and sent him to the sacred basilica. There he stayed with prayer and fasting and assiduously sought the aid of the saint. And when he had stayed for a long time in this faith, all his trembling was removed, and he recovered his senses as he had had them before. Forgetting his parents, even to this day he gives service for the benefit he received.

27. But a certain Charivaldus while hunting fell into a like ambush and lost the use of one side, and his hand and foot were paralyzed. He was carried to the glorious church by the hands of his servants, and subjected himself for almost a whole year to continuous fasts and prayers. When the health of all his members was recovered, he returned rejoicing to his own people. And for this reason we advise that none should seek anything from the soothsayers because they never profit the sick. For a little of the dust of the basilica has more power than those men with their witless remedies.

28. Who can ever find out or know what miracles continually occur or have occurred by means of the dust or wax from that place, or by means of any object which can be taken from the sepulcher? However, I have thought it a crime to leave unmentioned one manifest miracle which I have learned from the faithful. A man full of faith sought to carry away secretly some pledge from the basilica of the saint, and although he tried it many times, he never could, since he did not take anything publicly. However, wishing to return, he came at night to that

[86] I.e. the Devil.
[87] *His*, Krusch, *App.*; cf. Bonnet, p. 528, note.

rope by which the statue is moved, and took from the rope a piece which he cut off with a knife. And when he had returned home, health was granted by this relic to many who were sick. Consequently it cannot be doubted that many escaped illness who in faith had the merit to kiss that pledge. Behold, saint, what you grant to the faithful who particularly seek your protection. They are saved by you, who devoutly bear away your pledges, and since your aid follows them, they are freed. But an active faith performs all these things, since the Lord saith:[88] "Your faith hath made you whole."

29. It seems too that it should not be unmentioned that the blessed man offers aid in defending his property wherever he rules.[89] King Charibert[90] hated the clerics, neglected the churches of God, despised the priests, and more and more descended to luxury. There came to his ears the tale that a certain place, which the basilica of St. Martin held for a long time, belonged to the jurisdiction of his treasury. Ancient times had given to that place the name of Navicellis.[91] When this evil counsel had been received, he swiftly sent slaves to subject that humble place[92] to his own power. And since he seemed to have that which he did not possess, he ordered hostlers to go to that place with the horsemen, and there without justice he gave instructions that the horses be fed. Therefore the slaves drew near and took the hay which had been stacked there as fodder for the horses. While the slaves carried out their orders zealously, and the horsemen stationed there began to dole out the hay, the horses were seized by madness. And raging in turn with broken reins, they leapt over the plains and fled. And after they had been dispersed, some were blinded, some hurled themselves headlong from cliffs, and some ran into enclosures of their own accord where they transfixed themselves on the points of stakes. Nevertheless the hostlers, when they recognized the anger of God, drove a few which they were able to handle outside the boundary of that property and

---

[88] *Luke*, 18.42.
[89] Cf. MacGonagle, p. 82.
[90] Cf. Dalton, I, pp. 51f.
[91] Nazelles; Longnon, p. 280.
[92] *Reicolam:* cf. Du Cange, V, p. 637, *s.v. rescula* and Bonnet, p. 461, note 2 (*reicula*).

brought them back after they had been calmed. They announced to the king that this place was seized most unjustly, and consequently they had suffered this. Then they added: "Let it go and you will have peace." He was filled with fury, and it is recorded that he said: "Whether it belongs to me justly or unjustly, while I reign the basilica shall not have it." Straightway by divine order he passed away.[93] However, when the most glorious king Sigibert came into his kingdom,[94] at the suggestion of the blessed bishop Eufronius[95] he restored to the dominion of St. Martin this property which even today is in the possession of his basilica. All who have power, hear these things! Clothe some so that you do not despoil others. Add to your resources in such a way that you do not bring loss to the churches! God is a swift avenger of his servants. And so we advise that those powerful men who read this should not be angered. For if they are angered, they will confess that it is said about them.

30. In like manner the blessed confessor appeared in the case of property unjustly taken from him. A certain Eustochius often unjustly attempted to drive the sainted bishop Eufronius from the inheritance of his relative Baudulfus, who had named the basilica of St. Martin as heir. The blessed priest was moved by constant injuries to give some of these things to Eustochius. When he was carrying them to his own home, his only son straightway fell into a fever, and after he had been seriously ill of the fever for a day and a night, died. As quickly as his father was made master of property which was not due to him, so quickly was death present for the son. Like Gehazi[96] he possessed gold and silver, but, what was of more consequence to him, he contracted leprosy of the soul and lost his son. Nor did he ever from that time on have another.

31. That I might restrain the audacity of faithless men I will not be silent about how divine vengeance proceeded quickly in the case of another man who committed perjury in the sacred portico. The necessities of life are contributed daily by the

[93] A. D. 567. On the death of Charibert see *GC*, 19.
[94] December, 561. For Sigibert cf. Dalton, I, pp. 60f.
[95] Eighteenth bishop of Tours (*HF*, 10.31).
[96] *II Kings*, 5.20–27 (*IV Reg.*, 5.20–27: *Giezi*).

faithful, for the list[97] of persons whom the saint, by his beneficence, feeds by the alms of the devout. The blessed poor have the custom that when many of them depart for other places, they leave there a guard who might receive what has been offered. Therefore a certain devout man with a view to benefit left a coin.[98] The guard picked this up and was not afraid to conceal it from his brothers. However, the poor gathered together at the sixth hour and asked the aforementioned guard what the blessed Shepherd, watching with his accustomed piety, had sent. For they had heard that something had been donated at that place. He stated on oath: "By this sacred place and by the miracles of master Martin no more has come here than one silver coin." He had not yet completed the words, and his words were still hanging on his lips, when immediately he fell trembling to the ground. After he had been taken to his own bed by the hands of others, he began to gasp violently. Then he was asked by those standing around what was wrong and replied: "I swore falsely about the coin which the poor sought, and for that reason swift vengeance tortures me; but I beg that you will take it and return it to the offering." When it had been returned, he immediately breathed his last. O unhappy man, who was caught by evil greed and perished in such a manner that he lost the prize of life and did not possess the curse of money so gained![99] But, cursed greed, "What do you not force mortal hearts to do?"[100] You who formerly had been envious of the widow who purchased the kingdom of heaven with two mites,[101] hurl this man to the depths

[97] *Matricolam* "list, register of the poor." Cf. *TLL*, VIII, cols. 474f., *s.v. matricula.*

[98] *Trians*, one-third of a *solidus*. The gold *solidus* (*nomisma* in the Byzantine East) was rarely coined. Its value was 1/72 of a pound of gold and 12 *solidi* would purchase a horse. Dalton, I, pp. 223-5; II, p. 495.

[99] *Captae*, Krusch, *App.* The reading *aptae* which Krusch had orginally adopted, and Ruinart's conjecture *adeptae*, are less intelligible than *captae*, which is based on *capte* (of the *editio princeps*). This passage is discussed in detail by Krusch, *NA*, 19 (1894), p. 38 and Bonnet, p. 404, note 3.

[100] Virgil, *Aen.*, 3.56-57: *quid non mortalia pectora cogis,/auri sacra fames.* The first five words are quoted by Gregory, for the next three he substitutes *exsecranda cupiditas.* This is a favorite passage with Gregory, as well it might have been in those lawless days: *HF*, 4.46 (the full passage); 6:36 (*auri sacra fames*): 8.22 (*sed quid pectora humana non cogat auri sacra fames*).

[101] *Mark*, 12.42.

for one coin. And you who hanged Judas with a noose for the sale of his Master,[102] sink this man into Hell for a small coin. These words are sufficient for restraining the boldness of evil men.

32. Therefore since these miracles have been related which were done for others, I will approach that which the present miraculous power of my patron performed for me, unworthy as I am. In the one hundred and sixty-third year after the assumption of the sainted and praiseworthy man, the blessed priest Martin, in the seventh year of the rule of the church of Tours by the blessed bishop Eufronius, in the second year of that most glorious king Sigibert,[103] I fell into illness with evil sores and fever. And when the use of drink and food were denied me, I was so harassed that I lost all hope of the present life and thought about the ground necessary for burial. For eager death continually besieged me, wishing to drive my soul from my body. Now I was almost lifeless, but when I called upon the name of the blessed priest Martin I grew stronger for a little while and with efforts yet weak I began to prepare for a journey. There possessed my soul the urgency to visit the place of the venerable sepulcher. Whence I was affected with such longing that I did not hope[104] to live if I started out more tardily. And I who had scarcely escaped from the burning of my illness began to be inflamed a second time with the fever of my longing. There was no delay; as yet quite weak I start on the journey with my attendants. After two or three halts I entered a wooded region, and a second time fell into a fever and became so ill that all thought that I should lose my life. Then my friends approached me and, seeing that I was extremely weary, said: "Let us return to our own homes, and if God wishes to call you, you will die in your own home; if however you escape, you will more easily complete the journey you have vowed. It is better to return home than to die in the wilderness." In truth, when I heard these words I wept vehemently and bewailing my misfortune spoke with them and said: "I adjure you through

[102] *Matthew*, 27.5

[103] A. D. 563. Sigibert became king in Dec. 561, Eufronius bishop after Nov. 11 in 556, Martin died Nov. 11, 401: cf. Krusch.

[104] *Optarem*, Krusch, *App.* Bonnet (p. 272, note 3) approved this reading instead of Krusch's former reading *oporterem*, but later (p. 438) suggested *me oportere* <*credere*>*m* or <*putare*>*m* or *me putarem*.

Almighty God and the day of judgment feared by all the guilty that you consent to the request I make. Do not stop the journey we have begun, and if I am worthy to see the basilica of St. Martin, I give thanks to my God; if otherwise, carry my lifeless corpse there and bury it, since it is my decision not to return home if I shall not have deserved to be present at his sepulcher." Then weeping together we proceeded upon the journey we had begun. With the guardianship of the glorious master going before us, we came to his basilica.

33. At that time one of my monks, by name Armentarius, was well learned in the spiritual writings, since it was so easy for him to understand the modulation of sounds that you would think that he did not learn them but wrote them. He was extremely vigorous in his service and faithful in the work committed to him. Poison infected him, and he had lost all of his senses from evil sores and was so afflicted that he was wholly unable to understand or do anything. In truth on the third night after we came to the sacred basilica, we arranged ourselves to watch. This we did. However, when morning came and the signal apprised us of the morning devotions,[105] we returned to our lodging. There, resting on our beds, we slept until almost the second hour. When I awoke all of my illness and the bitterness of my heart had departed, and I realized that I had recovered my former health. Rejoicing, I called the household servant who was caring for me. However, Armentarius rose quickly, stood in my presence, and said: "Master, I will obey your commands." I thought that he was still out of his senses and said: "If you can, call the servant." And he said: "I will do whatever you order." Thunderstruck, I asked what had happened and he said: "I realize that I am quite well; but there is one lapse in my mind, because I do not know whence I came here." And beginning then he served me as had been his custom before his illness. Then exulting and weeping for joy I gave thanks to Almighty God for myself and for him because, by the intercession of our patron, He had made me whole in body, and him whole in mind, and because that one meeting had by faith been of advantage even to that other man who was out of his mind and did not have the sense to seek aid. But also I will not

---

[105] *Ad matutinas*, Krusch, *App. Sc. cursus*; cf. Krusch, *Index, s.v. matutinus*.

omit this fact: forty days after that same day I first took pleasure in drinking wine, although I had disliked it until then because of my illness.

34. On our return we carried three wax candles for a blessing from the blessed sepulcher. It is a long story to tell how many miracles occurred from these wax candles in the case of those ill because of chills and other sicknesses. But I will relate one miracle out of many. Each year a hailstorm had been wont to lay waste a certain field in our possession and to rage so violently that, when it had come, it left nothing in that same place. Then I chose one tree[106] which was taller than the rest amid the vineyards and placed some of the sacred wax upon it. After that day up to the present time, the storm has never struck there, but when it comes, it passes over that place as though afraid.

35. Moved by faith, a certain one of our men without my knowledge took a venerable piece of wood from the railing of a couch which is in the monastery of the sainted master. This he kept in his own lodgings for protection. But his family began to be seriously ill, because, I believe, the relic was not honored and cherished as was fitting. And when he did not know at all what was the matter, and they got no better but daily grew worse, he saw in a vision at night an awe-inspiring figure which said to him, "Why are you so afflicted?" He said, "I certainly don't know whence this has come." The figure said to him: "The wood which you took from the couch of the master Martin, this you keep negligently with you, and for this reason you have incurred these ills. But go now and take it to deacon Gregory and let him return it." He without delay showed it to me, and I took it with the greatest veneration and placed it in a worthy place. And the whole family in his house became well so that from that time on nobody there fell into any illness.

36. Moreover, it happened at a certain time that I was traveling on foot in Burgundy with zeal to visit my venerable mother. When we were going through the forests which are located across the Bèbre[107] River, we fell among robbers. They surrounded us

---

[106] *Arborem unum*, Krusch, *App.* Bonnet (p. 504, note 6) lists *arbor* as feminine in accordance with Krusch's former reading *arborem unam*.

[107] *Berberem fluvium*: cf. Longnon, p. 160. It flows into the Loire (*Liger*) on the left.

and wished to rob and kill us. Then I fled to my accustomed source of aid and prayed for the help of St. Martin. He straightway worthily stood by me and terrified[108] them so much that they were not able to do anything against us. But in turn those who had come that they might inspire fear[109] became afraid and began to flee very swiftly. But I, not unmindful that the apostle said we ought to fill our enemies with drink and food, ordered drink offered to them.[110] They did not expect this at all, but fled as fast as they could. You would believe that they were driven away with clubs or unwillingly forced to race against the speed of their own horses; and so, by the gift of the Lord and the aid of my patron, we came to our destination. It would take a long time to tell, let alone to write out, from what tribulations and hardships he snatched me, in what necessities his pity stood by me, or what bitterness in me he quelled by his miraculous power.

37. What shall I say about those who have dysentery, since a remedy was found as quickly as it was sought in faith? For I saw a woman so gravely ill from dysentery for five months that when necessity forced her she had to be carried by hand to the necessary places. When at the same time she had lost the comfort of food and the strength of her body by excessive diarrhea, I am a witness that she kept vigil at the basilica. When day had returned after the darkness of night and she as a remedy had drained a cup of dust scraped from the blessed tomb, she went home on her own feet, although she had been held up by others when she arrived.

38. Or what shall I relate about those possessed of demons or suffering from chills, from whom all dangers are soon removed by the aid of their patron, provided only that frugality and faith have been truly joined? So many of those suffering from chills while they were shaken by the force of a very bad fever, lay all day between the altar and the sacred tomb. At evening they drank of the dust of the sacred tomb and immediately regained their health. For Paulus, who was possessed, and was said to hold

[108] Cf. Bonnet, p. 422.
[109] *Qui venerant ut timetentur:* Bonnet correctly considers *ut* (the reading of 3 mss) necessary (p. 687, note 5); cf. Krusch, *App.*
[110] *Romans,* 12.20.

a legion of demons, at the insistence of the Enemy ascended a device which was near the sacred chamber and is said to have said: "The vessel which I live in is in flames."[111] And he hurled himself down headlong, and so lightly dropped to the pavement because of the miraculous power of the blessed one, that he injured not one of the limbs of his accursed body.

39. A certain Leomaria, blind and crippled, living but ill for a long time, made frequent visits using the hands of others for the journey when she went to the basilica of the blessed man. At last while she was lying at the sacred door, looked on with favor by his pity she received sight and the use of her limbs. O that there should be proclaimed in public what each one singly received in private after he has prayed in faith, and that the knowledge of many should understand the secret, that health is gained when it is openly sought by prayer and faith. But if all these things were made public, as we have said, I think that not only books but even the universe itself, as the evangelist says of the Lord,[112] could not hold them.

40. And since my narrative seeks an end, I will tell yet one more famous miracle to you before the book receives its end. A certain young man, named Securus, as he came from the womb of his mother, had a withered hand and foot and the joints of all his limbs were so dried that he seemed some kind of monster. He was also bound by the yoke of slavery. When his masters saw after seven years that he could not be profitable in any way, they carried him and placed him before the blessed sepulcher so that he might at least be fed by those who passed by, since he could not be fed by his own labor. And after he lay there for many days, his foot which was crippled was straightened and his withered hand was made whole as blood flowed through his veins. After he had received the aid of the blessed confessor, his whole body was so restored[113] that you would think he had been born again. The

---

[111] Various conjectural additions of a verb seem unnecessary to me and I have retained Krusch's older text (ms 5 adds *parcat*, ms 5a *pereat*). Krusch suggested *ruas: NA*, 19 (1894), p. 38. Later he rejected this in favor of *parcat* (*App.*). Neither these readings, nor *parcatur* (*editio princeps*), nor *pereatur* (Bonnet, p. 413, note 4) should stand, since the text is quite clear as it is.

[112] *John*, 21.25.

[113] <*Re*> *formatus:* Bonnet, p. 715, note 3.

boy was bought by Count Justinus[114] and set free, and afterwards he was baptized and even today lives unharmed under the patronage of the holy Church. Who will ever be able to seek out or tell these things systematically so that the praise will be sufficient? Nonetheless in so far as we could we wished to search them out and write them down faithfully. When this is read in praise of the most holy priest, we hope to receive this in payment, namely that perchance forgiveness of sins might be granted to us. For the poet says: "Perchance it will be a pleasure at some time to remember even these things."[115]

---

[114]This is probably Gregory's brother-in-law, as was assumed by Dalton (I, p. 6). He is mentioned also in *GM*, 70 and *Mart.*, 2.2.
[115]Virgil, *Aen.*, 1.203.

9
The Lives of
the Fathers

Introductory Note. The seventh book of the *Miracula* has more historical interest than any of the others. The accounts of individuals are more lengthy than the brief accounts of the martyrs and confessors, and Gregory is less preoccupied by miracles than in the four books on St. Martin and in the book on St. Julian. In his history of the Franks Gregory often digressed to give details about eminent churchmen—these digressions are rather similar to the connected biographies given here.[1] This work was being written at the same time as the history, and cross-references to it occur in the history.[2] In one case the same passage was used in both works.[3]

It consists of 20 chapters which are quite varied in length—the lives of St. Gallus and of St. Nicetius of Lyons are especially long. Not only is there a general preface, but each chapter has its own prefatory remarks. The most interesting of the lives are those of St. Quintianus, bishop of Rodez and Clermont (4); St. Gallus, bishop of Clermont, his paternal uncle (6); St. Gregory, bishop of Langres, his maternal great-grandfather (7); St. Nicetius, bishop of Lyons, his maternal great-uncle (8); and St. Nicetius, bishop of Trèves (17). The second and third of these (i.e. chapters 6–7) are translated below.

---

[1] E.g., the account of the bishop Salvius (*HF*, 7.1) or the account of Pope Gregory the Great (*HF*, 10.1).
[2] E.g. *HF*, 2.21 to *VP*, 3; *HF*, 4.36 to *VP*, 8.3; *HF*, 4.37 to *VP*, 10; *HF*, 5.12 to *VP*, 12.
[3] *HF*, 4.5 and *VP*, 6.6.

St. Gallus of Clermont

Those on the pinnacle of worldly nobility always gaze eagerly at lusts, rejoice in honors, are puffed up by attentions, beat the forum with lawsuits, feed on plunder, are delighted by lies, long for large amounts of gold which corrupts,[4] and while they possess little, burn the more to accumulate much. For them the heaping up of gold brings a thirst to possess the heights, as Prudentius says:[5] "For the hunger for gold becomes greater as gold is gained." Whence it happens that they rejoice in the delights of the pomp of this life and in empty honors, and nothing recalls them to the memory of eminence which will endure. They do not look to that which is unseen provided that they possess that by which they think that their souls are satisfied. But there are those who have released themselves by the talent of a keener mind from these bonds, as birds fly out of traps and head for the higher realms. So they hate and abandon earthly possessions and with all their strength they fit themselves for that which is heavenly. Such was St. Gallus, an inhabitant of the city of Clermont, since splendor of birth and the loftiness of senatorial rank and the resources of wealth could not take him away from the worship of God. The love of his father, the fondness of his mother, the love of his nurses, the attentions of his servants could not keep him from the love of God. But since he counted all these ties as nothing and hated them as filth, he vowed himself to the love and service of God and subjected himself to monastic restrictions. For he knew that the flame of youthful fervor could not otherwise be mastered unless it was placed under the canonical control and the most severe discipline. For he knew that thus he would rise from the lowliness of this life to higher things, and through endurance he would ascend to the glory of lofty heights. Afterwards the result proved this.

(1) St. Gallus from his youth began his devotion to God and diligently with his whole soul cherished the Lord and all which he knew was loved of God. His father was named Georgius[6] and his

---

[4] *Rubiginosi auri talenta:* cf. Sidonius, *Ep.*, 5.7.5: *robiginosi aura marsupii.*

[5] *Hamartigenia,* 257: *auri namque fames parto fit maior ab auro:* cf. Juvenal, *Sat.*, 14.139: *crescit amor nummi, quantum ipsa pecunia crevit.*

[6] Gallus was the brother of Gregory's father Florentius.

mother Leucadia. She was descended from the family of Vettius Epagathus who, as the history of Eusebius testifies, was martyred at Lyons.[7] Both were from noble senatorial families so that none could be found better born or nobler in Gaul. When his father wished to betroth him to the daughter of a certain senator, he took with him one servant only and sought the monastery of Cournon[8] which is situated six miles from the city of Clermont. There in a suppliant manner he pleaded with the abbot that he might deem him worthy to shave the hair of his head. But he saw the intelligence and culture of the boy and asked him his name and inquired about his family and country. He replied that he was called Gallus, was a citizen of Clermont and the son of Georgius the senator. When the abbot realized that he had been born of the highest rank, he said: "My son, your desires are good, but it is necessary first that knowledge of this be taken to your father; and if he shall consent, I will do what you ask." Then the abbot sent messengers to the father to ask what he should order done about the boy. A little saddened, he said: "He was my first-born and for that reason I wished him to marry; but if the Lord deign to enroll him in His service, let His will rather than ours be done."[9] And he added: "Fulfill whatever the child has suggested to you at the inspiration of God."

(2) Then the abbot learned this at the return of the messengers and made the boy a monk. He was of outstanding chastity, and, as he sought nothing improper when older, so even then he kept himself from youthful exuberance. He had a voice of remarkable sweetness with its smooth modulation, he paid continual attention to his reading, he delighted in fasts and abstained much from food. When the blessed bishop Quintianus[10] came to the same monastery and heard him sing, he did not allow him to be kept there longer but took him to the city and, like the heavenly

[7]. Vetti Epagati: Eusebius, Hist. Eccl., 5.1.9: Οὐέττιος 'Επάγαθος (i.e. Vettius Epagathus). He was among the 48 martyrs who perished at Lyons in the days of Pope Eleutherius: GM, 48; cf. AASS, 2 Jun., I, p. 160.

[8] Monasterium Crononensim: cf. Longnon, pp. 498f.

[9] Cf. Acts, 21.14.

[10] St. Quintianus was bishop of Rodez (Rutena) in 506 and 511, but was driven out of his city (HF, 2.36). He was appointed bishop of Clermont in 515 (HF, 3.2, cf. Dalton, II, p. 505) and died in 525 (below VP, 6.3). His day is November 13. Gregory wrote a rather full account of his life (VP, 4).

Father, nourished him in spiritual sweetness. After his father died, his voice became more and more mature[11] as each day passed, and he likewise acquired very great favor among the people. Men announced this to King Theodoric;[12] no sooner was this said than he had Gallus summoned and cherished him with such great affection that he loved him more than his own son. He was cherished also by the queen[13] with a like love not only as an honor to his voice, but also to the chastity of his body. For at that time king Theodoric enrolled many monks from the citizens of Clermont whom he ordered to attach themselves to the church of Trèves and to render service to the Lord. In truth he did not allow the blessed Gallus to be separated from himself at all. When it happened that the king was going to Cologne, he also went with him. However, there was a certain shrine where the neighboring barbarians made offerings of the first fruits and gorged themselves disgustingly with food and drink. And there they worshipped images as God and carved the parts of the body in wood when pain touched them.[14] When St. Gallus heard this, he immediately hastened thither with only one monk. Since none of the stupid pagans was there, he kindled fire, applied it, and set fire to the shrine. But when they saw the smoke of their temple rising to heaven, they sought the author of the fire and, when they had found him, pursued him with drawn swords. He fled and hid himself in the king's palace. After the king found out what had been done, since the pagans were uttering threats, he soothed them with soft words and so calmed their wicked wrath. The blessed man was often wont to recall this with tears and say: "Woe to me that I did not stay and meet my end in this cause."[15] At that time he was performing the duties of a deacon.

(3) Finally, when the blessed bishop Quintianus had passed from this life at the order of the Lord, St. Gallus was staying at that time in the city of Clermont.[16] The citizens of Clermont

[11] *Componeretur*, Bonnet (p. 294, note 3) who followed ms 4.

[12] One of the sons of Clovis: cf. Dalton, I, pp. 46–47.

[13] Suavegotha, daughter of King (later St.) Sigismund (*HF*, 3.5; cf. Dalton, II, pp. 506f.

[14] It was customary at shrines, such as those of Asclepius, to dedicate a replica of the part of the body which had been healed.

[15] By doing this, he would have gained the crown of martyrdom.

[16] In 525.

assembled at the home of his uncle Inpetratus,[17] bewailing the death of their priest and seeking the one who ought to be put in his place. After they had discussed this for a very long time, everyone returned to his lodgings. After their departure St. Gallus called one of the clergy and, inspired by the Holy Ghost, said: "Why do these men mutter? Why do they run hither and thither? Why do they draw back? Their work is fruitless. I will be bishop; the Lord will deign to grant this honor to me. When you have heard that I am returning from the presence of the king, take and saddle the horse of my predecessor, meet me and offer it to me. But if you scorn to listen to this, beware lest you repent afterwards." And when he had said this, he lay down on the bed. And then the cleric was angered against him because he disapproved of many things, and so he dashed him against the frame of the bed and injured his side. Then he left, greatly disturbed. After he left, the priest Inpetratus said to the blessed Gallus: "Son, listen to my counsel. Don't delay, but go to the king and announce to him what has happened here.[18] And if the Lord inspires him to grant this sacred office to you, we give great thanks to God; but if otherwise, you will commend yourself to the man who shall have been ordained." So he departed and announced to the king what had happened to the blessed Quintianus. At the same time also Aprunculus,[19] bishop of Trèves, passed away; and the clergy of that city met and asked King Theodoric for St. Gallus as their bishop. He said to them: "Depart and seek another; for I have deacon Gallus reserved for another post." Then they chose and received St. Nicetius as bishop.[20] The clergy of Clermont when the wish of the people[21] was known came to the king with great gifts. And now at that time the evil seed had begun to bear fruit that this sacred office should be sold by kings or bought by the

---

[17] *Abunculi* (i.e. *avunculi*) "maternal uncle." He was the brother of Leocadia, Gregory's paternal grandmother.

[18] *Contigerint*, Krusch. Bonnet preferred *contigerit* (p. 501, note 1). The translation of either would be the same.

[19] His day is April 22: *AASS, 22 Aprilis*, III, pp. 30f.

[20] For St. Nicetius, bishop of Trèves, cf. *VP*, 17. He should not be confused with St. Nicetius, bishop of Lyons, brother of Gregory's maternal grandmother (*VP*, 8).

[21] *Cum consensu insipientium*, i.e. *consensu populi: insipiens* is not used here in a derogatory sense. Cf. Forcellini, *s.v. insipiens* 2 and *Rom.*, 1.14: *Graecis ac barbaris, sapientibus et insipientibus debitor sum.*

clergy.[22] Then they heard from the king that they would have St.
Gallus as their bishop. When the priest had been ordained, the
king ordered that the citizens[23] should be invited to a banquet
given at the public expense and that they should celebrate in
honor of the future bishop Gallus. This was done. He was wont to
relate that for the bishopric he gave no more than one coin[24] to the
cook who served at the lunch. After this the king gave him two
bishops as companions[25] and sent him to the people of Clermont.
That cleric named Viventius who had injured Gallus' side on the
bed frame, hastened in great shame to meet the pontiff according
to his instructions and at the same time presented him with the
horse which he had ordered. And when both had entered the
bath, Gallus mildly reproached him because of the pain in his side
which he had received because of this cleric's attack of pride.
Thus he heaped great shame on him since he treated him not with
wrath but only with a spirited jest. After this he was received in
the city with much singing and was ordained bishop in his own
city.

(4) After he had assumed the office of bishop, he administered
it with such humility and such love for all that he was cherished
by everybody. In truth he was patient beyond the manner of men
so that, if it be right to say it, he should be compared to Moses for
the different attacks he underwent. So it happened that when at
banquet he was struck on the head by his own priest, he was so
calm that he did not make a harsh reply. But by enduring
patiently everything which occurred, he raised himself up in the
judgment of God by whom he sought to be nourished. When a
certain priest Evodius,[26] of a senatorial family, had attacked him

[22] In Merovingian Gaul the ordinary procedure for episcopal election was the
nomination of a candidate by the clergy and people. They met under the
presidency of a metropolitan who was usually accompanied by other bishops.
This nomination (*consensus*) was delivered to the king who authorized the choice
by a diploma (*praeceptio*). He might refuse the nomination and ask for another,
or substitute a nominee of his own. On the election of bishops in these days, cf.
Duchesne, *L'église*, pp. 524–41; Dalton, I, pp. 288–300.

[23] I.e., of Theodoric's capital city.

[24] *Treans:* one-third of a *solidus.*

[25] A free rendering of *ad solatium eius.*

[26] Son of Hortensius, a senator (*HF*, 4.35). His own sons were Salustius, count of
Clermont (*HF*, 4.13) and the priest Eufrasius (*HF*, 4.35).

at a banquet at the church with many quarrelsome lies, the bishop rose and visited the holy places of the sacred basilicas. When this had been reported to Evodius, the priest swiftly ran after him, threw himself at his feet there and sought forgiveness and begged he should not condemn him in his prayers to the Almighty Judge. But he raised him up benignly, mercifully forgave what he had said, convinced him that he should not further attack the priests of the Lord because he would never be worthy to become bishop.[27] Later events proved this. For when Evodius had been chosen bishop in Javols,[28] and had been placed in the bishop's chair, everything was prepared for his ordination as bishop, but the whole people rose against him so suddenly that he was scarcely able to escape with his life. Afterwards he passed away while still a priest.

(5) However, at the city of Arles a great gathering of bishops met at the order of King Childebert after bishop Marcus had been charged by evil men and driven from the city.[29] At this synod the blessed bishops found that the charge was false which had been muttered against him, and restored him to his city and his bishop's chair. Finally at this time the deacon Valentinianus who is now priest and singer, came into the service of St. Gallus. When another bishop was saying mass, that deacon because of pride rather than through fear of God wished to sing. But St. Gallus forbade him, and said to him: "My son, when the Lord orders it, let us celebrate the solemn rites, and then you ought to sing. Now let the clergy of him who consecrates mass, sing." But he asserted that he could then. The priest said to him: "Do as you wish; but you will not accomplish what you wish." When he was unmindful of the pontiff's order and appeared, he sang so unmelodiously that he was mocked by all. However, when another Lord's Day arrived and the famous pontiff was saying mass, he ordered him to appear and said: "Now in the name of the Lord you will accomplish what you wish." When he had done this, his voice

---

[27] St. Quintianus had prophesied that no man descended from Hortensius would become a bishop (HF, 4.35; VP, 4.3).

[28] In Gabalitano, cf. Longnon, pp. 528f. This was within the years 536–540 (Krusch).

[29] A. D. 549: the fifth council at Arles (Krusch). On Childebert I, one of the sons of Clovis, cf. Dalton, I, pp. 47f.

rang forth[30] so that he was praised by all. O blessed man, to whom such grace was granted that not only the souls but also the voices of men[31] were under his sway, for he kept these voices from song when he wished, and permitted them to sing when it pleased him.

(6) The Lord also displayed other great miracles through him. For when the defender[32] Julianus, a man of very sweet disposition who was later a priest, was seized by the quartan fever and was in severe pain, he sought the bed of the sainted priest. When he lay on it, covered by his blanket, and slept for a little while, he was so completely cured that he was never afterwards seized by this ailment.

When, however, the city of Clermont was burning with a very great fire and the saint found this out, he entered the church and for a long time with tears prayed to the Lord. Then he rose, took and opened the Evangel, and approached the fire. When this had been prepared, straightway at sight of him the whole blaze was so thoroughly extinguished that not even hot ashes remained in it.

About this time the city of Clermont was shaken with a great earthquake; but we know not why this happened. However, we do know this, that it injured not one of the people.

When, however, that pestilence[33] which they call the plague of the groin was raging through different regions and most of all was devastating the province of Arles, St. Gallus was frightened not for himself but for his people. And when he was praying day and night that he should not while alive see his people laid waste, there appeared to him in a vision at night an angel of the Lord

---

[30] *Praelata*, a reading of ms 4 which Krusch mentioned as preferable although he printed *praeclara* in his text: Bonnet approved *praelata* (*addendum* to p. 400, note 3).

[31] *Sicut animae ita etiam et voces hominum*, ms 4 (cf. Bonnet, *add.* to p. 314, note 1).

[32] *Defensor:* for this office cf. Leclercq in *DACL*, IV, cols. 406–27 (esp. 422f.) *s.v. defensor civitatis.*

[33] Much of what follows (*lues illa . . . stadia 360*) is identical with part of *HF*, 4.5. This verbal duplication in two passages in Gregory is rare. Even here the quoted words of the angel vary in the two versions. There are minor variations in spelling and reading in the two passages. For the bubonic plague in the sixth century, cf. Dalton I, pp. 421f. It is mentioned frequently in Gregory's history (4.31; 6.14; 7.1; 9.21, 22; 10. 1, 25).

with hair and raiment as white as snow who said to him: "The pity of God looks with favor upon you, O priest, as you make supplication for your people; and for this reason fear not, for your prayer has been heard; and lo! you and your people will be freed from this affliction, and none, while you live, will perish in this region from this plague. Now fear not; be afraid after eight years."[34] Whence it was manifest that after these years had passed he would depart from this life. However, when aroused, he gave thanks to God for this consolation, because He deigned to comfort him through a heavenly messenger. Then he instituted services of prayer in the middle of Lent during which they went to the basilica of the blessed martyr Julian singing and traveling on foot,[35] a journey of about three hundred and sixty stades.[36] However, although this pestilence consumed the other regions, as we have said, it did not touch the city of Clermont because of intercession through the prayers of St. Gallus. Whence I think that his grace was not small since he earned this, namely, that he, a shepherd placed there, should not see his sheep devoured, since the Lord was their defender.

(7) But let us come to that time when the Lord ordered him to be taken from this world. When he was weighed down with illness, and confined to his bed, the fever within so wasted away all his members that he lost his hair and at the same time his beard. However, when he knew through the Lord's revelation that he would depart after three days, he called together the people, and after breaking bread he administered communion to all of them with holy and pious will. Then came the third day, the Lord's Day, and it brought terrible grief to the citizens of Clermont. While the sky was growing light, he asked what they were singing in the church. They said that they were singing the benediction. And when he had sung the fiftieth Psalm and the

---

[34] The plague was in 543, Gallus died in 551 (Krusch).

[35] These *rogationes* in the middle of the *quadragesima* with their accompanying procession to Brioude were revived by the bishop Cautinus (*HF*, 4.13): cf. Dalton, I, p. 339.

[36] The Greek stade was about one-eighth of a mile, but we cannot be sure of the use of the word in Gregory: cf. Dalton, II, p. 517. Du Cange (VI, *s.v.* 3 *stadium*): *mensurae species, sed ignota prorsus*. On the church of St. Julian at Brioude cf. Longnon, pp. 492–6.

benediction, and had finished the chapter of the alleluias, he completed his matins.[37] When this duty had been performed he said: "We say farewell to you, brothers." And saying these things and stretching out his limbs, he sent his soul, intent on Heaven, to the Master. He passed on in the sixty-fifth year of his life in the twenty-seventh year of his service as bishop.[38] Then he was washed and clothed and carried into the church until his fellow bishops might gather to bury him. And there a great miracle was shown to the people, because the saint of God, by drawing up his right foot on the bier turned himself to that side which was toward the altar. While this was being done, those rites which occur after Easter were celebrated. He lay in the church for three days with a great crowd of people continually in attendance and singing. When the bishops arrived on the fourth day, they lifted him up and carried him from the church to the basilica of St. Laurentius[39] and buried him. And now in truth it can scarcely be told how great was the mourning in his funeral procession, what crowds of people were there. Women followed in garments of mourning as if they had lost their husbands, and likewise men with heads covered as is the custom at funerals for wives, also the very Jews with burning torches followed in tears. All the people with one voice said: "Woe unto us since we will never be worthy after this day to have a priest like him." And because, as we have said, his fellow bishops were far away and had not been able to come more quickly, as is the custom of the rustics, the faithful placed a piece of earth on the blessed body that it might not swell from the heat. After his funeral rites a certain woman, who was truly a very pure virgin, as I have diligently inquired, and devoted to God, by name Meratina, gathered up this piece of sod, when it was cast down by the others, and placed it in her own garden. When water was poured on it, the Lord granting increase, it

---

[37] Id est officium, quod Laudes appellamus, absolvit. In quibus eosdem psalmos hodieque, ut hic designantur, canimus, etc. (Ruinart).

[38] He was born in 487, ordained bishop in 525, and died in 551 (Krusch). Ruinart sets the date of his death ca. 554, but not on July 1, the day on which he is celebrated. According to Ruinart and Krusch, Fortunatus erred by poetic license in his dating in his epitaphium domini Galli episcopi Arvernae (Carm., 4.4). The Bollandists who included Gregory's account and Fortunatus' poem, dated his life as follows: born 489, ordained bishop 527 or 528, died 554: AASS, 1 Julius, I, 91-7.

[39] On the basilica of St. Laurentius cf. Longnon, p. 487.

became fruitful. The sick, who took herbs from this piece of sod and drank their juice, were cured. Also faithful prayer above the sod merited approval. Afterwards it was lost through lack of care when the virgin moved away. Finally at his sepulcher many miracles were displayed. For those sick with the quartan and with divers fevers, once they touch the blessed tomb with faith, straightway drink the draught of health.

Therefore the singer Valentinianus whom we recalled above,[40] who now is a priest, when he was fulfilling the office of deacon, was seized by the quartan fever, and for many days suffered severe weakness. It happened, however, that on the day of the attack of this fever he planned to travel around the holy places and pray. When he came to the sepulcher of this saint, he prostrated himself and said: "Be mindful of me, most blessed, sainted priest. I was raised, taught, and encouraged by you. Be mindful of your own student whom you cherished with a singular love and rescue me from this fever by which I am held." When he had said this, he collected the herbs which for honor to the priest had been scattered on the tomb; and because they were green, he put them to his mouth, bit them off with his teeth, and sucked their juice. That day passed and he was not stricken by his illness. Then he was restored to such good health that he did not again endure those attacks which are commonly called seizures. That this happened, I learned from the mouth of the priest himself. For there is no doubt but that miracles occur at the tombs of the slaves of the Master because of the power of Him who called Lazarus from the tomb.[41]

St. Gregory of Langres[42]

There are men of outstanding sanctity who, though born from the earth, have been carried to the heavens by the palm of perfect blessedness. The bond of true charity binds them, the fruit of alms enriches them, the flower of chastity adorns them or the agony of certain martyrdom crowns them. In them is the desire to

[40] VP, 6.5.

[41] John, 12.17.

[42] Gregory's life of St. Gregory of Langres was published by the Bollandists, but the text was interpolated: AASS, 4 Januarius, I, pp. 168f.

begin the task of perfect justice so that they might first of all offer a body without spot as a habitation prepared for the Holy Spirit. Thus they reach the heights of other virtues. And they themselves become their own persecutors since they suppress the vices in themselves and they triumph like proved martyrs, after the course of their lawful contest has been completed. None will be strong enough to accomplish this without the aid of God, unless he be protected by the shield and the helmet of the Lord's help. Let him assign this which he has done not to his own glory, but to the glory of the divine name in accordance with the words of the apostle:[43] "Let him who boasts, boast in the Lord." For in this the blessed Gregory gained all glory. For, although he was born to the lofty power of the senatorial order, he subjected himself to humility, and, casting aside all cares for this life, he dedicated himself to God alone Whom he cherished in his breast.

(1) Then St. Gregory, who was of the foremost senators and well taught in letters, attained the position of Count of the city of Autun. In this office he governed that region for forty years[44] with justice as his companion, and he was so severe and rigorous against malefactors that scarcely any of the guilty were able to escape him. He had a wife named Armentaria, born of a senatorial family, whom he is said to have known only for the sake of propagating children. And the Lord granted him sons from her.[45] Nor did he burn for any other woman as men do in the fervor of youth.

(2) After the death of his wife he turned to the Lord, and was elected by the people and was ordained bishop of the city of Langres.[46] His abstinence was great, but, lest he be thought

[43] *I Corinthians*, 1.31.

[44] From 466/7 to 506/7 (Krusch).

[45] St. Gregory and Armentaria were the grandparents of Gregory's mother, Armentaria. Their two sons were Gregory's grandfather, whose name we do not know, and St. Tetricus, who succeeded his father as bishop of Langres. Dalton is confused when in one place he called Tetricus the grandfather of Gregory (I, p. 4) and in a note on the same page speaks of Gregory's grandmother as a daughter of St. Gregory (I, p. 4, note 1). Gregory's maternal grandmother was a daughter (whose name we do not know) of Artemia and Florentinus, and a sister of St. Nicetius, bishop of Lyons, and of Duke Gundulf. For St. Nicetius cf. *VP*, 8 (the life which immediately follows this one); for Gundulf cf. *HF*, 6.11: *matris meae avunculum*.

[46] In 506 or 507.

boastful, he used to place thin barley loaves secretly under wheaten bread. Then he broke the wheaten bread, and offered it to others, but he himself, without the knowledge of others, ate the barley bread. He did likewise in the case of wine, for when the cupbearer offered water to him he ordered the water to be poured secretly for the sake of pretense and chose opaque glassware to conceal the colorlessness of the water. Now in fasts, in alms, in prayers and watching he was so thorough and devoted that, although he was placed in the middle of worldly life, he gleamed as a new hermit.

He had his regular residence in the town of Dijon, where his house was next to the baptistery[47] in which the relics of many saints were kept. There he used to rise from his bed at night without the knowledge of others and go to pray with only God as his witness. When the door had been unlocked by divine power, he sang attentively. But when he had done this for a long time, at last his action was discovered and made known by a deacon. When this man realized what was being done he followed at a distance so that the blessed man could not realize it and waited to see what he was doing. The deacon learned that, when the saint of God came to the door of the baptistery and knocked on it with his hand, the door opened though nobody was visible. Then after his entrance there was silence for a very long time. Afterwards, for a space of somewhat more than three hours, what seemed to be the sound of many voices was heard. I believe that, since the relics of many saints were housed in the same place, they revealed themselves to the blessed man and rendered song to the Lord in unison. After the completion of his prayers, he returned to his bed, and placed himself carefully upon it so that none might know about it. In truth the doorkeepers[48] found the door of the baptistery locked and opened it in the accustomed way with their own key. Then when the signal was given, the saint of God rose again for the Lord's work as did the others. For when those possessed of demons confessed him on the first day of his

[47] This *baptisterium* may have been the *basilica* S. *Johannis* where Gregory was buried, but it was more probably the *oratorium* S. *Vincentii* which existed as late as the 17th century near the *ecclesia* S. *Stephani*: Longnon, pp. 211f.

[48] *Obseratores* "those who lock, i.e. doorkeepers": a conjecture by Bonnet who translates "portier" (p. 196, note 7).

bishopric, the priests asked him that he deign to pronounce a benediction on the possessed. He avoided this strenuously lest he incur vain-glory, and he cried out that he was unworthy to be a servant in making manifest the miracles of the Lord. But none the less, since he could no longer conceal this, he ordered that they be led to him, and without touching them he merely made the sign of the cross in front of them and with a word ordered the demons to depart. They straightway heard this and freed those bodies which they had held fast with their own evil. For in his absence many drove out demons from those possessed by stopping them and making the sign of the cross with the staff he was wont to carry in his hand. Also if anyone who was sick took anything from his bed, they were immediately cured. Moreover Armentaria, his grand-daughter, at a certain time in her youth was seriously ill from the quartan fever and, though treated zealously by the doctors, she could not obtain relief. She was often urged by the blessed confessor himself that she should give herself to prayer. When on a certain day she sought his bed and was placed on it, the whole fever was cured so completely that from that time she was never ill from fever.

(3) In truth when St. Gregory had walked to the city of Langres for the sacred day of Epiphany,[49] he was stricken by a moderate fever and departed this life and passed over to Christ.[50] After his passing his blessed face was so glorified that it seemed like roses to those who saw it. For this rosy flush appeared, and in truth the rest of his body gleamed as white as the lilies so that you would think that he was prepared for the glory of the coming resurrec-tion. The bier grew heavy for those carrying it to the town of Dijon, where he had ordered that he be buried. When they were

[49] *Ad sanctum diem epifaniorum*, Krusch (*diem* was omitted on p. 688, 19 by a typographical error; cf. p. 883, 38f.). Ruinart felt that this phrase must mean that he died on the day of Epiphany and consequently revised the text to *per* (i.e. *propter*) *diem sanctam Epiphaniorum* (a text which Bordier also printed). Bonnet (p. 591, note 3) suggested *per diem sanctum epifaniorum*. However *ad* (omitted by ms 1*a*) expresses purpose. Since Gregory ordinarily had his residence at Dijon rather than at Langres (*VP*, 7.2; *HF*, 3.19, and cf. Longnon, pp. 210f.), he had made the trip from Dijon to Langres on foot to celebrate Epiphany, but died at or near Langres on January 4, two days before Epiphany. This interpretation answers Ruinart's objection to the text in the mss.

[50] In 539 or 540 (Krusch).

on the plain, which is on the north not far from the town, they did not hold it up but placed it on the ground, and gathering their strength there for a little while, they raised it up after a little time and bore it to a church that was within the walls.[51] When the bishops gathered on the fifth day, it was carried from the church to the basilica of the blessed John. And lo! those bound in prison began to call out to the blessed body, saying: "Have pity on us, most pious master, that now dead and possessing the heavenly kingdom you may deign to free those whom you did not free while living. Be present, we pray and have pity on us." When they cried out these things and others, the body became so heavy that the pall-bearers could not hold it up. They they placed the bier upon the ground and waited for the miraculous help of the blessed priest. While they were waiting, the doors of the prison were suddenly unlocked, and the pole to which the feet of the prisoners were fastened broke in the middle. The locks were knocked off, the chains were broken, and all were freed likewise and flocked to the blessed body, since nobody held them back. Then the bearers raised up the bier, and the prisoners followed among the rest and afterwards were freed by the judge without any penalty.

(4) After this the blessed confessor declared himself by many miracles. For a certain devout man said that he had seen the heavens open on the day of his burial, nor is there any doubt that after his angelic deeds he was enrolled in the starry throngs. A certain prisoner was being led to the aforesaid town by that road over which the blessed body was carried from Langres. And as the soldiers went along on horseback and dragged the prisoner behind them, they came to the place where the limbs of the blessed confessor had rested. While they were passing it, the prisoner called upon the name of the blessed priest and sought that he should in mercy free him. While he was praying, the nooses were loosened from his hands. He realized that he had been freed, but he kept quiet and hid his hands and his captors thought that he was still bound. However, when they had entered the gate of the town and had come to the forecourt of

---

[51] *Ecclesia S. Stephani:* this church became a cathedral in 1731 but is now a grain-exchange: Longnon, p. 211.

the church, he leapt away and cast off the thong of his bonds,[52] and was freed by the aid of the All-powerful Lord and by the intercession of the blessed pontiff.

And wonderful too is the miracle by which his blessed body appeared glorious when it was moved after a long time. Since the blessed priest had been buried in a corner of the basilica and that place was small and the people were not able to approach it as their devotion demanded, St. Tetricus, his son and successor,[53] realizing this and seeing that miracles were continually being performed there, placed foundations before the altar of the basilica and erected an apse. This he constructed with fine work and built it in a curve, and when it was built and the old wall had been destroyed, he built an arched doorway.[54] When the work had been completed and decorated, he dug a crypt in the middle of the apse. Since he wished to transfer the body of his blessed father to this place, he called the priests and abbots together for this duty. They held vigils and prayed that the blessed confessor should permit himself to be moved to the place which had been prepared. When morning came, with choruses singing they took the sarcophagus and carried it to the apse which the blessed bishop had built. While they were arranging this place of burial with care, suddenly, by God's order as I believe, the sarcophagus broke open in one part. And lo! his blessed face appeared so untouched and unharmed that you would think that he was not

---

[52] *Trahentium in ora* has been omitted as an inconsistent interpolation: cf. Bonnet, p. 749, note 1.

[53] Gregory planned to write an account of the life of St. Tetricus, since his name is listed as the title of chapter 105 in the table of contents of *GC*. However there is no text for chapters 105–107, and the probability is that he had not completed these chapters at the time of his death: cf. Krusch, *ad GC*, 105 and Bonnet, p. 432, note 6. St. Tetricus was bishop of Langres from 539/540 to 572/573. His day is March 18. He was buried in the basilica of St. John. Cf. Krusch *ad VP*, 7.4.

[54] St. Tetricus added an apse to one of the short sides of the earlier church (*basilica S. Johannis*) which apparently had been rectangular, as Bordier suggested. When Gregory says *disruptoque pariete, arcum aedificat*, he apparently refers to an arched doorway in the center of the apsidal wall. His language is somewhat obscure because of his brevity. Bordier's translation of these four words—"il abattit la muraille droit qui terminait l'ancien édifice et compléta sa construction en ouvrant à la place de cette muraille une grande arcade"—goes beyond the meaning of the Latin. The *reliquiae* of St. Gregory were later transferred to the basilica of St. Benignus the martyr which was outside the walls of Dijon (Longnon, pp. 211ff.).

dead but sleeping. Whence he rightfully appeared glorious after his passing whose flesh was not corrupted by wantonness. For great is the untouched condition of body and heart which shows grace at the present time and grants eternal life for the future. And concerning this the apostle Paul says:[55] "We follow peace and sanctification without which no one will see the kingdom of God."

(5) While a certain girl was combing her hair on the Lord's Day, because, I believe, of the violation of the sacred day the comb she held clung to her hands in such a way that the teeth were fixed in her fingers and palms and caused her great pain. Then she went to the basilicas of the saints with tears and prayers, and prostrated herself at the sepulcher of the blessed priest Gregory, since she trusted his miraculous power. And when for a very long time she had urgently summoned the aid of the blessed confessor, the comb fell off and her hand was immediately returned to its original task. Those possessed of demons confessed him, and often were cleansed at his tomb. Many times since his passing we have seen them transfixed at those walls by the staff which we mentioned above so that you would think that they were held by strong and very sharp stakes.

(6) We have learned of many other miracles at the same place but lest they cause boredom we have touched but a few of the many. He died in the thirty-third year of his service as bishop at the age of ninety,[56] and he has often declared himself by manifest miracles.

[55] *Hebrews*, 12.14: *pacem sequimini et sanctificationem, sine qua nemo videbit regnum Dei* (Gregory); *pacem sequimini cum omnibus et sanctimoniam, sine qua nemo videbit Deum* (*Vulg.*). Ms 2 brings Gregory's quotation into harmony with the Vulgate.

[56] St. Gregory was born 450/451, became count of Autun in 466/467, bishop of Langres in 506/507, and died in 539/540. He was count for 40 years and bishop for 33: his extreme youth when appointed count is another indication of the importance of his family.

10
The Seven Sleepers
of Ephesus

Introductory Note. Stories of sleepers who wake after many years hold a perennial interest. The most famous of these stories is that of the martyrs of Ephesus. By Gregory's time it was already current in the Eastern Mediterranean. He became familiar with a version which was translated for him by a Syrian named John. It is not certain whether this version was in Greek or not. If it had been in Greek, Gregory's probable ignorance of Greek would be proved by his need of a translator, but it was probably in Syriac.[1] Gregory had already included a brief version in the first book of his *Miracula*.[2] Later a longer version formed an independent work. It was not included in Gregory's list of his own works, and was first definitely assigned to its proper place by Bruno Krusch in his monumental edition of 1885 on the basis of two earlier printed editions.[3] In 1893 he published a revision based on four manuscripts.[4] In 1920[5] in the *Appendix* of his edition, working with eight manuscripts and with Bonnet's notes, he issued an *editio nova* which now gives scholars a better text for this story than is available for any of the other hagiographic writings of Gregory. The translation below follows Krusch's edition of 1920.

We do not have the earlier version upon which Gregory based his version, but an earlier Greek version, sometimes attributed

---

[1] Krusch, *Anal. Boll.*, 12 (1893), pp. 373f., cf. Bonnet, p. 53, note 5.
[2] *GM*, 94.
[3] Pp. 847 (introduction), 848–53 (text and notes).
[4] *Analecta Bollandiana*, 12 (1893), pp. 371–77 (introduction), 377–87 (text and notes). Morf followed this text (pp. 16–21): although this selection was issued by Heraeus in 1922, Morf had completed it in 1914.
[5] Pp. 757–61 (introduction), 761–69 (text and notes).

to Symeon Metaphrastes, and early Syriac versions do exist. Krusch's conclusive discussion of the interrelation of the various versions is based partly on two elaborate discussions of the origin and tradition of the famous story by Koch and Huber.[6] Later it appears in Paul the Deacon,[7] as well as in the Koran, in Vincent of Beauvais, in Jacobus a Voragine, and in many other authors.[8] There is even a translation into Irish preserved in a manuscript of the 13th century.[9]

The narrative is laid in the reigns of Decius (A.D. 249–251) and Theodosius II (A.D. 408–450).[10] The attack on Christianity in the middle of the third century was the first great ecumenical persecution.[11] It started in 250 with the issue of a general edict by Decius ordering all citizens of the Empire to perform public acts of worship to the state gods. Certificates of compliance were issued, and some of these have been recovered on Egyptian papyri. One says in part:[12] "We have always followed the practice of sacrificing to the gods, and now while you are present we have sacrificed, have made libations, and have tasted the offerings in accordance with the regulations and we request you to certify this."

This is an excellent example of Gregory's ability to tell a story rapidly and vividly, but is not wholly typical since it is more or less a translation. In particular the inclusion of scriptural language is different from Gregory's regular pattern. Gregory is affected by the language of the Bible, and often uses quotations or fragmentary phrases, but these are not so frequent within straight narrative. Here he has embodied fragments of verses, cento-like, in his sentences. The notes below list thirteen such fragmentary half-quotations. This gives a flavor to the Latin which has been

[6] J. Koch, *Die Siebenschlaeferlegende, ihr Ursprung und ihre Verbreitung,* Leipzig, 1883; M. Huber, *Die Wanderlegende von den Siebenschlaefern,* Leipzig, 1910.

[7] *Hist. Langob.,* 1.4.

[8] Cf. Koch, pp. 98–104, 162–64, *et passim.*

[9] Krusch, *App.,* p. 760.

[10] Koch definitely established that the story refers not to Theodosius the Great but to his grandson (pp. 69f.).

[11] Cf. A. E. R. Boak, *A History of Rome to 565 A.D.* (3rd ed., New York, 1943), p. 413.

[12] *P. Mich.,* 157 (lines 8–15): J. G. Winter, *Papyri in the University of Michigan Collection:* III. *Miscellaneous Papyri* (Ann Arbor, 1936), pp. 132–33. *P. Mich.,* 158 (*op. cit.,* 134f.) is a similar *libellus.*

partially reproduced by a limited use of biblical language in the English translation.[13]

"The Passion of the Seven Sainted Martyrs Sleeping at Ephesus"

1. In the time of the Emperor Decius, when throughout all the earth the persecution of the Christians was being stirred up and deadly sacrifices were being offered to vain idols, there were in the palace of the king seven important men, born of noble lineage, Achillidis, Diomedis, Diogenus, Probatus, Sambatus, Stephanus, and Quiriacus. They often saw the savage crimes of the emperor when he ordered deaf and dumb idols to be worshipped instead of God Eternal. Stirred by God, they hurried to baptism and from the source of regeneration were named[14] Maximianus, Malchus, Martinianus, Constantinus, Dionisius, Johannis, Serapion.[15] Then Decius, when he arrived at the city of Ephesus, ordered that the Christian race be sought out with such zeal that he might be able, if heaven allowed, to snuff out the very name of the religion. At last sacrifices are prepared and he sacrifices and with beguiling words and with threats of terror stirs up his own men to sacrifice. All were sacrificing victims; the whole city reeked with the smell of the dreadful ceremonies. When the seven champions of Christ saw this, with tears they prostrated themselves in prayer and, sprinkling dust on their heads, urgently called upon the compassion of the Lord, that looking down from His holy heaven He[16] should not allow the people for long to be destroyed in this frowardness.

[13] This revision of a translation already published (McDermott, pp. 289–92) is used by the kind permission of Professor M. S. Enslin, editor of *The Crozer Quarterly*.

[14] *Compuncti divinitus ad baptismum convolant appellatique sunt regenerationis fonte* (on the basis of ms 2). This difficult passage is typical of the improvement made by Krusch in the text of his *editio nova*. Krusch originally printed: *c. d. a. baptismi gratiam convolaverunt, a. s. r. f.* Bonnet (p. 243, note 4) preferred to follow the printed text of Mombritius: *appellatique sunt renati regenerationis fonte* (this reading was criticised by Krusch, *NA*, 19, 1894, pp. 44f.). Krusch (*An. Boll.*) revised his text on the basis of ms 1b: *c. divino nutu lotique s. r. f.* Morf, whose text follows Krusch's text in *An. Boll.*: *compuncti divino nutu lotique s. r. f.* (with the suggestion of *ablutique*).

[15] Gregory first reconciled the two series of names found in variant versions as the names of the seven before and after baptism (Krusch, *App.*, p. 759).

[16] *Psalms*, 33.13 (*Ps.*, 32.13).

2. When this was discovered, persecutors of the Christian name came to the prince saying: "The orders of your realm, O king, traverse the ends of the whole earth,[17] and none dares go against your command, and all taste the daily sacrifices to the immortal gods save seven men whom you foster and cherish with singular affection." To them the emperor said: "And who are these?" They replied: "Maximianus, son of the prefect, with his accomplices." And immediately, while the emperor raged, they were led into his presence loaded with fetters, having their faces suffused[18] with tears and dust on their heads just as they had been while praying in the sight of the Master.[19] Looking at them, the emperor said: "Does such great treachery of an evil mind possess you that you dare infringe upon our dignity and refuse due burnt offerings to the immortal gods? For I say to you on my honor that you will undergo divers kinds of torture for your contempt of our gods." The men replied, saying: "Our God is the one, true God, the Creator of heaven and earth and sea, to Whom we offer the due sacrifice of daily praise,[20] for Whose honor we are prepared to die. We know that those names which you urge us to worship, under the name of gods, are absolutely nothing, because they are able to make no use of life, since they are fashioned with limbs by the art of artisans. And so those who worship them are by the sanction of the prophets condemned to become like them—both those who made them and those who worship them."[21]

3. Then the emperor raged and, when all men had been removed, said: "Depart, gallows birds,[22] from our presence, until, practising penitence for the crime of this obstinacy, you shall be received in our palace and reconciled by the mercy of the gods.

---

[17] *Psalms*, 72.8 (*Ps.* 71.8). It is interesting to note this reflection of the language of the Bible in the mouth of the persecutors.

[18] *Suffusus*. This reading of ms 2 was anticipated by Bonnet's conjecture of *suffusos* (which appears in mss 1b, 1c, 3a, 3b, 3e) based on *eius*, *effusos* (p. 156, note 2).

[19] *Iudith*, 4.15 (*Vulg.*). The book of *Iudith* is not included in the American Revised Version.

[20] *Psalms*, 50.14 (*Ps.*, 49.14).

[21] *Psalms*, 135.18 (*Ps.*, 134.18).

[22] *Furciferi* "yoke-bearers" (the yoke was a wooden brace put on a slave's neck as a punishment), often applied to slaves in comedy, became a taunt with a double meaning when applied to Christians: cf. Prudentius, *Peristephanon*, 2. 317.

Until then you shall enjoy the flower of youth because it is not fitting that such physical charm and beauty be subjected to torture." And when the iron had been stricken from their necks, he ordered them to go free until he should return to Ephesus. When the seven men had received permission to go and the emperor had departed to another city, they went to their own homes. And when the treasures in their homes had been examined, they took their gold and silver and all their garments and furniture, and having distributed it to the poor, went to a cave in Mount Chilleus, carrying with them a little[23] money for the purchase of the necessities of life. And they chose Malchus to go secretly to the city, buy food, and hear what the emperor was decreeing daily concerning the Christians.

4. Then when the saints freed from prison were enclosed under barriers, and were free for continual prayer, that most worthless emperor returned to Ephesus, and when according to his wont Christians were sought out, he asked about Maximianus and his comrades. Their parents, however, said they were hidden in a certain cave in Mount Chilleus from which they could easily be routed out if a regal order of the emperor should go forth. When the men, at Malchus' announcement, learned this, extremely terrified they prostrated themselves on the ground[24] and with tears prayed that the Master, guarding them under his protection, should free them from the sight of that most unjust emperor. While they were praying, God in his providence, because they were needed for the future, heard their prayer and caught up their souls. And they lay on the ground as though sleeping in sweet sleep.

5. Then the emperor, troubled, said to his men: "Go, therefore, and stop up the mouth of the cavern lest those rebels against the gods have a way to go forth." While those men were going who were to stop up the mouth of the cave, two men went ahead of them, Theodorus and Ruben, Christians, who because of the emperor's threats were praying to Christ only in secret. They wrote on lead tablets the whole history of the saints and placed

---

[23]*Parumper.* This reading of mss 1a, 1b, 1c, was conjecturally restored as a synonym of *parum* by Bonnet (p. 277, note 3).

[24]*Iudith,* 7.4.

these inside in the entrance to the cavern, without the knowledge of any, saying: "Whenever God wishes to reveal the blessed limbs of His champions to the peoples, let these tablets teach what they have endured in His name." And when those came who had been sent, they rolled up great stones, closed the entrance of the cave, then went away saying: "Let them grow weak with hunger and devour themselves with their own jaws,[25] who considered it of little worth to offer due libations to our gods."

6. After this when Decius was dead, in the following times the height of power came to Theodosius, son of Arcadius. In his time that unclean sect of the Sadducees[26] arose, wishing to destroy the hope of resurrection, saying that the dead do not rise.[27] The fountainheads of this heresy were the bishops Theodorus and Gaius,[28] who wished to join the soul of the emperor himself to this unbelief. Whence it happened that the emperor, much afflicted for this reason and prostrate on the ground, prayed to the Lord that he should make known to him what he should fitly believe. There was at that time in Ephesus a certain Dalius, extremely rich in flocks, who, going around Mount Chilleus, ordered his servants, saying: "Prepare enclosures here for our sheep, because this place is suitable for feeding the flocks." For he did not know what had occurred in the cave. However, while the servants were working and rolling out huge rocks, they came to the mouth of the cave and found great stones.[29] Rolling these away, they constructed a wall. Nevertheless they did not enter the cave.

7. Then the Lord ordered the breath of life to return to the

---

[25] *Deuteronomy*, 32.34. *Hic fame deficiant propriisque se morsibus devorent* (Gregory); *consumentur fame, et devorabunt eos aves morsu amarissimo* (*Vulg.*); "*They shall be* wasted with hunger, and devoured with burning heat and bitter destruction" (*ARV*).

[26] Since the Sadducees denied the resurrection of the body (*Act.*, 23.8: *Sadducaei enim dicunt non esse resurrectionem*), the name is applied to a heresy which took that position. For this doctrine of the Sadducees cf. G. H. Box in Hastings, *Encyclopaedia of Religion and Ethics*, XI (1920), p. 45, *s. v. Sadducees*.

[27] *I Corinthians*, 15.16.

[28] Since the Greek and Syriac versions name Theodorus bishop of Gali, Gaii, or Aegaei, and do not mention Gaius, it is obvious that Gregory mistook the place name for a personal name and invented the second bishop (cf. Krusch). Nothing further is known of Theodorus than is told in this story: cf. W. Ensslin, *RE*, II.V.2 (1934), col. 1911, *s. v. Theodoros* no. 139.

[29] *Joshua*, 10.18.

bodies of the saints, and they arose and greeted each other after their custom and, thinking they had slept only one night, they sat down strong and vigorous. For not only were their bodies comely and very beautiful, but even their garments were untouched and unharmed, just as they had been put on by them a great many years before. And turning to Malchus they said: "Tell us, brother, we ask, what the emperor has said this night, or if we have been sought out, that we might know." To them he said: "You have been sought out that you might sacrifice to the gods." To him Maximianus said: "All of us are prepared to die for Christ. But now take pieces of silver and go to purchase food and listen carefully and report to us what you have heard." And so he took the money and left. For these were silver pieces stamped with the name of Decius. However, approaching the gate of the city he saw the sign of the cross above the gate and thunderstruck he marveled, saying to himself: "Was the heart of Decius changed[30] yesterday after the setting of the sun when I left the city so that he should protect those entering through the gate with the sign of the cross?" And he entered the city and heard men swear by the name of Christ and saw a church and a priest who was hastening to and fro through the city, and he examined new walls, and marveling even more he said to himself, "Think you that you have entered another city?" And approaching the market he brought forth his pieces of silver, asking that they give him food.

8. But they examined the stamp of his silver and said: "This man has found ancient treasures, for, behold, he offers silver from the time of Decius." Malchus, in truth, hearing these things, was turning over his thoughts in his heart, saying: "What mean these things? Do I see a vision?" However the men took him and led him to the bishop Marinus and the prefect. To him the prefect said: "Whence are you and from what region have you come?" He said: "From Ephesus, if indeed this is the city of the Ephesians, which I remember seeing yesterday." The prefect said: "Whence have you these pieces of silver?" He replied: "I took them from the home of my father." The prefect said: "And where is your father?" And he named his parents, but nobody recognized them. The prefect said: "Tell us, whence have you these

[30] *Exodus*, 14.5.

pieces of silver? For they are from the time of Decius, who has been dead for years. From this it is manifest that you have come to deceive the wise men of the Ephesians and for this reason ought to be subjected to torture until you disclose the truth." And Malchus, moved, said with astonishment and tears: "I would ask you one thing if you think it worthy. Where is the Emperor Decius who persecuted Christians in this city?" Marinus the bishop replied: "Dealy beloved son, there is not a man in this city who recalls the time of Decius; for he died many years ago."

9. Malchus hearing this turned and said to the bishop: "I thought that I with my brothers had slept only one night, but, as I learn, the course of many years has passed during our sleep. And now the Lord has aroused me with my brothers that every age might know that the resurrection of the dead will come to pass. Therefore follow me and I will show you my brothers who have arisen with me." Then the astonished bishop with the prefect and all the people followed Malchus and came to the cave. While Malchus was telling his brothers what had happened to him in the city, the bishop entered and found a box sealed with two silver seals. He went outside and calling together the whole multitude of the city with the prefect he opened the seals and found the two lead tablets on which had been written the whole passion of these men, as I have related above. And they learned that those things were true which were said by Malchus.

10. Then having entered, they found the blessed martyrs sitting in a corner of the cave, and their countenances were flourishing like the rose and shining in virtue like the sun;[31] for their garments and bodies had not been destroyed. Then Marinus the bishop with the prefect fell at their feet[32] and worshipped them, and all the people glorified God who deemed it proper to show such a miracle to his servants. In truth the saints told the bishop and all the people what had happened to them in the time of Decius. Then the bishop with the prefect sent messengers to the Emperor Theodosius, saying: "Hasten quickly if you wish to see a great miracle which is manifest in your times, by the gift of God. For if

[31] *Revelation*, 1.16.
[32] *Luke*, 8.47.

you come, you will find out that the hope of resurrection is verily
so in accordance with the solemn promise of the evangelical
covenant."

11. The Emperor Theodosius hearing this arose from his couch
of mourning and extending his hands to God, said: "I thank
you, Lord Jesus Christ, the Sun of justice, Who have deemed it
proper to sprinkle the shadows of mortals with the light of Your
truth; I thank You who did not permit the lamp of my confession
to be veiled by the vile fog of false advocacy." When he had said
these things and his horsemen had mounted, he came with the
greatest haste to Ephesus. Then the bishop with the prefect and
the whole multitude of the city came out to meet the emperor.
Then while they were ascending the mountain, the sainted
martyrs came out to meet Augustus,[33] and their faces gleamed
with virtue like the sun. And Augustus fell to the earth and
worshipped them, glorifying God. And rising he kissed them and
wept on the neck of each one of them, saying: "I see your faces as
if I saw my Lord Jesus Christ when He called Lazarus from the
tomb,[34] to Whom I offer unlimited thanks because He has not
withdrawn from me the hope of resurrection."

12. Then Maximianus replied: "Know, emperor, that the Lord
ordered us to rise again to strengthen your faith. Therefore
trusting always in Him learn that the resurrection of the dead will
come to pass, since today you see us after our resurrection
speaking with you and telling the greatness of God." And they
spoke many other things with him, and having stretched themselves on the ground again slept, handing over their souls to the
immortal King Almighty God. The emperor seeing these things
fell upon their bodies and weeping kissed them, and taking off his
own raiment placed it upon them, ordering golden coffins to be
made in which they might be buried. But on that night the saints
appeared saying: "Do not do this, but leave us above the earth;
whence a second time the Lord will arouse us on the great day of
the resurrection of all flesh." Then the emperor built above them a
great basilica and constructed there a place of refuge for the

---

[33] I.e. Theodosius.
[34] *John*, 12.17.

poor, ordering that they be fed at public expense. And when the bishops had been called together he celebrated a festival of the saints, and all glorified God in whose Trinity is perfect honor and glory for age upon age. Amen.

Here ends the passion of the seven sainted martyrs sleeping near Ephesus, translated into Latin by the bishop Gregory, with the interpretation of John the Syrian. The day of their passion is observed on the fourth of August.[35]

---

[35] *IIII id. Ags.* "August 4": August 4 and October 22 or 23 are listed in the *Menologia Graeca;* July 27 in the *Menologia Latina* (Krusch).

11
The Seven Wonders of the World

Introductory Note. Gregory in his account of his own works lists a single book *On the Offices of the Church.*[1] This work was lost and consequently could not be printed in earlier editions including that of Dom Ruinart. Haase discovered the work without Gregory's name attached to it[2] in a manuscript of the royal library of Bamberg and issued the *editio princeps* in 1853. There is no doubt that Haase's assignment of the work to Gregory is correct. The work falls into two distinct parts: an introductory section on the seven wonders of the world which is translated in full below, and the body of the essay which is a brief account of enough astronomy so that the clergy could perform certain ceremonies at the proper time of night (*vigiliae, nocturnae solemnitates*). The astronomical material shows the state of learning in Merovingian times. According to Galle, a noted astronomer who aided Haase in his edition, Gregory's data are

[1] *HF*, 10.31: *de Cursibus etiam ecclesiasticis unum librum condidi.* Haase's edition is elaborately and excellently annotated: Krusch (p. 857) said that he left scarcely anything for his successors to add. In my translation I have followed the text of Krusch (pp. 854-72). Manitius (pp. 221-23) gives an unusually full account of this essay.

[2] In the ms it is between the *de metris* of Mallius Theodorus and the *de natura rerum* of Isidore of Seville and bears the heading: *in Christi nomine incipit de cursum stellarum ratio, qualiter ad officium implendum debeat observari.* Another fragmentary ms (*Sangallensis*) containing most of the introduction was discussed by Krusch: *NA*, 12 (1887), pp. 303-08. In the title given by Gregory *cursus* has the meaning "office, duty," but in the title in the ms *cursus* has the meaning "course": cf. Bonnet, p. 241, note 3. The second is the ordinary classical meaning: for the first cf. Du Cange, II, pp. 720f., *s. v.* 2 *cursus.*

surprisingly accurate. This latter section is especially interesting since the Bamberg manuscript is illustrated by drawings of the constellations—these drawings are roughly sketched in the editions of Haase, Bordier, and Krusch.[3] The introductory section exists in four other manuscripts, and parts had already been published as *incerti auctoris* by Mai and Haupt.[4] The whole introduction was published with a commentary in 1882 by Omont, who was unaware of Haase's edition.[5]

The list of the seven wonders of the world was probably made in Hellenistic times. An extant treatise ascribed to Philo of Byzantium lists them as follows: (1) the hanging gardens of Babylon; (2) the pyramids near Memphis; (3) the chryselephantine statue of Zeus at Olympia by Phidias; (4) the colossal statue of Helios at Rhodes; (5) the walls of Babylon; (6) the temple of Artemis at Ephesus; (7) the Mausoleum at Halicarnassus.[6] Usually the lighthouse (*pharos*) in the harbor of Alexandria is found instead of the walls of Babylon. Many variations were inserted by later authors because of chronology, piety, or patriotism. Gregory's treatment of the list is peculiarly interesting. In Gregory only the colossus of Rhodes, the *pharos* of Alexandria, and the walls of Babylon remain from the earlier lists. "The sepulcher of a Persian king" in Gregory probably represents the Mausoleum. Of the three additions, Noah's ark and Solomon's temple are natural

[3] Krusch (*App.*, opp. p. 770) reproduced fol. 79r of the ms on which some of the drawings appear. This page runs from the end of 16 to the beginning of 20.

[4] A. Mai, *Scriptorum veterum nova collectio*, III.2 (1828), p. 239 (paragraphs 13–14); M. Haupt, *Ovidii Halieutica etc.* (Leipzig, 1838), pp. 67–73 (paragraphs 9–16).

[5] H. Omont, "Les sept merveilles du monde au moyen âge," *Bibliothèque de l'école des Chartes*, 1882, pp. 50–55. This was part of a longer article (pp. 40–59) in which Omont discussed the seven wonders and published several medieval versions. The first version published by Omont (pp. 47–50) was attributed by him to Bede (but cf. Krusch, p. 855). This version shows several marked similarities to Gregory's list.

[6] For the *de septem orbis miraculis* of Philo cf. Omont, pp. 40–43. The text of Philo was edited with commentary by Orelli (Leipzig, 1816) and appended to the Didot edition of Aelian and Porphyrius by Hercher (Paris, 1858). The last chapter (on the Mausoleum) is lost, but the subject is certain since Halicarnassus in Caria is mentioned in the preface. This work is undoubtedly not by the engineer and physicist who lived in the second century B.C., but by a larger rhetorician who either bore the same name or to whose small work the more famous name was attached.

additions in the list of the pious bishop, but the addition of the theater of Heraclea is unusual. Haase's suggestion that "he has certainly omitted those in which mention is made of the pagan gods"[7] is a partial explanation, since Gregory does not seem to realize the religious significance of a Greek theater, nor does he indicate that the colossus was a statue of the Sun.[8]

Gregory was not content merely to give a list in which there are two biblical structures, "constructed," as he says, "at God's command." To this list he added "seven wonders" created by the hand of God. A notable feature of this second list, which was surely compiled by Gregory himself,[9] is the pious application of the various wonders. The whole introduction is remarkable for frequent citation of pagan and Christian sources.

"The Course of the Stars," Chapters 1–16

(1) 1.[10] Many philosophers, free for the study of literature, wrote of seven wonders[11] as more marvelous than others. Of these it has pleased me to pass over certain ones and to recall others at which we must marvel the more. Such is the appearance or the construction of these wonders.

(2) 2. And so we list Noah's ark as the first wonder. And the mouth of God told what it should be.[12] Its length was three hundred cubits, its width fifty, its height thirty. We read that the ark had a second and a third story,[13] and all of the work in it was finished to a cubit. It had a window and[14] a door in its side. In it all species of the birds of heaven and the beasts of earth and[14]

---

[7] P. 29 (note on *Curs.*, 1).

[8] Pliny, *NH*, 34.41: . . . *Solis colossus Rhodi, quem fecerat Chares Lindius* . . .

[9] Cf. Krusch, p. 855. Manitius' statement (p. 219) that it was copied from an earlier author is implicitly denied by his general discussion of the work.

[10] Krusch divided the essay into 47 paragraphs; i.e. intro. 1–16, body of essay 17–47 (indicated by the numbers in parentheses): Haase into 73 paragraphs; i.e. intro. 1–37, body of essay 38–73. Both numbering systems have been inserted in this translation, but cross-references are to the numbering of Krusch.

[11] *Miracula* "wonders": usually "miracles" in Gregory, but in this essay the meaning varies.

[12] The description is based on *Genesis*, 6.15–20. The cubit is about 18 inches.

[13] St. Jerome, *adversus Iovinianum*, 1.17 (*PL*, 23, col. 247).

[14] *Sive* "and": cf. Bonnet, pp. 315f.

reptiles as well as eight human beings[15] were preserved throughout the flood for the renewal of the world.

(3) 3. We list as the second wonder Babylon, of which the description in Orosius is this:[16] "Because of the remarkable smoothness of the plain it could be seen from all sides, and was most pleasing in its likeness to a camp,[17] laid out with equal ramparts on four sides. Scarcely credible is the story of the strength and size of the walls, fifty cubits thick and four times as high. And its circuit was four hundred and seventy stades. The wall of baked brick had bitumen as mortar. 4. In it were a hundred bronze gates. Throughout its length, moreover, barracks for its defenders were placed at regular intervals on each side at the top of its battlements, and there was space between to drive a four-horse chariot. The houses built against it on the inside were of eight stories, remarkable for their menacing height." After the renewal of the human race this city was first built by the giant Nebroth.[18]

(4) 5. The third wonder is the temple of Solomon which was marvelous not so much for the size of the structure as for its decoration.[19] "And he built the walls of the house on the inside with boards of cedar from the floor of the house even to the top of the walls and to the coffered ceilings and he faced it on the inside with timbers and he covered the floor of the house with boards of fir. And at the back of the temple he built it of twenty cubits with cedar boards from the floor to the upper parts and he made the inner part the house of the mercy seat[20] in the Holy of Holies. 6. Then the temple itself was of forty cubits in front of the doors of the mercy seat. And the whole house was covered on the inside

[15] I.e., Noah, Shem, Ham, and Japheth and their wives.

[16] Orosius, *historiae adversum paganos*, 2.6.8-10. Here, as often Gregory is careless in his quotation: cf. Bonnet, p. 20, note 4; p. 98, note 7. He also quotes portions of this passage elsewhere (*HF*, 1.6), and used this history of Orosius as a source for much of his earlier material (cf. *HF*, 2, *Praef.*) There is an excellent translation by I. W. Raymond: *Seven Books of History Against the Pagans*, New York, Columbia U. Press, 1936 (*Records of Civilization*, 26).

[17] The Roman *castra*, even when hurriedly constructed for a single night, was laid out in a rigidly prescribed and formal pattern.

[18] Orosius, 2.6.7 (*Nebrot*).

[19] *I Kings*, 6.15-35 (*III Reg.*, 6.15-35). The variations from the text of the Vulgate indicate Gregory's use of an older Latin version for this passage: cf. Krusch, p. 855, note 6; Bonnet, pp. 54-61 (for a specific point cf. p. 423, note 1).

[20] *Oraculum* "oracle (classical), mercy seat (ecclesiastical)."

with cedar and had its turnings and its joinings fashioned and carved in high relief, nor did any stone appear in the wall. 7. He made a mercy seat in the middle of the inner part of the house that he might place there the ark of the covenant of the Lord. The mercy seat was twenty cubits in length and twenty cubits in width. And he covered it and clothed it with the purest gold, but the altar he covered with cedar. And he sheathed the house before the altar with the purest gold and fastened the metal sheets with golden nails. There was nothing in the temple which was not sheathed with gold, and he covered the whole altar of the mercy seat with gold. 8. And he set in the mercy seat two Cherubim of the wood of the olive which were ten cubits in height; one of the Cherubim had wings five cubits in length, that is, it was ten cubits from the tip of one wing to the tip of the other wing. The second of the Cherubim likewise had a like measure of ten cubits, and he placed the Cherubim in the middle of the inner part of the temple and covered them with gold. 9. And he carved all the walls throughout the circuit with various cuttings and turnings, and in them he carved Cherubim and palms and varied pictures, reliefs which seemed to project and fly off. But the pavement of the house he covered inside and outside with gold. 10. And he constructed the entrance of the temple with square posts of olive wood and two doors of fir on each side, and he carved on them figures of Cherubim and the likeness of palms in high relief, and he covered them with gold. 11. And each door was double and each part closed in turn. And he carved Cherubim and palms in extremely high relief." He did many other wonderful things within, which would take long to relate.

(5) 12. The fourth wonder is the tomb of the Persian king carved with wonderful workmanship from one hollowed amethystine stone, engraved in low relief, and on the outside there were likenesses of men, beasts, and birds in high relief. It had also trees with leaves and fruit carved in high relief.[21]

---

[21] This confused account probably goes back to a description of the Mausoleum (Haase). This tomb of Mausolus, king of Caria, was finished about 353 B.C. by his widow Artemisia. The architect Pythios published an account which is now lost. It was a temple-type building on a high base, topped by a pyramid and a chariot group. The sculptural decoration was elaborate. It was not rock-cut. Cf. D. S. Robertson, *A Handbook of Greek and Roman Architecture* (2nd. ed., Cambridge, 1943), pp. 150f., fig. 65, pp. 335, 358 (bibliography).

(6) 13. The fifth wonder is the statue, cast in bronze and gilded, which is on the island of Rhodes.[22] Its height is so immense that scarcely can one throw a stone to its head. Many say too that a man could climb through its leg to its head, if he had an entrance through which he might go. They assert also that the head of this statue could hold 330 bushels of wheat.[23]

(7) 14. The sixth wonder is the theater in Heraclea which is said to have been carved from one mountain so that the whole of it was built from one side, not only the walls on the outside but those on the inside, as well as the arches, pits, steps, and seats. And the whole structure was completed from one rock. In addition it was faced with Heraclean marble.[24]

(8) 15. The seventh wonder is the Pharos of Alexandria,[25] which is said to have been built on four crabs of remarkable size. Nor could they have been small since they support an object so immense in height and width. For they say that were a man to lie

[22] Pliny says that the statue which was made by Chares of Lindos was 70 cubits high and was erected by the funds raised from the sale of the siege machinery of Demetrius Poliorcetes who abandoned it when he gave up the siege of Rhodes in disgust (*HN*, 34.41). Pliny adds: *pauci pollicem eius amplectuntur, maiores sunt digiti quam pleraeque statuae.* The siege was lifted in 304 B.C., Chares started the statue in 302 and finished it in 290, it was toppled over by an earthquake between 227 and 222: cf. C. Robert in *RE*, III.2 (1889), cols. 2130f. *s. v. Chares* no. 15, and E. A. Gardner, *A Handbook of Greek Sculpture* (rev. ed., London, 1915), pp. 482–4). The size of the statue was tremendously exaggerated in medieval times when it was pictured as bestriding the harbor of Rhodes.

[23] *Choros duos et viginti.* The *cor* was a Hebrew dry measure containing about 20 cubic feet or 15 bushels. Cf. Isidore, *Origines*, 16.26.17: *Corus triginta modiorum mensura impletur.*

[24] Gregory is inextricably confused here, since none of the many cities named Heraclea, in honor of Heracles, contained a noteworthy theater nor does any early list of the Wonders contain this item. It is mentioned otherwise only in the list of Pseudo-Bede (Omont, *loc. cit*). The Greek custom of building a theater on an natural slope, as the theater of Dionysus was built on the south slope of the Acropolis at Athens, surely gave rise to some features of this story. Examples of this type of architecture may be found in the rock-cut tombs and temples of the Egyptians, and the Graeco-Oriental temples at Petra. Heraclean marble (from Heraclea Latmi in Caria) is mentioned by Vitruvius (10.2.15) in connection with the building of the Artemisium at Ephesus. Two other passages in Gregory mention marble from Heraclea (*GM*, 64: *columnis Pharis Heraclisque*, cf. Krusch's note; *GC*, 100: *marmore Heracleo*), both times in conjunction with Parian marble.

[25] This great lighthouse was built on the island of Pharos in the harbor of Alexandria about 290 B.C. by Sostratus of Cnidus for Ptolemy I or Ptolemy II.

on a claw of one of the crabs he would not be able to cover it.[26]
16. Moreover the Pharos is lit at night with faggots[27] supplied by
public funds so that ships wandering at nighttime by wind and
wave might know, if they cannot see the stars, in what quarter
they should set their sails.

(9) 17. But it is certain that these wonders, although some were
constructed in accordance with the order of God and some by
man's invention, were none the less established by men, and for
this reason some have perished and some are close to destruction.
In truth there are other wonders which our Almighty God renews
each day in this universe with His own hands, or presents again
after the circle of the year is completed. Some are displayed as
enriching gifts, as the tide of the ocean and the fruitful earth.
18. Others are for the indication of virtue, as the sun, the moon,
the stars, the phoenix: and certain of these reprove sinners and
represent the fires below, as Aetna and the spring of Grenoble.
These are the wonders which in no age grow old, by no accident
fall, by no loss are diminished, except when the Master shall have
ordered that the universe be destroyed.

(10) 19. The first of all, then, is the tide of the ocean-sea by
which each day it is enlarged so that it fills its shores, and then
withdrawing again it offers dry land. And then a great supply of
fish and different kinds of seaweed[28] is collected by people
walking on dry land. God has prepared this first miracle for the

---

Representations on coins and reliefs as well as later Arabic accounts are so vague
that any reconstruction is problematical. It seems to have had four square
stepped-back stories. It was reconstructed and reduced in height by the Byzantine
emperior Anastasius in the fifth century A.D., and lasted until the fourteenth
century. Cf. Robertson, *op. cit.*, pp. 184f., 335. *Pharos* or *pharus* was soon used for
the lighthouse on the island (e.g., Caesar, *Bell. Civ.*, 3.112.1) and then for any
lighthouse (e.g., Suetonius, *Tiberius*, 74). Gregory uses *pharus* or *farus* (i.e.,
lumen) "light" ten times (Krusch, *Index*, p. 956).

[26] Since both in the original structure of Sostratus and in the reconstruction
under Anastasius the lowest story seems to have been a square, the *cancri* are
probably apocryphal additions to the description. Du Cange (II, p. 86, *s. v.* 2
cancer) defines *cancer* as *arcus, fornix, quod cancri forcipem referat*, but Gregory
seems to understand *cancer* literally. In *TLL* (III, col. 229.14–18) this passage is
cited and the word is defined as "a base constructed in the shape of a crab."

[27] Robertson (p. 185) suggested that the original fuel of the lantern may have
been naphtha or petroleum.

[28] *Liguminum*, i.e., *legumina* "leguminous plants, seaweed."

human race that it might be notable in wonder and in accordance with His virtue.[29]

(11) 20. The second is like the first. To be sure, when seeds, grains of wheat, and the fruit of trees are cast in the earth and hidden in the furrows of the plough, with the coming of summer they spring up with stalks. And the stalks are crowned with leaves and ears, and within are bursting with milky sap. And the Master, the Sower of spiritual doctrine, changed this and, speaking in parables about the increase of His word, when it fell among peoples, said:[30] "Such is the word of God, as often as a man casts down seed, it grows day and night; for of its own accord the earth bears fruit, first the blade, then the ear, then the full grain in the ear." 21. Likewise the apostle Paul used this figure for the resurrection, saying:[31] "But the seed does not live, unless it die first. Such too is the resurrection of the dead: it is sowed in weakness, it arises in virtue," and so forth. 22. Like too is the nature of trees which, I think, signify the resurrection itself. Although in winter they are bare of leaves and like the dead, in truth in the springtime they are clothed with leaves and ornamented with flowers, and in summer they are filled with fruit. Although this wonder has this metaphorical meaning, nevertheless it offers a present benefit to the peoples, that man may realize that he receives food from Him Who created man from nothing.

(12) 23. The third wonder is that which Lactantius relates about the phoenix.[32] He says: "Its body is large and its plumage and

---

[29] *Congruum suae virtuti:* this conjecture, which Haase printed in his textual notes, is surely correct. Bonnet (p. 546, note 1) adopted it, but Haase and Krusch printed *congruum servituti* in accordance with the mss.

[30] *Mark*, 4.26–28 (with omissions).

[31] *I Corinthians*, 15.36, 42, 43 (with omissions).

[32] An elegiac poem of 85 couplets survives under the title of *de Phoenice*. In some of the mss it is attributed to Lactantius. Although there is nothing inherently improbable in this attribution, the authorship has been much discussed. It was included by J. W. and A. M. Duff in *Minor Latin Poets* (Loeb Classical Library, revised edition, Cambridge, Mass. and London, 1935), pp. 643–49 (intro.), 650–65 (text and translation). Citation of the text of the *Phoenix* below is from this edition. Gregory has digested ideas from this poem rather haphazardly. For the tremendous vogue of the story of the phoenix cf. Tuerk in Roscher, *Ausfuehrliches Lexikon der griechischen und roemischen Mythologie*, III. 2 (Leipzig, 1902–09) cols. 3450–66 (in literature), 3466–72 (in art) *s. v. Phoinix*. Baehrens noted differences between Gregory's summary and the extant poem and concluded that

claws and eyes are beautiful. It neither consorts nor mates[33] with any other bird. For it is obvious that men do not know whether it is masculine, feminine, or neither. After is has lived a thousand years,[34] 24. it seeks a spot which surpasses in loftiness all places in the world, where green foliage lasts through spring and winter. In the middle is a great spring which flows abundantly and is very clear in its gentleness. On the bank of the spring a noble tree surpasses the rest of the tress of the grove in height. 25. On the tip of the tree the bird builds for itself a nest or a sepulcher from different types of colored material.[35] Sitting in the midst of its nest, it drags the sweet-smelling branches with its beak and covers itself with them. Then it begins to pour forth sweet song with different melodies, and leaping from its nest dives into the waters of the spring. 26. When it has done this thrice and four[36] times, it again mounts to its nest and drags over it the sweet-smelling branches which it has brought in. However, when the

Gregory summarized Lactantius' *de Phoenice* which is now lost and that the extant poem is not by Lactantius: *Poetate Latini minores*, III (Leipzig, 1881), pp. 248–52. Max. Leroy made an elaborate study of the relation of the passage in Gregory with the poem *de ave Phoenice* "Le chant du Phénix, l'ordre des vers dans le *carmen de ave Phoenice*," *L'Antiquité classique*, 1 (1932), pp. 213–31. He considered it the work of Lactantius and reached the conclusion that Gregory's summary which antedates the mss of the poem represents the original order of the ideas better than do the mss of the poem. On the basis of his comparative study he concluded that one page of the ms had been copied in the wrong place and rearranged the poem. Although Leroy's solution is ingenious and his analysis of the poem is valuable, Gregory's carelessness in quoting and summarizing other authors makes such a hypothesis unnecessary. Leroy used Krusch's text without change (p. 214) except for the insertion of extra cross-references to the poem. Krusch had noted 14 passages, Leroy noted 44. He also included (p. 215, note 4) examples of verbal similarity.

[33] Bonnet (p. 746, note 1) preferred *non iuncta consortio nec vincta* (ms 1) *coniugio* to Krusch's text *n. i. c. n. iuncta c.*: the translation is the same for either text.

[34] The life cycle of the phoenix is most frequently given as 500 years, but other figures are found—540, 654, 1000, 1461 (i.e., *magnus annus*, Tacitus, *Annales*, 6.28) etc.: cf. Roscher, *loc. cit.*, cols. 3451, 3460–2.

[35] *Pigmentorum* "colors, colored materials": it is obvious from Lactantius (line 79: *colligit huic sucos et odores divite silva*) that the reference is to flowering branches.

[36] *Ter quaterque*: Bonnet pointed out that *tertio* is ordinarily used by Gregory, that the *terque quaterque* in *GM*, 105 is due to imitation of Virgil, and that the phrase here may be due to imitation of Lactantius from whose poem some lines are missing (p. 450, note 6). The last suggestion is unnecessary: cf. 37–38 where the

sun first flashes forth, its brilliance brings fire, and the nest catches fire, and the bird is wholly burnt. Then the dust and ashes are gathered together and are collected into one mass as if in the likeness of an egg. 27. And from it the bird rises again. When its life is resumed, it is fed while it is a fledgling but no man takes care of its feeding. Nourished only by the dew of heaven, it is called back again to its old figure and appearance. Born again with the same feathers and color it flies forth, just as it had been before its death." 28. This miracle strongly foreshadows and shows the resurrection of man. Just as man, made of clay and reduced to dust, must be aroused again from the very ashes at the sound of the trumpet.

(13) 29. The fourth is Mt. Aetna, granted to the island of Sicily, where it burns with living fires, belches forth strong flames, and vomits sulphur terribly in that region. Of it Publius the Mantuan in the third book of his *Aeneid* so speaks:[37] "The port was huge and unmoved by the approach of the winds but Aetna thunders nearby with horrifying desolation, and at times it sends forth a black cloud smoking with pitch-black eddies and white-hot ash, and it raises up balls of flame and licks the stars." 30. And if any objects are cast into the openings, whence the flames come, they are soon belched forth. And Julius Titianus recalled this mountain in these words and said:[38] "The four largest mountains in Sicily are Eryx, Nebrodes, Neptunius, and Aetna. When they saw[39] that Aetna often whirled flames from its summit, they were forced to believe that they saw the end of the world close at hand.[40]

phrase *ter quater* starts both lines. Leroy (p. 216, note 9) says that *ter quater* in Lactantius means "twelve times," and that Gregory's *ter quaterque* "many times" is due to failure to comprehend the distinction. This is possible, but I would take *ter quater* in Lactantius as poetic license for the Virgilian *terque quaterque* (e.g. in *Aen.*, 1.97), as the Duffs do in their translation "thrice and again." Virgilian influence is strong in Lactantius' poem: e.g. lines 15–20 are modeled on *Aen.*, 6.273–281. Bonnet's suggestion (*loc. cit.*) of -*ve* for -*que* in Gregory is unnecessary.

[37] *Aen.*, 3.570–574.

[38] This Julius Titianus was a writer whose work on geography was mentioned by Servius (*ad Aen.*, 4.42). Haupt's conjecture of *Titus Livius* led Weissenborn to include the passage as *fr.* 4 from the 14th book of Livy (*Livi ad urbe condita*, vol. VI, Leipzig, 1851, p. vi). In the later edition of Weissenborn it was eliminated (2nd ed., by H. J. Meuller, vol. X.2, Berlin, 1881).

[39] *Vident*, (from mss 2 and 3).

[40] *Eisque se sentire orbis prope finem credendum. Quamquam id cum primum*

However, when first it was announced at Rome that Aetna was on fire, expiatory sacrifices were made as in the case of unnatural events."

(14) 31. The fifth wonder is that of the springs of Grenoble, from which water and fire flow simultaneously.[41] For you may see flames flying over the waters, you may drain water from the middle of a fire and not be burned, you drink it nor are you in flames, you carry it nor are you set on fire by the flame. But should you touch a wax taper or a pitchy torch to it, straightway when they have touched the flames, they are kindled. Also if you put your hand in, it is not burnt. 32. Hence a certain Hilary says:[42] "If the fires truly burn, why, waters, do you live? If waters truly extinguish, why, fires, do you live? The hand of God[43] has hidden hostile fire in the bosom of the waters and orders a common source for both," and so forth. 33. Oh wonderful mystery of divine power! One spring produces fire and water, verily that all may learn that the solace[44] of a glorious life and the judgment of eternal death attend His power, and might understand that no power is given to flames to destroy the human body which, if guilty of sin, must accept the penalty of eternal fire after the judgment.[45]

(15) 34. Although the sixth wonder was created by the work of God before these, nevertheless in this listing it is placed late: it is that God, the Creator of all, has ordered that everything be illuminated by the sun. Not without great wonder do we see that the sun itself like a slave brings light to the world every day, that it traverses the east and the west, that it fructifies the earth with its heat and causes fruits to arise.

etc. Eisque se sentire is my conjecture for *idque sentire* of the mss. *Finem* is Haase's conjecture for *fide. Credendum* is from ms 3; *credentium* of other mss would mean a *lacuna* as Haase noted. The text cannot be reconstructed with certainty. Perhaps Gregory misunderstood or garbled the quotation.

[41] The only reference to these springs in ancient times is that of St. Augustine: *de civitate Dei*, 21.7. 2: cf. Omont, *loc. cit.*, p. 46.

[42] Omont (p. 46) identifies him as St. Hilary of Poitiers whom Gregory often mentions; but Mai, Haase, and Krusch note that St. Hilary of Arles is listed in an anonymous life as author of "verses on a flaming spring." Riese (*Anthologia Latina*, II, 2, 2nd. ed., 1906, p. 37, no. 487) assigns it to Hilary of Arles.

[43] *Alta manus* "the hand of God."

[44] *Refrigerium* "cooling, solace," cf. *Mart.*, 4, *Praef.*

[45] A free translation; cf. Haase and Bonnet (p. 512, note 10).

(16) 35. The seventh wonder is that the moon in thrice five days either increases to a full moon or decreases to a new moon. We marvel too at the fact that the stars rise in the east and set in the west; while some appear in the middle of the sky, some towards the north turn in a circle and do not travel a straight path; while some are visible through the whole year, others have specific months in which they appear.[46]

---

[46] With this sentence the introductory section on the seven wonders of the world ends, the second half of this paragraph forms a transitional introduction to the main topic of the essay (i.e. the determination of the proper time for the night offices by observation of the stars).

IV
Conclusion

12
From *The Life of St. Barbatus*

The short preface and condensed translation that follow are taken from Thomas Hodgkin, Italy and Her Invaders, *Vol. VI, The Lombard Kingdom (Oxford, 1895), pp. 293–299. Hodgkin bases his translation on the text of the life printed by G. Waitz in the* MGH, Scriptores rerum Langobardi-carum. *The events involving the Byzantine emperor Constans II (641–668) occurred around 663 and shortly thereafter. Constans, possibly anticipating a massive Moslem offensive against Europe, moved to Italy in 663 and established himself in Sicily shortly before he was assassinated in 668. The seventh century witnessed a new increase in Byzantine interest in south Italy, and the activities of St. Barbatus are particularly interesting in this light.*

This narrative is derived from two documents published in the great Bollandist collection of the Acta Sanctorum under the date 19th of February. One of these lives, we are told, is extracted from an ancient codex written *in Lombard characters* belonging to the Benedictine monastery of St. John at Capua. The other, an expanded and paraphrastic copy of the first, comes from the archives of the church at Benevento. Waitz, who has edited the life of the saint in *Scriptores rerum Langobardicarum (MGH)*, mentions eleven mss, most of which he has consulted, and three of which are 'litteris Beneventanis exarati.' He considers that even the earlier form of the history cannot have been written before the ninth century, and follows Bethmann in rejecting as valueless the later and paraphrastic form which he attributes to the tenth or eleventh century. From some slight indications (chiefly the description of the invading Emperor as 'Constantinus qui et Constans appellatur'), I should be disposed to believe that there is a foundation of contemporary tradition for the earlier document. The following is a greatly condensed translation of the Life:—

'Barbatus (who was born in the year 602) became famous when Grimwald held the reins of the Lombard kingdom, and his son Romwald ruled the Samnites.

'The Lombards, though baptized, worshipped the image of a viper; and moreover, they devoutly paid homage in most absurd fashion to a certain "sacrilegious" tree not far from the walls of their city. From the branches of this tree was hung a piece of leather; and all those who were to take part in the ceremony, turning their backs to the tree, rode away from it at a gallop, urging on their horses with bloody spurs. Then suddenly turning round, they hurled their lances at the leather, which quivered under their strokes; and each one cut out a little piece thereof, and ate it in a superstitious manner for the good of his soul.[1] And as they paid their vows at this place, they gave it the name *Votum*, which [says the scribe] it still bears.

'All these superstitious practices greatly distressed the soul of Barbatus, who told the people that it was vain for them thus to try to serve two masters. But they, in their blind and beastlike madness, refused to abandon this equestrian form of worship, saying that it was an excellent custom, and had been handed down to them by their ancestors, whom they mentioned by name, and declared to have been the bravest warriors upon earth.

'However, by his miracles, Barbatus began to soften the hearts of the rude people, who even by drinking the water in which he had washed his hands after celebration of the Mass, found themselves healed of their diseases.

'Then "Constantius, who is also called Constans," desiring to restore the kingdom of Italy to his obedience, collected an innumerable multitude of ships, arrived at Tarentum, and ravaged

---

[1] The second scribe amplifies the simple *corium* (leather) of the first into *putredo corii*, and *ignominiam corii*, and makes the trite reflection, 'Nam quid despicabilius credendum est quam ex mortuis animalibus non carnem sed corium accipere ad esum comestionis ut pravo errori subjecti Longobardi fecerunt?'

nearly all the cities of Apulia. He took the very wealthy city of Luceria after severe fighting, and by the labour of his robber-bands levelled it to the earth. Then he went on to Beneventum, where Romwald abode, having a few very brave Lombards with him, and the holy father Barbatus remained there with them. Terrible was the attack of Constans, who harassed the defenders with ever-fresh bands of assailants. This lasted long, but Romwald, magnanimous and unterrified, made a brave resistance, now fighting from the walls, now making a sudden sally and hasty return into the city, for he was not strong enough to fight in the open plain. Still, though he had slain many of the assailants, his own ranks were thinned, and the inhabitants began to weep and wail, thinking that they would soon be destroyed by the robber-bands of Constans. As for Romwald, he, growing weary of fighting, gave a counsel of despair to his soldiers [2]—"It is better for us to die in battle than to fall alive into the hands of the Greeks, and so perish ignominiously. Let us open the gates of the city, and give them the hardest battle that we can." Perceiving this discussion, St. Barbatus said, "Never let so many brave young men be given over to destruction, lest they perish everlastingly. Good were the boldness of your hearts, if your minds were not so empty, and your souls so weak." Said Romwald, "What dost thou mean by emptiness of mind, and weakness of soul? Prithee, tell us." Thereupon Barbatus, promising them the palm of victory, if they would follow his counsels, preached a long sermon against idolatry, and exhorted his hearers to the steady and serious worship of Christ.[3]

Thereupon Romwald said, "Only let us be delivered from our foes, and we will do all that thou biddest us, will make thee bishop of this place, and in all the cities under our rule will enrich thee with farms and 'colonies.'"

'Barbatus answered, "Know for certain that Christ, to Whom ye have now turned in penitence, will set you free, and the assaults of Caesar and his people shall not penetrate the streets of Beneventum, but with changed purpose they shall return to their own borders. And that thou mayest know that I am telling thee

[2] I take some sentences here from the later MS.
[3] So far the later MS.

the very truth, which shall shortly come to pass, let us come together under the wall. There will I show thee the Virgin Mary, the most pious Mother of God, who has offered up her health-giving prayers to God for you, and now, having been heard, comes to your deliverance.

'After public prayers and solemn litanies, and after earnest private prayer offered up by Barbatus in the Church of the Virgin, the people, with Romwald at their head, assembled at the gate which is still called Summa. Then Barbatus desired them all to bow down to the dust, for God loveth a contrite heart, and went, in conversation with Romwald, close under the wall. Then suddenly appeared the Mother of God, at sight of whom the Prince fell to the earth and lay like one dead, till the holy man lifted him from the ground and spoke words of comfort to him whom had been permitted to see so great a mystery[4].

'On the following day the besieger, who had refused to be turned from his hostile purpose by an immense weight of silver and gold and a countless quantity of pearls and precious stones, now, receiving only the sister of Romwald, turned his back on Beneventum and entered the city of Neapolis. The blessed Barbatus at once took a hatchet, and going forth to Votum, with his own hands hewed down that unutterable tree in which for so long the Lombards had wrought their deadly sacrilege: he tore up its roots and piled earth over it, so that no one thereafter should be able to say where it had stood.

'And now was Barbatus solemnly chosen bishop of Beneventum. Of all the farms and "coloniae" wherewith Prince and people offered to endow him, he would receive nothing, but he consented to have the house of the Archangel Michael on Mount Garganus, and all the district that had been under the rule of the bishop of

---

[4] It is interesting to observe how the story grows in minuteness as time goes on. In the earlier MS. the words are simply—
'pariterque subeuntes murum visa Dei genitrice in faciem decidit Princeps, nimioque pavore perterritus et paene exanimis solo consternatus jacebat.'
In the later MS. this becomes—
'Barbatus ... cum Romualt subiit civitatis murum, et ecce apparuit subito candidae nubis fusio praecipuo plena splendore quae confixa per gyrum turris obumbrabat cacumen, quod eminebat super ipsam portam praefatam, et in medio nubis, delectabilis visio perfuso lumine rutilabat Virginis puerperae vultu et coelorum Reginae perennis.'

Sipontum transferred to the See of the Mother of God over which he presided[5].

'Still Romwald and his henchmen, though in public they appeared to worship God in accordance with the teaching of Barbatus, in the secret recesses of the palace adored the image of the Viper to their souls' destruction; wherefore the man of God, with prayers and tears, besought that they might be turned from the error of their way.

'Meanwhile Romwald's wife, Theuderada, had forsaken the way of error, and was worshipping Christ according to the holy canons. Often when Romwald went forth to hunt, Barbatus would come to visit her, and discourse with her concerning her husband's wickedness. In one of these interviews she, heaving a deep sigh, said, "Oh! that thou wouldest pray for him to Almighty God. I know that it is only by thine intercession that he can be brought to walk in the path of virtue."

'*Barbatus.*—"If thou hast, as I believe, true faith in the Lord, hand over to me the Viper's image, that thy husband may be saved."

'*Theuderada.*—"If I should do this, I know of a surety that I should die."

'*Barbatus.*—"Remember the rewards of eternal life. Such death would not be death, but a great gain. For the faith of Christ thou shalt be withdrawn from this unstable world, and shalt attain unto that world where Christ reigneth with His saints, where shall be neither frost nor parching heat, nor poverty nor sadness, nor weariness nor envy, but all shall be joy and glory without end."

'Moved by such promises she speedily brought him the image of the Viper. Having received it, the bishop at once melted it in the fire, and by the help of many goldsmiths made of it during the prince's absence a paten and chalice of great size and beauty, for the offering up of the body and blood of Jesus Christ.

'When all was prepared, on the sacred day of the Resurrection, Romwald, returning from hunting, was about to enter Beneventum, but Barbatus met him, and persuaded him first to come and assist in celebration of the Mass in the church of the Mother of God. This he did, receiving the communion in the golden vessels made,

[5] Sipontum had probably lain desolate since its ravage by the Sclavonians in 642.

though he knew it not, from the image of the Viper. When all was done, the man of God approached the prince, and rebuked him sharply for tempting God by keeping the Viper's image in his palace. Should the terrible day of the Divine vengeance come, in vain would he flee to that idol for protection. Hearing these words, Romwald humbly confessed his sin, and promised to give up the image into the bishop's hands. "That thou needest not do," said the saint, "since it has already been changed into the vessels from which thou hast received the body and blood of the Lord. Thus what the Devil had prepared for thy destruction is now the instrument through which God works thy salvation."

'*Romwald.*—"Prithee tell me, dearest father, by whose orders the idol was brought to thee.'

'*Barbatus.*—"I confess that I, speaking in much sorrow to thy wife concerning thy spiritual death, asked her for the image, and received it at her hands."

'Thereat one of the bystanders burst in, saying, "If my wife had done such a thing as that, I would without a moment's delay cut off her head." But Barbatus turned to him and said, "Since thou longest to help the Devil, thou shalt be the Devil's slave." Thereupon the man was at once seized by the Devil and began to be grievously tormented by him. And that this might be a token and a warning to the Lombard nation in after times, the saint predicted that for so many generations [the biographer is not certain of the exact number] there should always be one of his descendants possessed by the Devil, a prophecy which, down to the date of the composition of the biography, had been exactly fulfilled.

'Struck with terror, all the other Beneventans abandoned their superstitious practices, and were fully instructed by the man of God in the Catholic faith, which they still keep by God's favour.

'Barbatus spent eighteen years and eleven months in his bishopric, and died on the eleventh day before the Calends of March (19th of February), 682, in the eightieth year of his age.'

This curious narrative, however little worthy of credence as a statement of facts, is a valuable piece of evidence as to the spiritual condition of the Lombards of south Italy in the seventh century. We may safely infer from it that conversion to Christianity was a much more gradual process in the south than in the north of Italy. Lupus of Friuli is neither saint nor hero in the pages of Paulus, but his daughter Theuderada is like another Clotilda or Theudelinda to the barbarous, half-heathen rulers of Benevento. In another Life, contained in the Acta Sanctorum, that of St. Sabinus (ix Februarii), we have a slight notice of Theuderada as a widow. After the death of her husband she ruled 'the Samnites' in the name of her young son [Grimwald II], and during her regency a certain Spaniard named Gregory came to Spoleto in order to find the tomb of St. Sabinus, who had died more than a century before (in 566). Not finding the sepulchre there, he persuaded the Princess Theuderada to go and seek for it at Canusium. She found the tomb, and on opening it perceived that pleasant odour which often pervaded the sepulchres of the saints. She also found in it a considerable weight of gold, which the biographer thinks had been stored there in anticipation of that invasion of the barbarians which St. Sabinus had foretold. Unmindful of the commission which Gregory had given her to build a church over the saint's tomb, she carried off the gold and returned in haste to Benevento. But when she arrived at Trajan's Bridge over the Aufidus, by the judgment of God her horse slipped and fell. She was raised from the ground by her attendants, but recognised in the accident the vengeance of the saint for her forgetfulness. She hastened back to the holy man's sepulchre, built a church with all speed, reared over his body a beautiful marble altar, and made chalice and paten out of the gold found in the tomb. To the end of his life Gregory the Spaniard ministered in the church of St. Sabinus.

Selected Bibliography

I

Barmby, James, ed. & trans. *Selected Epistles of Gregory the Great*. Select Library of Nicene and Post-Nicene Fathers of the Christian Church, Second Series, Vols. XII–XIII. reprint ed. Grand Rapids, 1956.

Blair, P. H. *The World of Bede*. London, 1970.

Davis, Henry, trans. *Gregory the Great: Pastoral Care*. Ancient Christian Writers, Westminster, Md., 1950.

Dudden, F. H. *Gregory the Great, his place in History and Thought*. London, 1905.

Hubert, J., J. Porcher & W. F. Volbach. *Europe of the Invasions*. trans. Stuart Gilbert & James Emmons. Arts of Mankind, eds. Andre Malraux and Andre Parrot. New York, 1969.

Kellett, Frederick William. *Pope Gregory the Great and his relations with Gaul*. Cambridge, 1889.

Klauser, T. *A Short History of the Western Liturgy*. New York, 1969.

McNeill, J. T. *A History of the Cure of Souls*. reprint ed. New York, 1951.

Zimmerman, Odo John, trans. *Gregory the Great: Dialogues*. Fathers of the Church Series, 39. Washington, D.C., 1959.

II

Addison, James Thayer. *The Medieval Missionary: A Study of the Conversion of Northern Europe, A.D. 500–1300*. London & New York, 1936.

Aigrain, René. *L'hagiographie: ses sources, ses methodes, son histoire*. Paris, 1953.

Beck, Henry G. J. *The Pastoral Care of Souls in Southeast France during the Sixth Century*. Rome, 1950.

Bitterman, Helen Robbins. "The Influence of Irish Monks on Merovingian Diocesan Organization." *American Historical Review* XL (1935): 232–245.

Butler, Cuthbert. *Benedictine Monachism.* New York, 1965.

Clark, J. M. *The Abbey of St. Gall* as a centre of literature and art. Cambridge, 1926.

Cuming, G. J. *The Mission of the Church and the Propagation of the Faith.* Studies in Church History, ed. G. J. Cuming, VI. Cambridge, 1970.

Daly, L. J., S. J. *Benedictine Monasticism.* New York, 1965.

Dubois, M. M. *Un pionnier de la civilisation occidentale, St. Columban.* Paris, 1950.

Duckett, Eleanor Shipley. *The Gateway to the Middle Ages: Monasticism.* paper ed. Ann Arbor, 1961.

———. *The Wandering Saints of the Early Middle Ages.* paper ed. New York, 1964.

Gazay, J. "De l'influence des moines irlandaises dans l'Eglise provencale au debut du moyen age." *Annales du Midi* XLVII (1935): 225–279.

Gougaud, Louis. *Gaelic Pioneers of Christianity: The Work and Influence of Irish Monks and Saints in Continental Europe, VIth–XIIth Centuries.* Trans. Victor Collins. Dublin, 1923.

Hillgarth, Jocelyn N., ed. *The Conversion of Western Europe, 350–750.* Englewood, 1969.

Hughes, Kathleen. *The Church in Early Irish Society.* Ithaca, 1966.

Knowles, David. *Christian Monasticism.* New York, 1969.

Lehane, Brendan. *The Quest of Three Abbots* [Saints Brendan, Columba, Columbanus]. New York, 1968.

Luff, S. G. "A Survey of Primitive Monasticism in Central Gaul, c.350 to 700." *The Downside Review* 70 (1952): 180–203.

Markus, R. A. "Gregory the Great and a papal missionary strategy," *Studies in Church History,* ed. G. J. Cuming, vol. 6. Cambridge, 1970: 29–38.

McCann, Justin, ed. & trans. *The Rule of St. Benedict in Latin and English.* London, 1969.

O'Briain, F. The Expansion of Irish Christianity to 1200: An Historiographical Survey." *Irish Historical Studies* III (1943): 241–266; IV (1944): 131–163.

O'Carrol, J. "Monastic rules in Merovingian Gaul." *Studies in Irish Literature and History.* Dublin, 1955.

O'Doherty, J. F. "St. Columbanus and the Roman See." *Irish Ecclesiastical Record* 42 (1933): 1 ff.

Prinz, Friedrich. *Frühes Mönchtum im Frankenriech.* Munich & Vienna, 1965.

Robinson, Charles Henry. *The Conversion of Europe.* London & New York, 1917.

Schroll, Sister Mary Alfred, O.S.B. *Benedictine Monasticism as Reflected in the Warnefrid-Hildemar Commentaries on the Rule.* New York, 1941.

Settimane di Studio del Centro Italiano di Studi sull'Alto Medioevo, IV. *Il monachesimo nell 'alto medioevo e la formazione della civiltà occidentale.* Spoleto, 1957.

———, XIV. *La conversione al cristianesimo nell 'Europa dell 'alto medioevo.* Spoleto, 1967.

Strunk, Gerhard. *Kunst und Glaube in der lateinischen Heiligenlegende.* Munich, 1970.

Sullivan, Richard E. "The Papacy and Missionary Activity in the Early Middle Ages." *Mediaeval Studies* 17 (1955): 46–106.

Uhlfelder, Myra L., trans. *The Dialogues of Gregory the Great, Book II: Saint Benedict.* Indianapolis & New York, 1967.

van der Meer, F. and C. Mohrmann. *Atlas of the Early Christian World.* Amsterdam, 1958.

Waddell, Helen. *The Desert Fathers.* Ann Arbor, 1966.

Zarnecki, George. *The Monastic Achievement.* New York, 1972.

III

BIBLIOGRAPHICAL ABBREVIATIONS

AASS: Acta sanctorum, Antwerp etc., 1643ff. *Note:* These volumes are arranged by months. The last volume is *Novembris,* IV (1925), containing Nov. 9–10. There is an index for Jan.–Oct. in *Octobris supplementum* in which the saints of Nov.–Dec. are listed (pp. 396–435). For a description of the inception and progress of this great work cf. H. Delehaye, *Works of the Bollandists through three Centuries, 1615–1915,*

Princeton, 1922. The late Father Delehaye was one of the editors of the last volume.

ARV: the American revision of the King James version: *The Holy Bible,* being the version set forth A.D. 1611, newly edited by the American Revision Committee, A.D. 1901.

CSEL: Corpus scriptorum ecclesiasticorum Latinorum, Vienna, 1866ff.

DACL: F. Cabrol and H. Leclercq, *Dictionnaire d'archéologie chrétienne et de liturgie,* 1903ff.

Du Cange: C. D. Du Cange. *Glossarium mediae et infimae Latinitatis.* Ed. by G. A. L. Henschel, 7 vols. Paris, 1840–50.

Forcellini: A. Forcellini. *Totius Latinitatis lexicon,* rev. ed. by V. de Vit, 6 vols. Leipzig, 1858–79.

Habel: E. Habel. *Mittellateinisches Glossar.* Paderborn, 1931.

MGH, AA: Monumenta Germaniae historica, auctores antiquissimi.

MGH, SRM: Monumenta Germaniae historica, scriptores rerum Merovingicarum.

NA: Neues Archiv der Gesellschaft fuer aeltere deutsche Geschichtskunde, Hannover, 1876ff.

PL: Patrologiae cursus completus, series latina, ed. J. P. Migne, 221 vols. Paris, 1844–64.

RE: Pauly-Wissowa-Kroll. Real-Encyclopaedie der classischen Altertumswissenschaft. Stuttgart, 1894ff.

TLL: Thesaurus linguae Latinae. Leipzig, 1900ff.

Vulg.: versio vulgata: Bibliorum sacrorum iuxta vulgatam Clementinam, nova editio, curavit Aloisius Gramatica. Milan, Hoepli, 1914.

ABBREVIATIONS FOR GREGORY'S WORKS

Cursu: de cursu stellarum ratio

Dorm.: passio sanctorum martyrum septem dormientium apud Ephesum.

GC: liber in gloria confessorum.

GM: liber in gloria martyrum beatorum.

HF, 1–10: historia Francorum, libri decem.

Iul.: liber de passione et virtutibus sancti Iuliani martyris.
Mart., 1–4: *de virtutibus beati Martini episcopi, libri quattuor.*
VP: liber vitae patrum.

EDITIONS OF THE TEXT
USED FOR THE TRANSLATION

Arndt, W., and B. Krusch. *Gregorii Turonensis opera. MGH,*
SRM, I. Hannover, 1885.
Note: Arndt edited *HF,* Krusch the other works, except *de*
miraculis beati Andreae, (pp. 821–46) edited by Max Bonnet;
Krusch drew up the elaborate indices for the whole volume
(pp. 884–963). These indices are cited as Krusch, *Index.* The
new edition by Krusch and W. Levison is complete (Hannover, 1937, 1942, 1951). All selections except the *Dorm.* have
been translated from the text of Krusch in this volume.
Wherever other readings have been used, the source is
specified in the notes. Citations of *HF* have been made from
Arndt. The introductions of both editors and many of
Krusch's notes have great value for the study of the life and
works of Gregory.

Krusch, B. and W. Levison. *Passiones vitaeque sanctorum aevi*
Merovingici cum supplemento et appendice. MGH, SRM,
VII. Hannover, 1920.
Note: pp. 707–72 by Krusch form the appendix of volume I.
In this appendix pp. 707–56 contain supplementary readings
from the mss and further discussion of text problems in the
first six books of Gregory's *Miracula.* This section is of vital
importance since Krusch frequently changed his text in
accordance with new information or new readings of the
mss, and his *editio altera* did not go beyond *HF,* 1–5. Pp.
757–69 contain *Passio VII dormientium, editio nova,* which is
the text here used for the translation of that work. Pp. 770f.
give supplementary notes on the *de cursu stellarum.* References to this section of his volume are cited as Krusch, *App.*

TEXTS AND TRANSLATIONS
OF THE WORKS OF GREGORY

Bordier, Henri Leonard. *Les livres des miracles et autres opuscules de Georges Florent Grégoire, évêque de Tours.* A revised text and translation, 4 volumes. Paris, 1857–1864.
Note: This is the only complete translation of the *Miracula.* It includes a revised text and an excellent French translation. This translation is at times helpful for interpretation of the Latin, more often for the choice of a felicitous word. Bordier translated only the *Miracula,* but included the text of the other works (except *Dorm.*). Of great value are the *testimonia* (pp. 212–276), bibliography (pp. 281–318), and index (pp. 321–73) in the fourth volume. In the first of these the *vita sancti Gregorii episcopi Turonensis* often assigned to Odo is included, as well as 27 pages of quotations from Fortunatus. The bibliography of 60 items (1511–1864) is invaluable since Bordier has included a full bibliographical note followed by his own critical opinion.

Brehaut, Ernest. *History of the Franks by Gregory, Bishop of Tours.* Selections translated with notes. Records of Civilization, I. New York, 1916.
Note: Pp. 249–262, contain 15 brief selections from the *Miracula:* the following items are also included in McDermott's translation: *GM, Praef.* (in part, p. 249); *Mart.,* 1, *Praef.* (pp. 254f.); 1.20, 32, 33 (pp. 255-7); 3, *Praef.* (in part, p. 258); *VP,* 6 (in part, pp. 260-2).

Dalton, O. M., trans. *The History of the Franks by Gregory of Tours.* 2 vols. reprint ed. Farnborough, 1967.
Note: The first volume comprises an introduction of wide scope which gives a broad view of the age of Gregory. Both volumes are invaluable for the interpretation and background of the minor works.

Giesebrecht, W. von. *Zehn Buecher fraenkischer Geschichte von Bischof Gregorius von Tours.* Fourth edition by S. Hellman, 3 vols.: I. books 1–4 (Leipzig, 1911); II. books 5–8 (Leipzig, 1913); III. books 9–10 (Leipzig, 1913): *Die Geschichtschreiber der deutschen Vorzeit.* Second ed., VIII, IX. 1-2.

Note: The index in volume III of this translation is very useful since it gives complete references in *HF* to the Frankish kings (pp. 173–210).

Haase, F. S. *Georgii Florentii Gregorii Turonensis episcopi liber ineditus de cursu stellarum*, etc. Vratislavae, 1853.
Note: This is the *editio princeps* of *Curs.* and contains an exhaustive commentary.

Krusch, B. "Gregorii Turonensis passio VII dormientium apud Ephesum." *Analecta Bollandiana* 12 (1893): 371–87.
Note: Krusch's second edition of *Dorm.*

Krusch, B. "Ueber die handschriftliche Grundlage von Gregors Miracula." *NA* 19 (1894): 25–45.
Note: This is a section of a larger article. In it Krusch gave many additional ms readings and discussed their significance. The findings here published were included in his *Appendix*, but with less discussion.

Morf, H. *Auswahl aus den Werken des Gregor von Tours.* Heidelberg, 1922: *Sammlung vulgaerlateinischer Texte*, 6.

Omont, H., and G. Collon. *Grégoire de Tours, histoire des Francs.* Texte des mss de Corbie et de Bruxelles. New edition by R. Poupardin. Paris, 1913.
Note: A full list of editions and translations of *HF* is given on pp. xxiv–xxx.

Ruinart, Theodoricus. *Gregorius Turonensis, opera omnia* etc. Paris, 1699.
Note: This magnificent folio edition by the great Benedictine scholar has been reprinted verbatim in *PL,* 71, Paris, 1849.

LIFE OF GREGORY
AND CRITICISM OF HIS WORKS

Bardenhewer, O. *Geschichte der altchristlichen Literatur.* V. Second ed., Freiburg, 1932: 357–67.

Bonnet, Max. *Le latin de Grégoire de Tours.* Paris, 1890.
Note: This volume and Krusch's text form the basis for the study of the Latin text of Gregory's minor works. After a perspicuous account of the works of Gregory, M. Bonnet analyzed in great detail the language of Gregory. He made

numerous additions to the apparatus of the text. Many conjectural readings that he proposed were later confirmed by new mss.

Buchanan, T. R. in Smith and Wace. *Dictionary of Christian biography.* II. London, 1880: 771-76 *s.v. Gregorius* (32) *Turonensis.*

Ebert, A. *Allgemeine Geschichte der Literatur des Mittelalters im Abendlande.* I. Second ed., Leipzig, 1889: 566-79. *Note:* Pp. 671-78 cover the minor works.

Hellmann, S. "Studien zur mittelalterlichen Geschichtschreibung: I. Gregor von Tours." *Historische Zeitschrift* 107 (1911): 1-43.

Kurth, Godefroid. *Études franques.* 2 vols. Paris, 1919. *Note:* This is a series of 18 essays, some reprinted with or without revisions and some new. The following are of especial significance for the study of Gregory. I. "Grégoire de Tours et les études classiques au VIe siècle" (vol. I, pp. 1-29), which is a greatly amplified version of an article published in *Revue des questions historiques,* 24 (1878), pp. 586-93. XIII. "Les sénateurs en Gaule au VIe siècle" (vol. II, pp. 97-116), first published here. XIV "De l'autorité de Grégoire de Tours" (vol. II, pp. 117-206), first published here. XV. "Les sources de l'histoire de Clovis dans Grégoire de Tours" (vol. II, pp. 207-71), which is a reprint of an article published in *Rev.qu.hist.,* 44 (1888), pp. 385-447.

Laistner, M. L. W. *Thought and Letters in Western Europe, A.D. 500-900.* Rev. paper ed. Ithaca, 1966.

Latouche, Robert. "Grégoire de Tours et les premiers historiens de la France." *Lettres d'Humanité* 2 (1943): 81-101.

Leclercq, H. in *DACL.* VI, 2. Paris, 1925: cols. 1711-53, *s. v. Grégoire de Tours.*

McDermott, William C. "Gregory of Tours." *Crozer Quarterly* 21 (1944): 277-92.

MacGonagle, Sara H. *The Poor in Gregory of Tours, a Study of the Attitude of Merovingian Society toward the Poor as reflected in the Literature of the Time.* Dissertation, Columbia University, 1936.

Manitius, Max. "Zur Frankengeschichte Gregors von Tours." *NA* 21 (1896): 549-57.

Manitius, Max. *Geschichte der lateinischen Literatur des Mittelalters*. I. Munich, 1911: 216–23 (on Gregory) *et aliter:* Mueller, *Handbuch der klassischen Altertumswissenschaft*, IX, II, I.

Osterhage, Georg. *Bemerkungen zu Gregor von Tours kleineren Schriften*. Progr. des Humboldts-Gymn. Berlin, 1895.

Roger, M. *L'enseignement des lettres classiques d'Ausone à Alcuin*. Paris, 1905. *Note:* Especially 100–10.

Vinay, G. *San Gregorio di Tours*. Turin, 1940.

Wattenbach, W. *Deutschlands Geschichtsquellen im Mittelalter bis zur Mitte des dreizehnten Jahrhunderts*. I. Seventh ed., revised by E. Duemmler. Stuttgart, 1904: 103–12 *et aliter*.

Wright, F. A., and T. A. Sinclair. *A History of Later Latin Literature*. New York, 1931: 100–10.

THE MEROVINGIAN BACKGROUND

Dill, Samuel. *Roman Society in Gaul in the Merovingian Age*. Reprint ed. New York, 1966.

Duchesne, L. *Fastes épiscopaux de l'ancienne Gaule*. I. Second ed., Paris, 1907; Vol. 2, Paris, 1900; Vol. 3, Paris 1915.

Duchesne, L. *L'église au sixième siècle*. Paris, 1925: 486–550 (ch. XIII, "L'église dans la Gaule franque").

Duckett, Eleanor Shipley. *The Gateway to the Middle Ages: France and Britain*. Paper ed. Ann Arbor, 1961.

Jacobs, A. *Géographie de Grégoire de Tours, le pagus et l'administration en Gaul*. Paris, 1858.

Laistner, M. L. W. *Thought and Letters in Western Europe, A.D. 500–900*. Rev. paper ed. Ithaca, 1966.

Lasko, Peter. *The Kingdom of the Franks: Northwest Europe before Charlemagne*. New York, 1971.

Latouche, Robert. *Caesar to Charlemagne: The Beginnings of France*. Trans. by Jennifer Nicholson. London & New York, 1967.

Lavisse, E., ed. *Histoire de France*. II, 1. Paris, 1903: 117–255 ("La période mérovingienne" by C. Pfister and C. Bayet).

Loebell, J. W., *Gregor von Tours und seine Zeit*. Second ed. with additions by Th. Bernhardt. Leipzig, 1869.

Longnon, Auguste. *Géographie de la Gaule au VIe siècle.* Paris, 1878.
Note: This work is based on Gregory and is invaluable for the study of his work. Part I (pp. 1–37) contains a discussion of the geographical terms (*civitas, urbs,* etc.), part III is "Description topographique de la Gaule d'après Grégoire de Tours" (pp. 153–622).

Marrou, Henri Irenée. *A History of Education in Antiquity.* Third ed. Trans. by George Lamb. London & New York, 1956.

Monod, Gabriel. Études critiques sur les sources de l'histoire mérovingienne. Part I. Paris, 1872: Bibliothèque de l'École des Hautes Études, VIII.
Note: The introduction is valuable (pp. 3–20); the section on Gregory is extensive and forms the basis for most later discussions of his life and works (pp. 21–146).

Morris, John. *The Age of Arthur: A History of the British Isles from 350 to 650.* London & New York, 1973.

Pfister, Christian. in *Cambridge Medieval History.* II. New York, 1913: 109–58, 728–32 (chs. IV–V), and in *Histoire du Moyen Age.* I. Paris, 1928: 181–209, 254–79, 297–393.
Note: This latter work is one section of G. Glotz, *Histoire générale.*

Stroheker, K. F. "Die Senatoren bei Gregor von Tours." *Klio* 16 (1941): 293–305.

Wallace-Hadrill, J. M. *The Long-Haired Kings and other Studies in Frankish History.* London, 1962.

―――― and John McManners, eds. *France: Government and Society.* London, 1957.
Note: Especially 36–60.

Wieruszowski, Helene. "Die Zusammensetzung des gallischen und fraenkischen Episkopats bis zum Vertrag von Verdun (843) mit besonderer Beruecksichtung der Nationalitaet und des Standes." *Bonner Jahrbuecher* 127 (1922): 1–83.